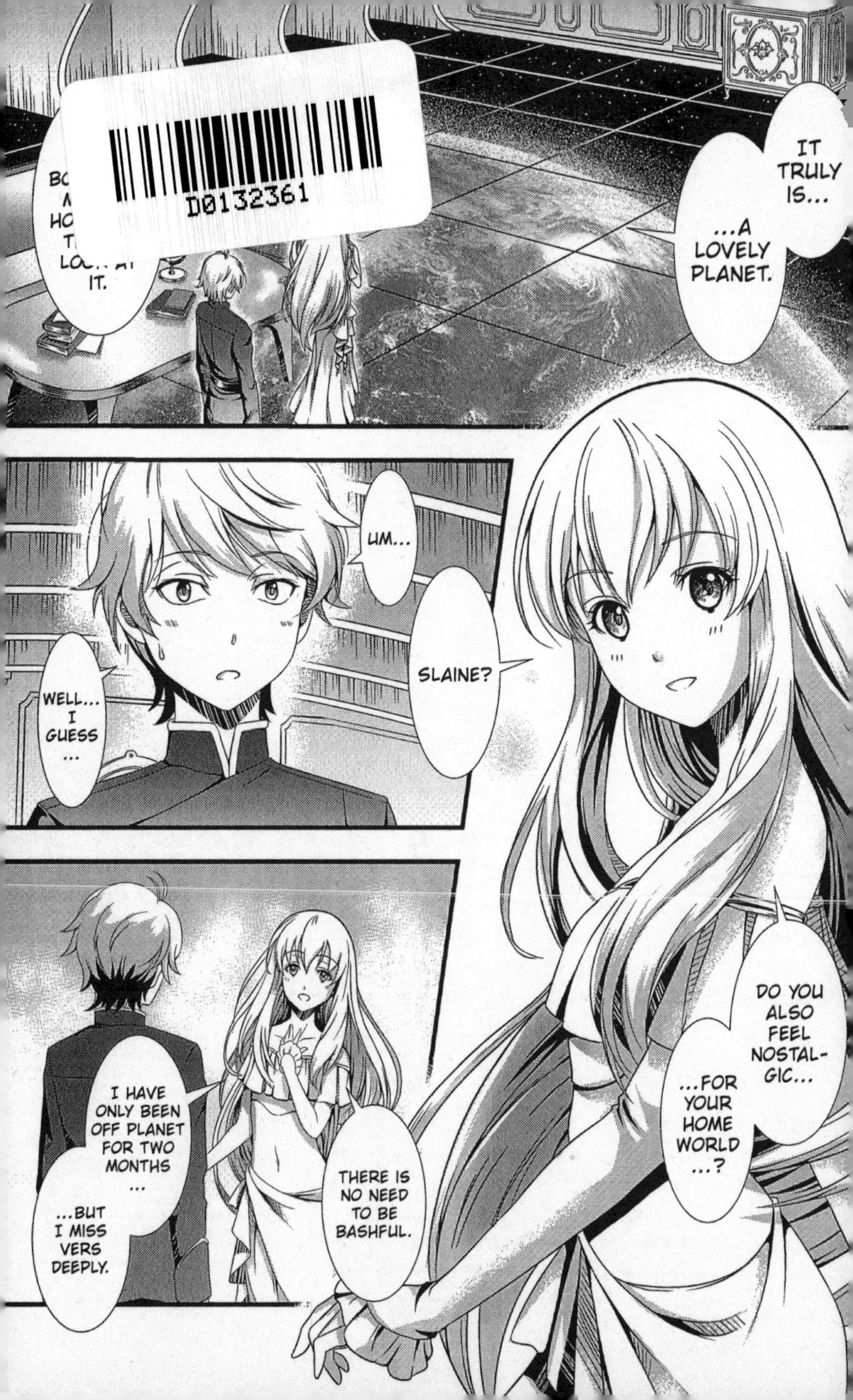
IT TRULY IS...
...A LOVELY PLANET.
DO YOU ALSO FEEL NOSTAL-GIC...
...FOR YOUR HOME WORLD ...?
UM...
SLAINE?
WELL... I GUESS ...
THERE IS NO NEED TO BE BASHFUL.
I HAVE ONLY BEEN OFF PLANET FOR TWO MONTHS ...
...BUT I MISS VERS DEEPLY.

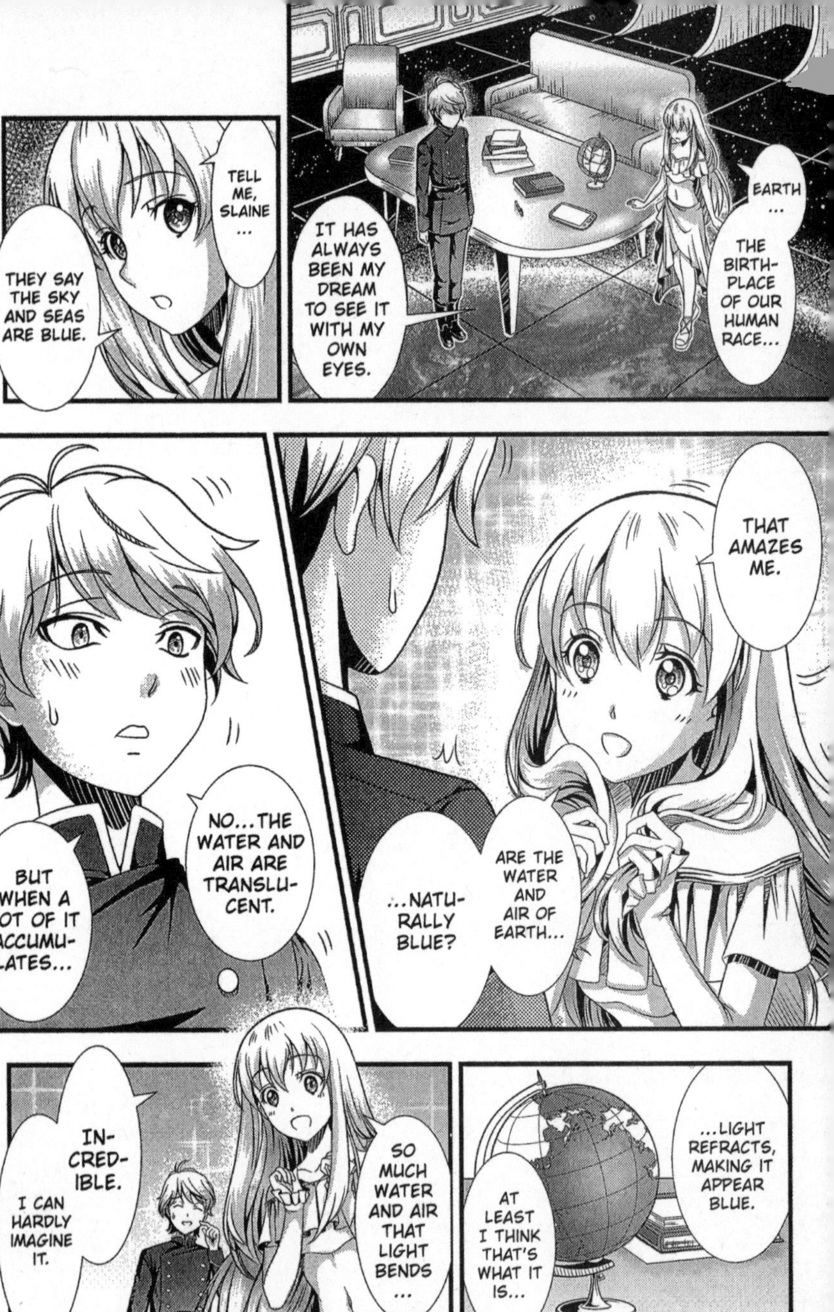
EARTH... THE BIRTHPLACE OF OUR HUMAN RACE...
IT HAS ALWAYS BEEN MY DREAM TO SEE IT WITH MY OWN EYES.
TELL ME, SLAINE...
THEY SAY THE SKY AND SEAS ARE BLUE.
THAT AMAZES ME.
ARE THE WATER AND AIR OF EARTH...
...NATURALLY BLUE?
NO...THE WATER AND AIR ARE TRANSLUCENT.
BUT WHEN A LOT OF IT ACCUMULATES...
...LIGHT REFRACTS, MAKING IT APPEAR BLUE.
AT LEAST I THINK THAT'S WHAT IT IS...
SO MUCH WATER AND AIR THAT LIGHT BENDS...
INCREDIBLE.
I CAN HARDLY IMAGINE IT.

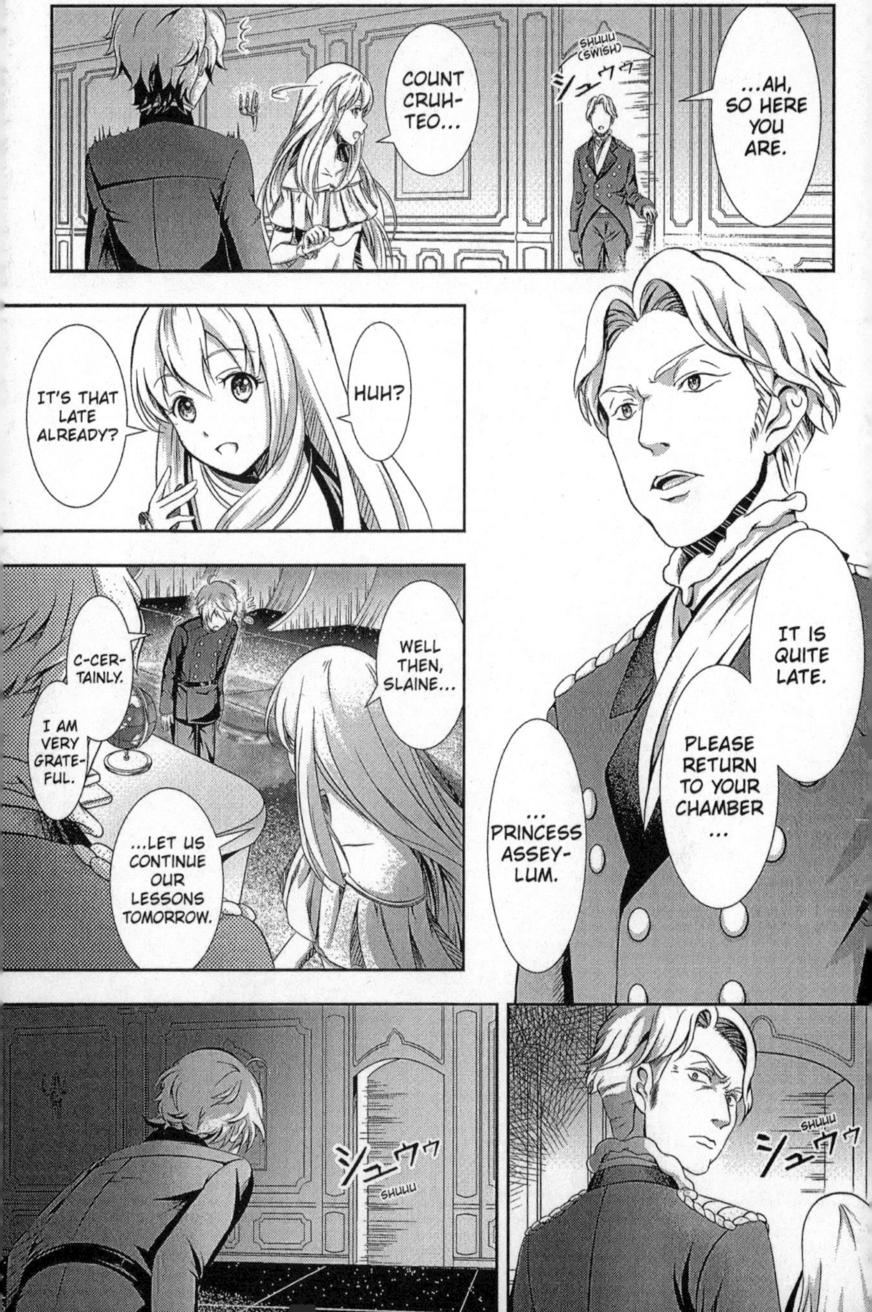
...AH, SO HERE YOU ARE.
SHUUU (SWISH)
シュウウ
COUNT CRUHTEO...
IT IS QUITE LATE.
PLEASE RETURN TO YOUR CHAMBER...
...PRINCESS ASSEYLUM.
HUH?
IT'S THAT LATE ALREADY?
WELL THEN, SLAINE...
...LET US CONTINUE OUR LESSONS TOMORROW.
C-CERTAINLY.
I AM VERY GRATEFUL.
SHUUU
シュウウ
シュウウ
SHUUU

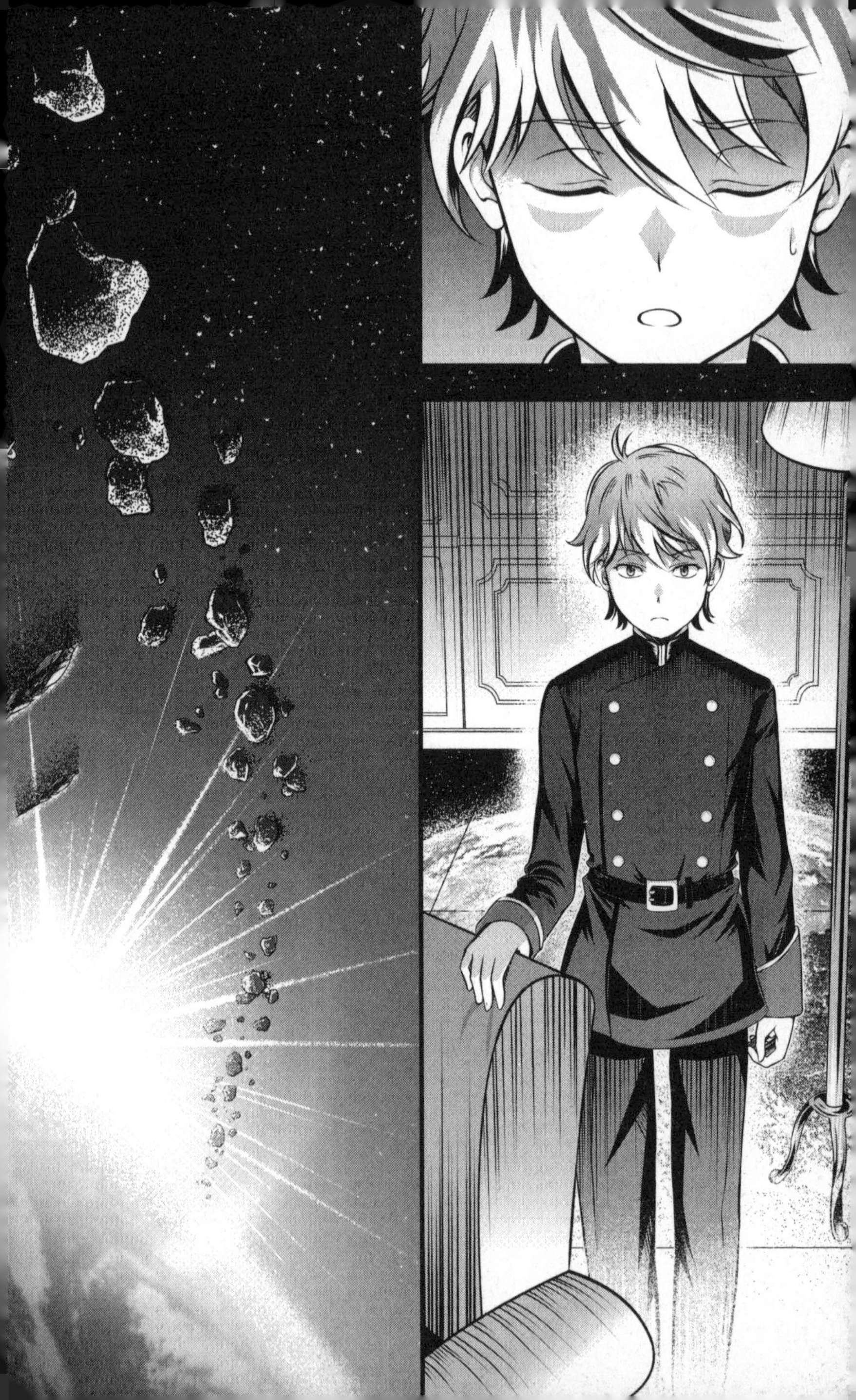

EP01 Princess of Mars — Princess of VERS —

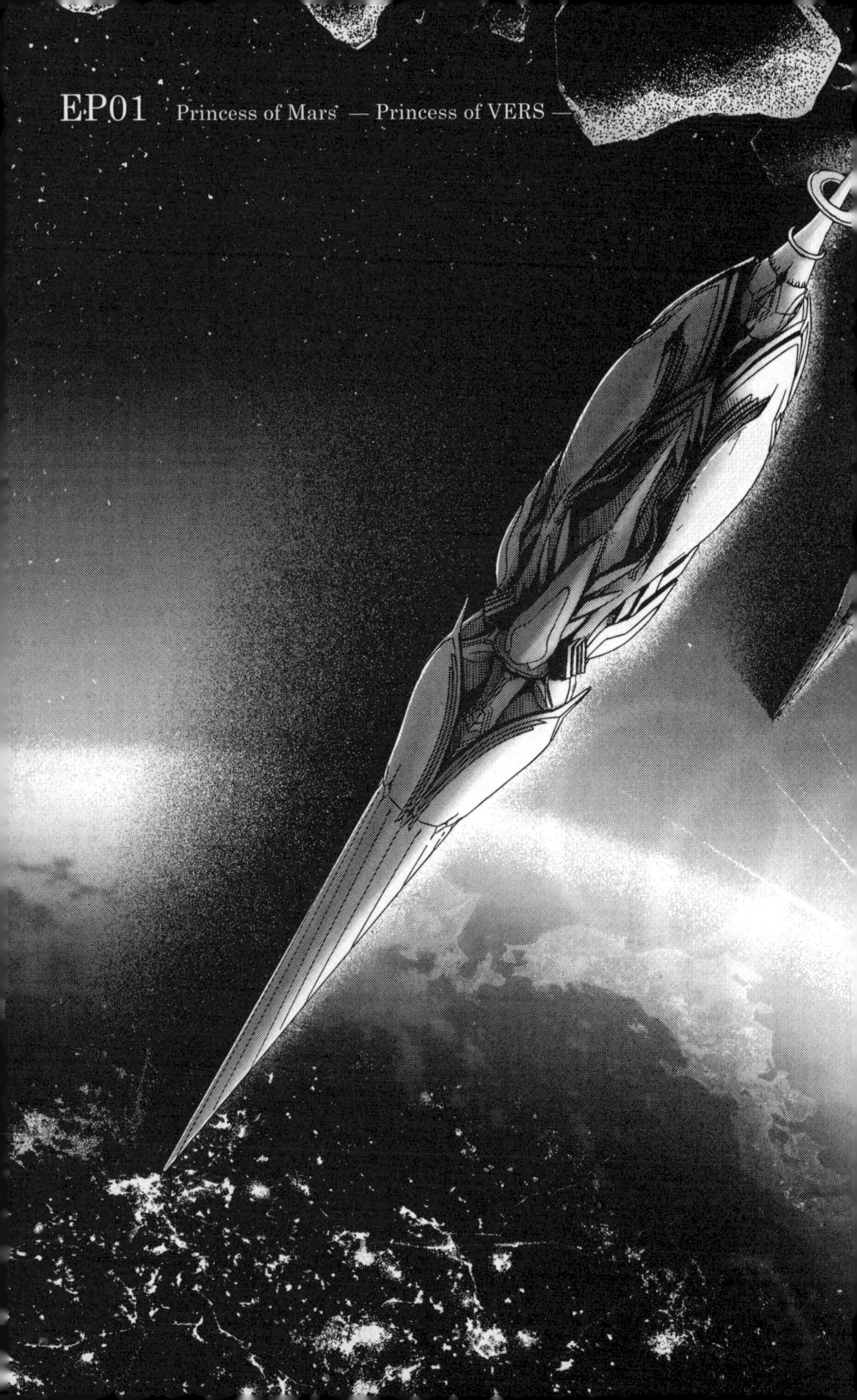

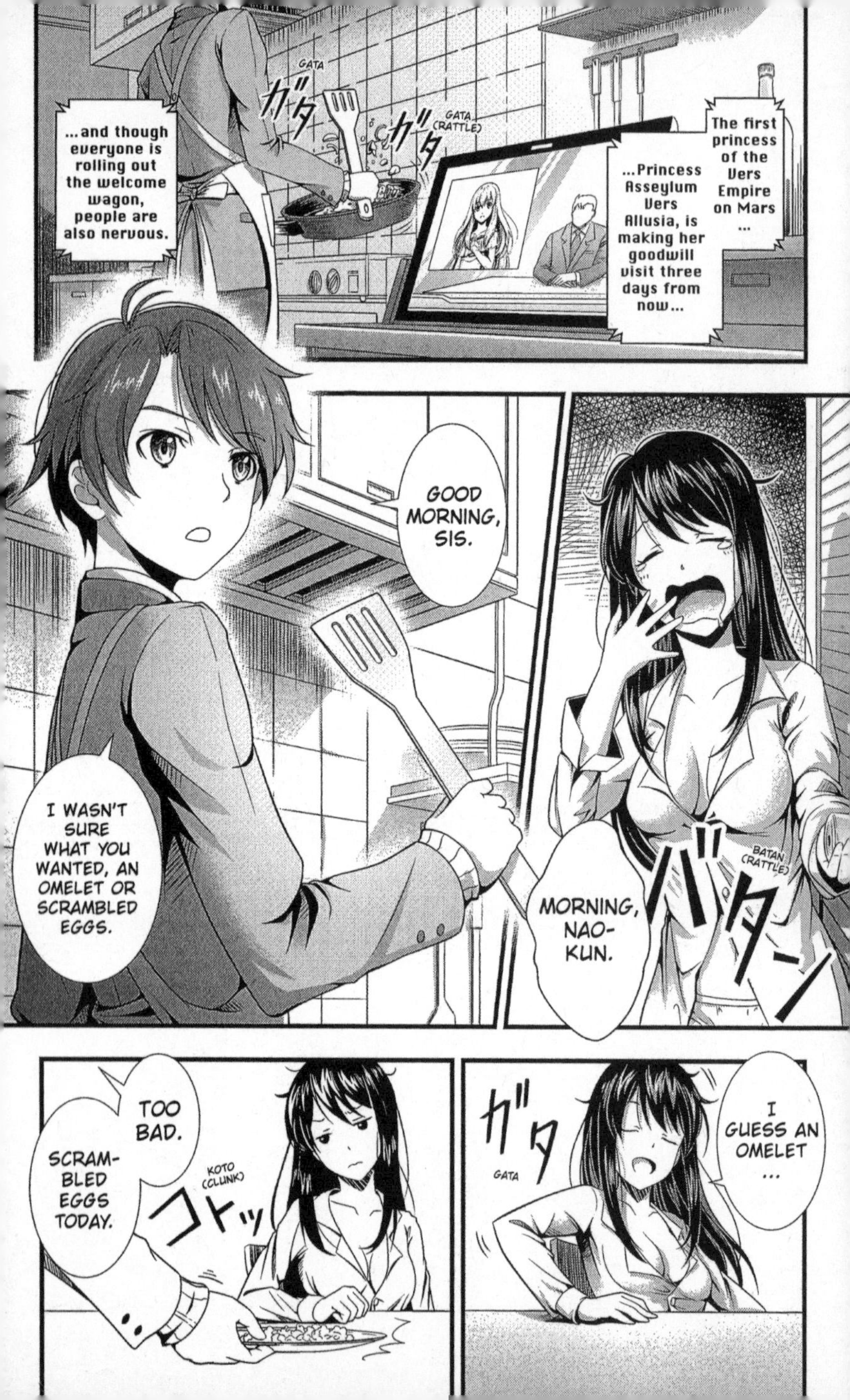
The first princess of the Vers Empire on Mars ...
...Princess Asseylum Vers Allusia, is making her goodwill visit three days from now...
GATA
GATA (RATTLE)
...and though everyone is rolling out the welcome wagon, people are also nervous.
BATAN (RATTLE)
MORNING, NAO-KUN.
GOOD MORNING, SIS.
I WASN'T SURE WHAT YOU WANTED, AN OMELET OR SCRAMBLED EGGS.
I GUESS AN OMELET ...
GATA
TOO BAD.
SCRAM-BLED EGGS TODAY.
KOTO (CLUNK)

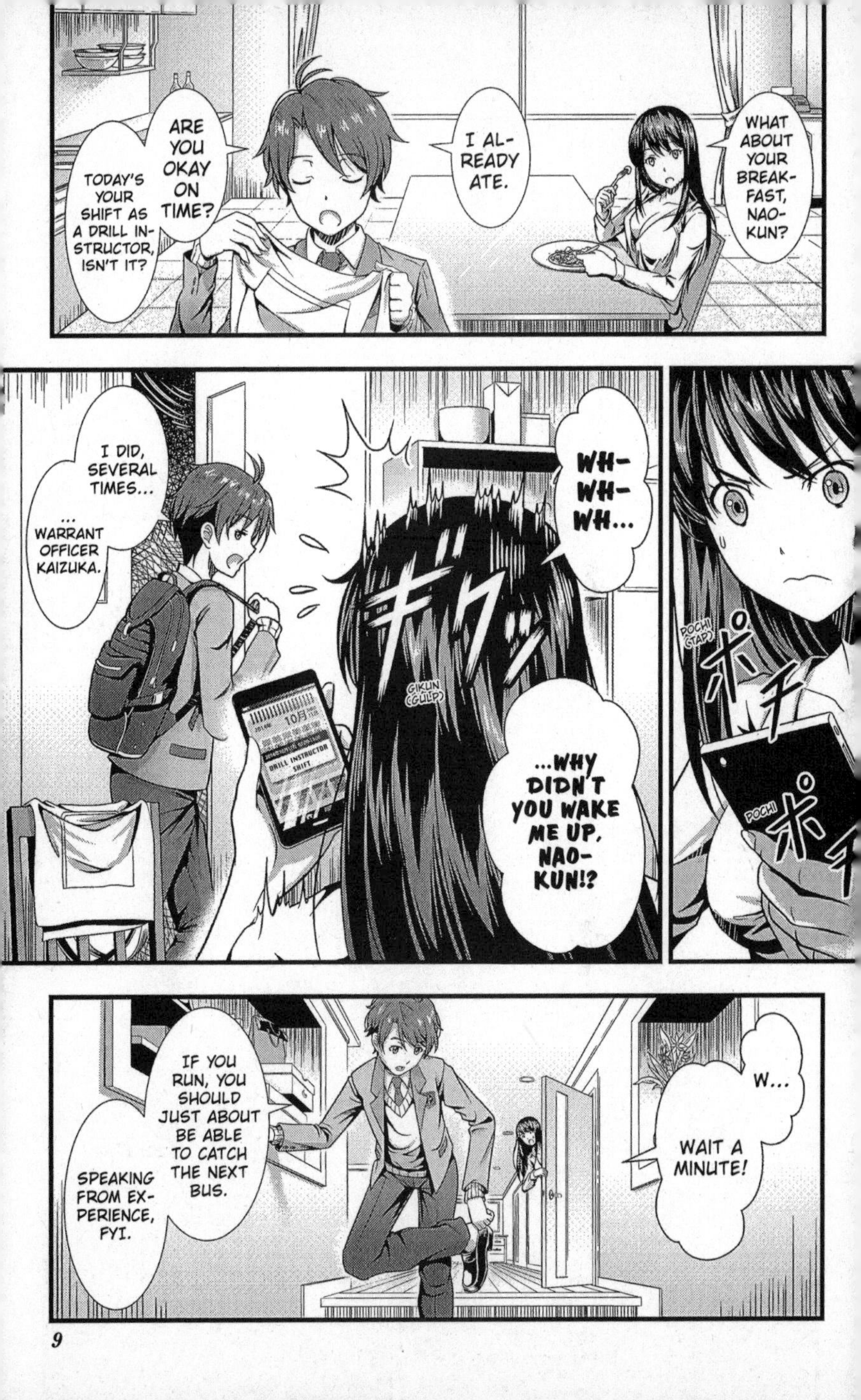
WHAT ABOUT YOUR BREAK-FAST, NAO-KUN?
I AL-READY ATE.
ARE YOU OKAY ON TIME?
TODAY'S YOUR SHIFT AS A DRILL IN-STRUCTOR, ISN'T IT?
POCHI (TAP)
POCHI
WH-WH-WH...
GIKUN (GULP)
...WHY DIDN'T YOU WAKE ME UP, NAO-KUN!?
10月
DRILL INSTRUCTOR SHIFT
I DID, SEVERAL TIMES...
...WARRANT OFFICER KAIZUKA.
W...
WAIT A MINUTE!
IF YOU RUN, YOU SHOULD JUST ABOUT BE ABLE TO CATCH THE NEXT BUS.
SPEAKING FROM EX-PERIENCE, FYI.

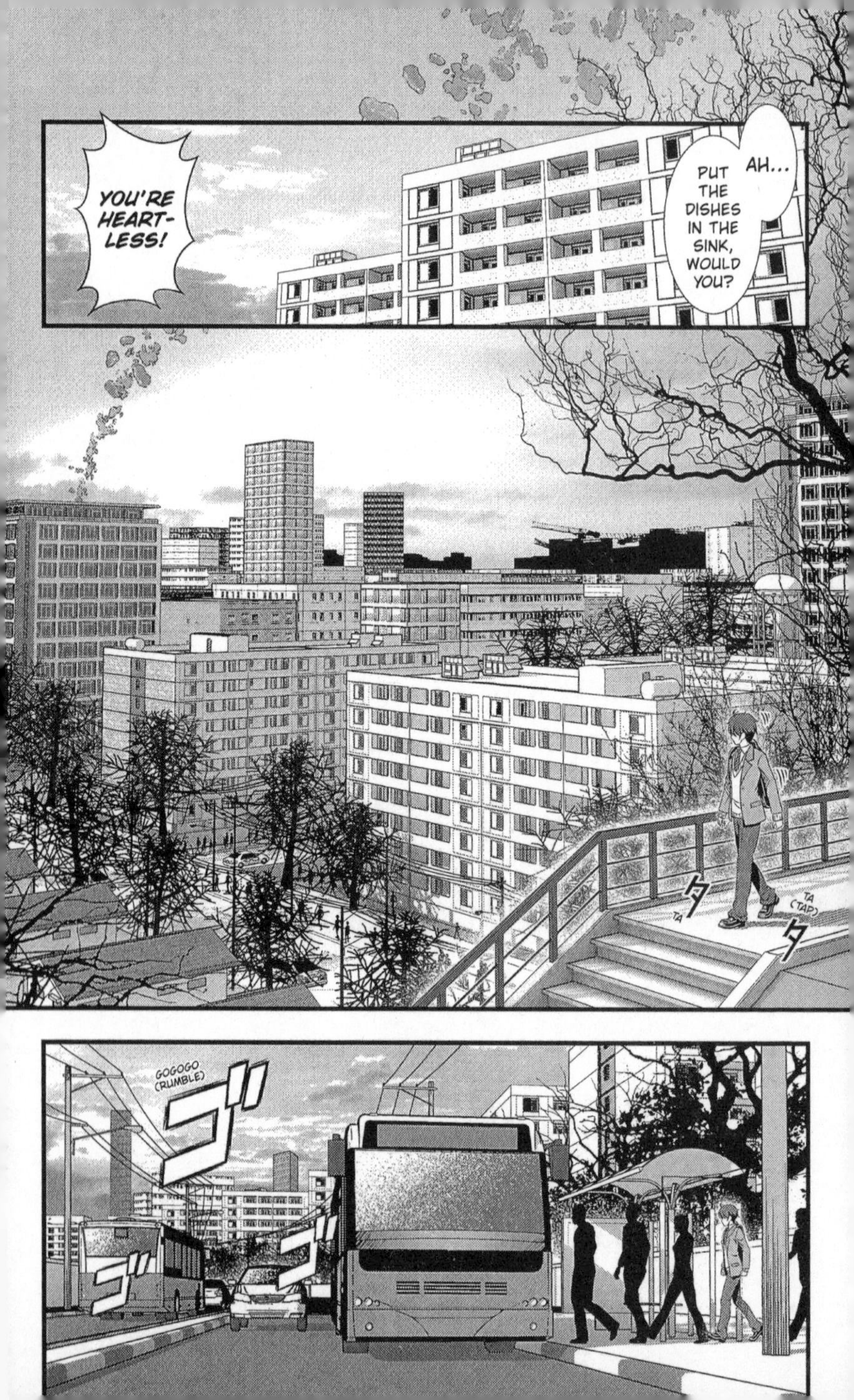
AH... PUT THE DISHES IN THE SINK, WOULD YOU?
YOU'RE HEART-LESS!
TA (TAP)
TA
GOGOGO (RUMBLE)

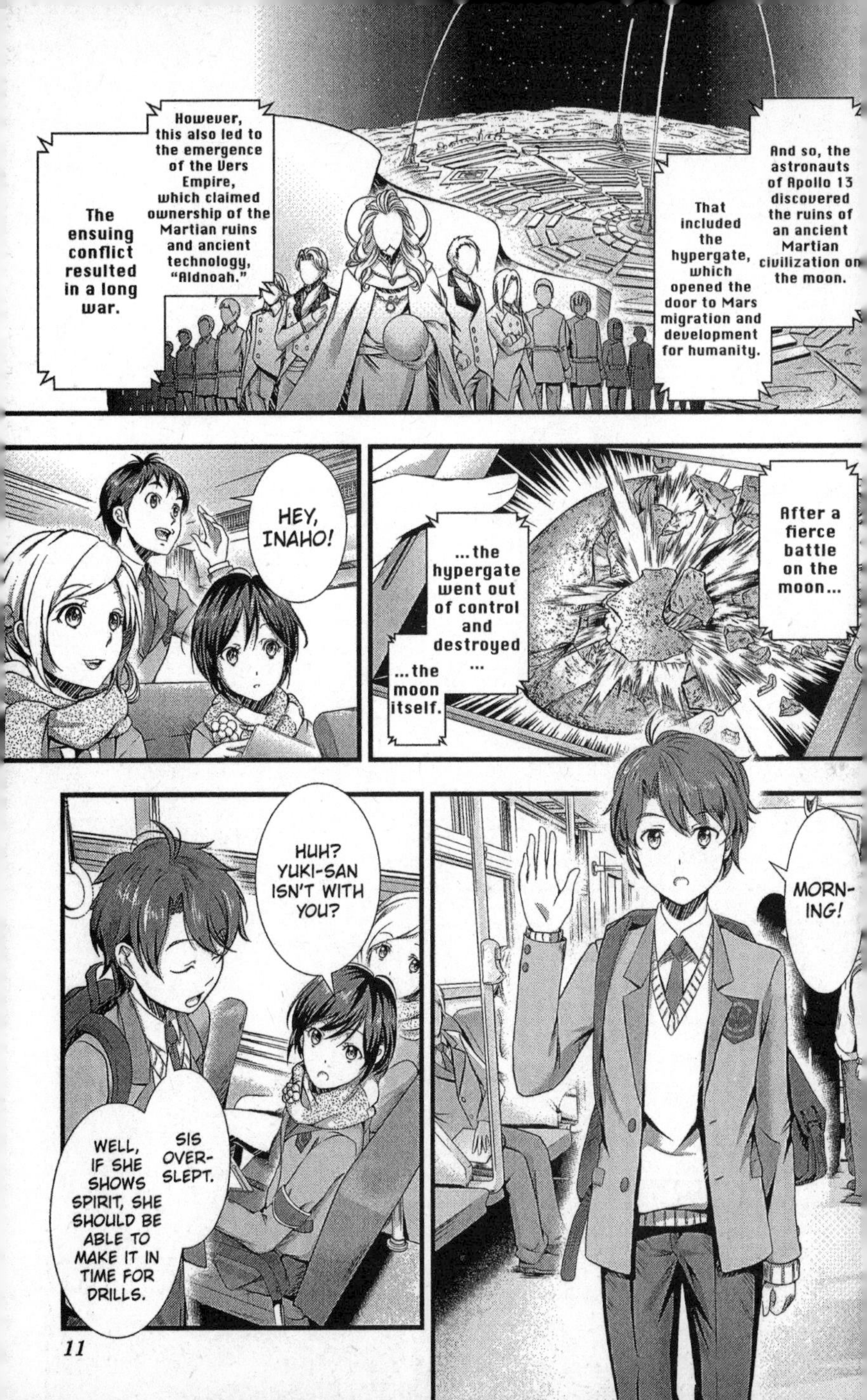
And so, the astronauts of Apollo 13 discovered the ruins of an ancient Martian civilization on the moon.
That included the hypergate, which opened the door to Mars migration and development for humanity.
However, this also led to the emergence of the Vers Empire, which claimed ownership of the Martian ruins and ancient technology, "Aldnoah."
The ensuing conflict resulted in a long war.
After a fierce battle on the moon...
...the hypergate went out of control and destroyed...
...the moon itself.
HEY, INAHO!
MORNING!
HUH? YUKI-SAN ISN'T WITH YOU?
SIS OVERSLEPT.
WELL, IF SHE SHOWS SPIRIT, SHE SHOULD BE ABLE TO MAKE IT IN TIME FOR DRILLS.

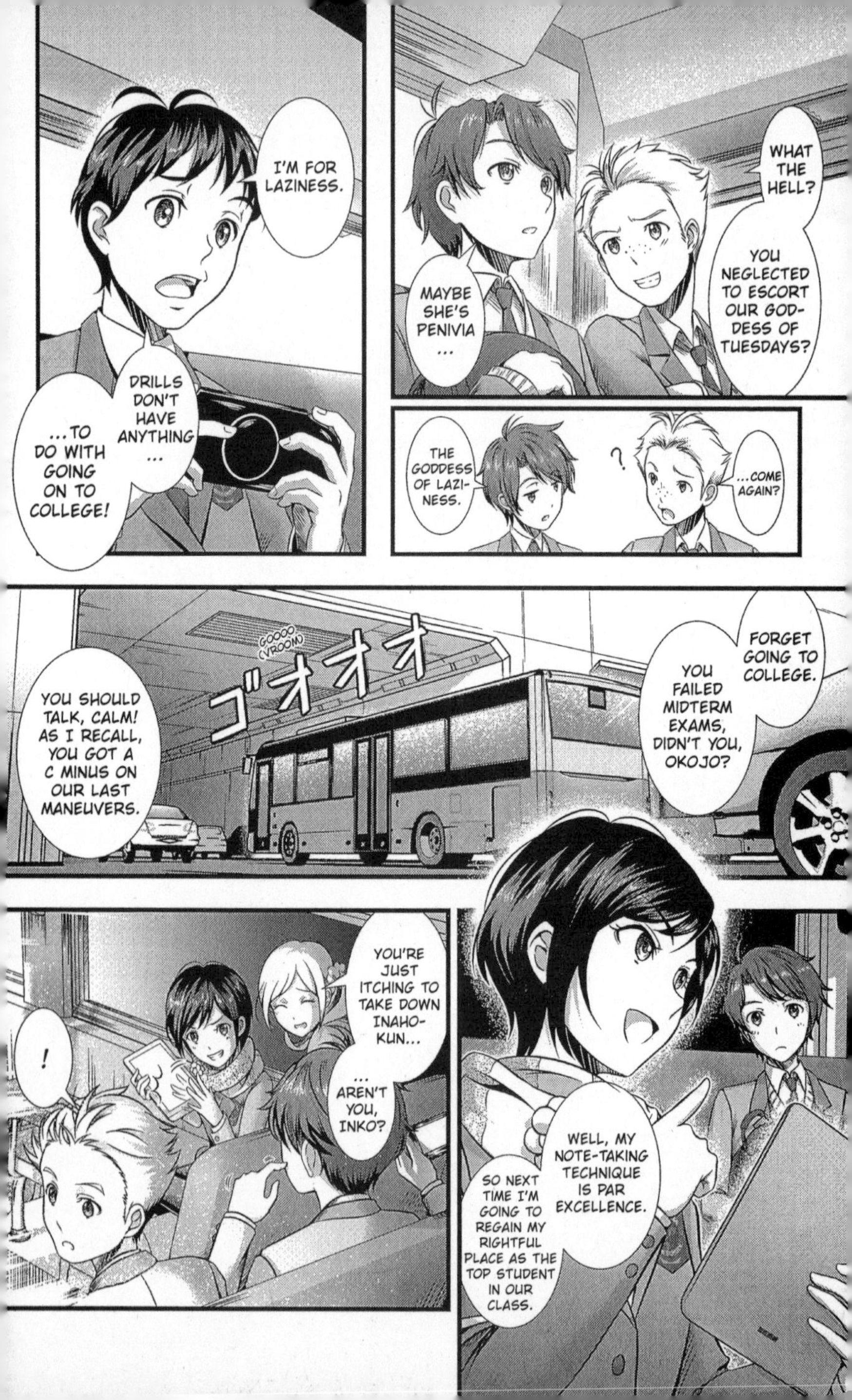
WHAT THE HELL?
YOU NEGLECTED TO ESCORT OUR GOD-DESS OF TUESDAYS?
MAYBE SHE'S PENIVIA...
...COME AGAIN?
THE GODDESS OF LAZI-NESS.
I'M FOR LAZINESS.
DRILLS DON'T HAVE ANYTHING...
...TO DO WITH GOING ON TO COLLEGE!
FORGET GOING TO COLLEGE.
YOU FAILED MIDTERM EXAMS, DIDN'T YOU, OKOJO?
ゴオオオ
GOOOO (VROOM)
YOU SHOULD TALK, CALM! AS I RECALL, YOU GOT A C MINUS ON OUR LAST MANEUVERS.
WELL, MY NOTE-TAKING TECHNIQUE IS PAR EXCELLENCE.
SO NEXT TIME I'M GOING TO REGAIN MY RIGHTFUL PLACE AS THE TOP STUDENT IN OUR CLASS.
YOU'RE JUST ITCHING TO TAKE DOWN INAHO-KUN...
...AREN'T YOU, INKO?
!

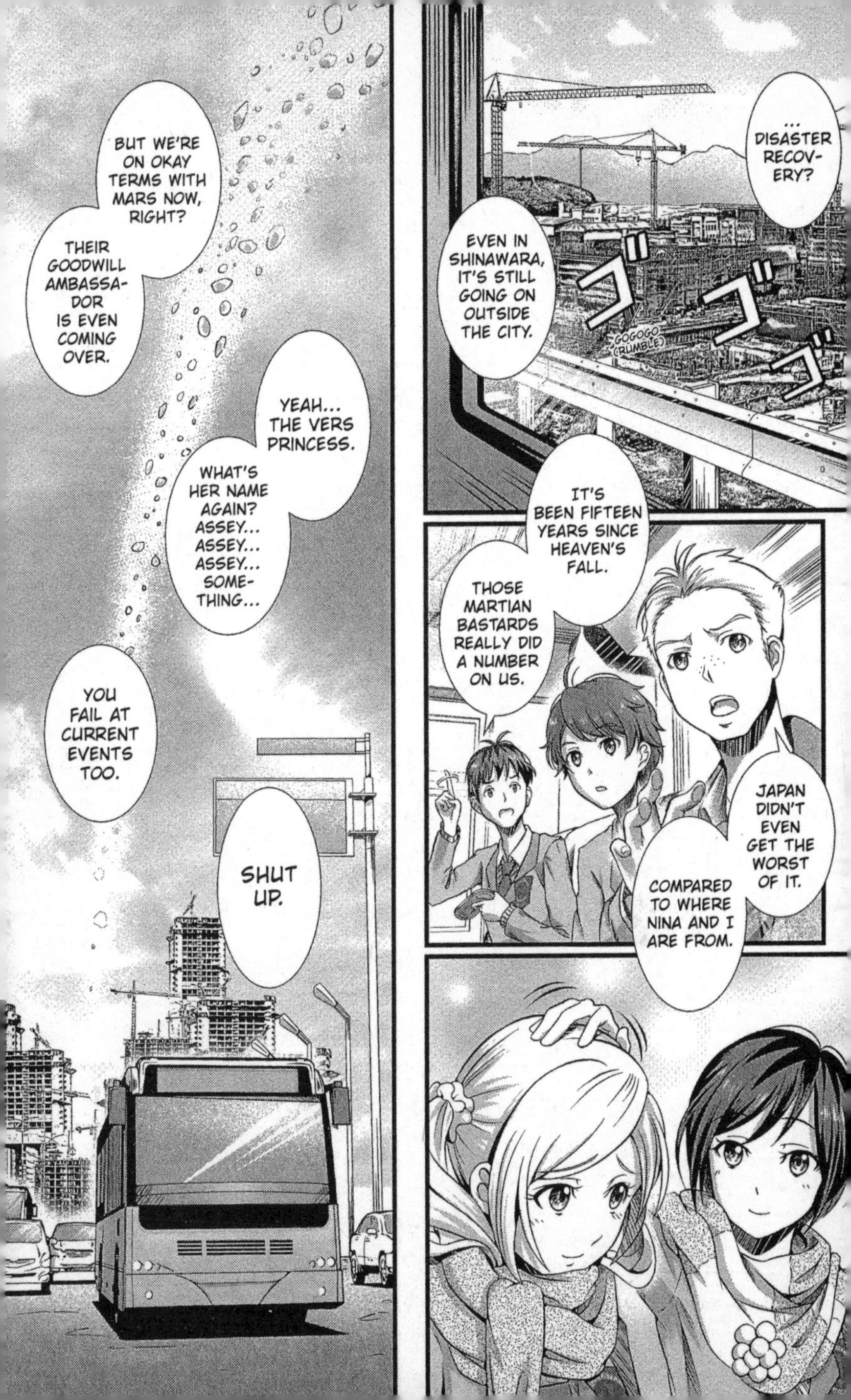
...DISASTER RECOVERY?
EVEN IN SHINAWARA, IT'S STILL GOING ON OUTSIDE THE CITY.
GOGOGO (CRUMBLE)
IT'S BEEN FIFTEEN YEARS SINCE HEAVEN'S FALL.
THOSE MARTIAN BASTARDS REALLY DID A NUMBER ON US.
JAPAN DIDN'T EVEN GET THE WORST OF IT.
COMPARED TO WHERE NINA AND I ARE FROM.
BUT WE'RE ON OKAY TERMS WITH MARS NOW, RIGHT?
THEIR GOODWILL AMBASSADOR IS EVEN COMING OVER.
YEAH... THE VERS PRINCESS.
WHAT'S HER NAME AGAIN? ASSEY... ASSEY... ASSEY... SOMETHING...
YOU FAIL AT CURRENT EVENTS TOO.
SHUT UP.

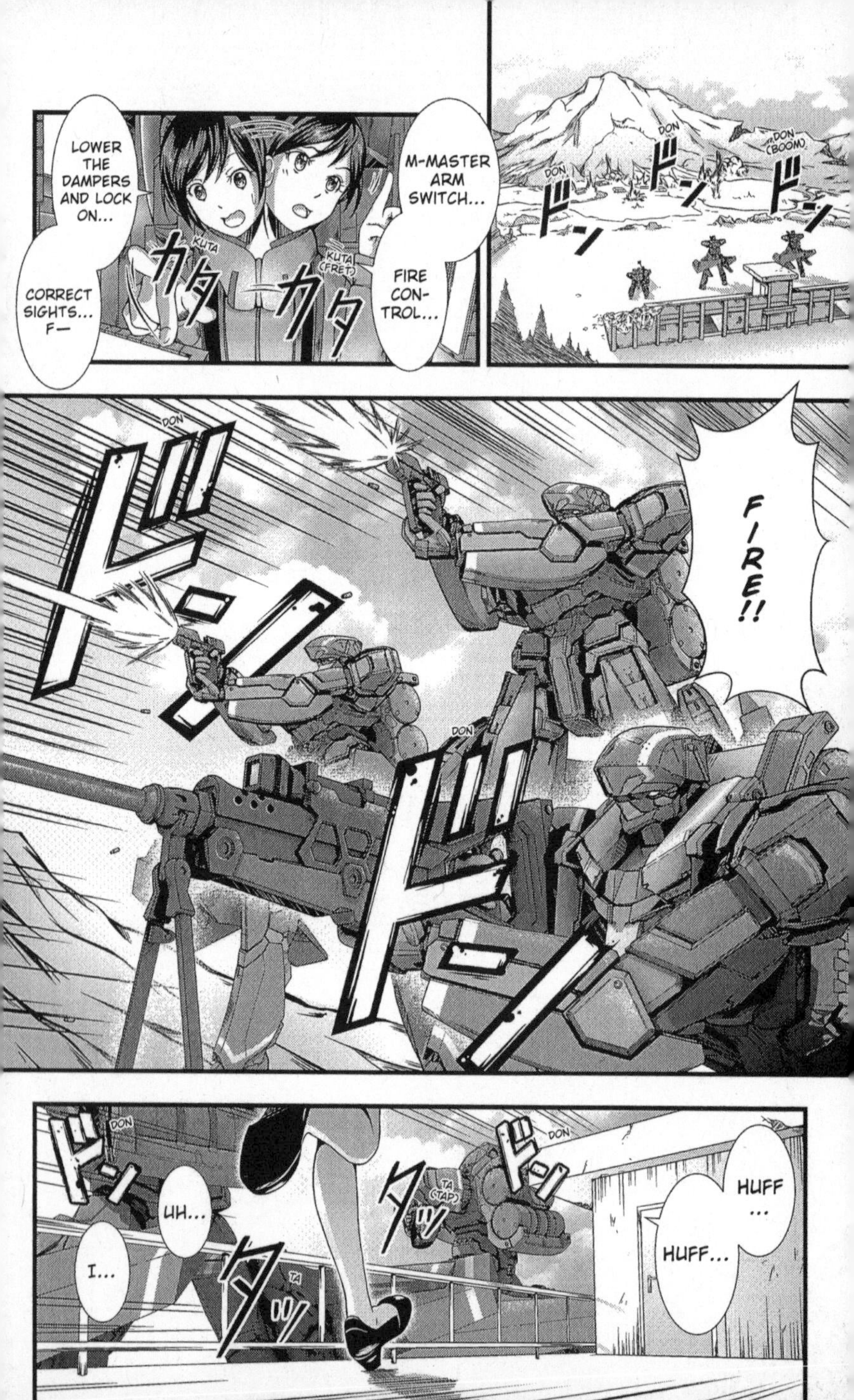
DON
DON (BOOM)
DON
M-MASTER ARM SWITCH...
FIRE CON-TROL...
KUTA (FRET)
KUTA
LOWER THE DAMPERS AND LOCK ON...
CORRECT SIGHTS... F—
FIRE!!
DON
DON
HUFF...
HUFF...
DON
TA (TAP)
UH...
I...
TA
DON

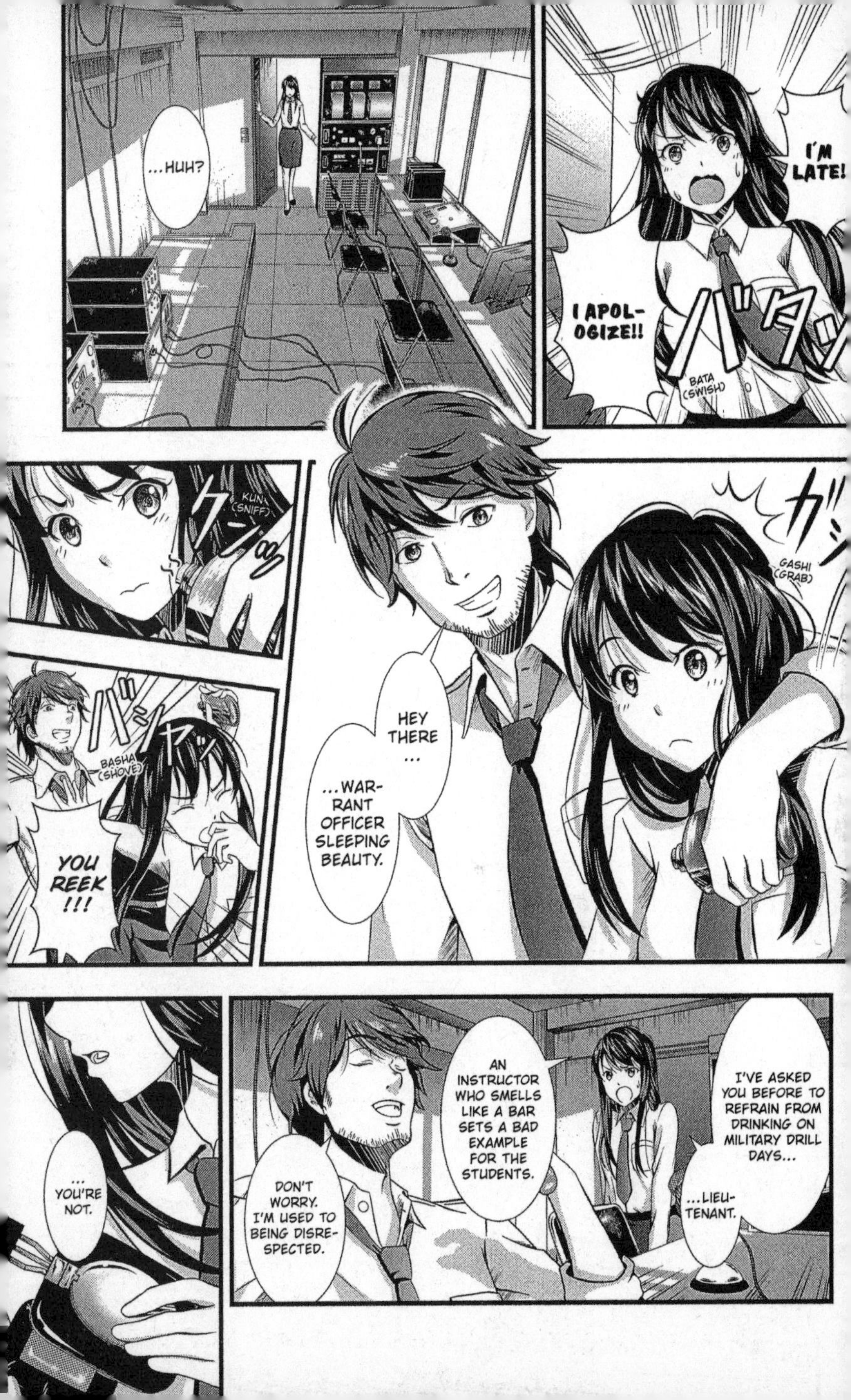
I'M LATE!
I APOLOGIZE!!
BATA (SWISH)
...HUH?
GASHI (GRAB)
HEY THERE...
...WARRANT OFFICER SLEEPING BEAUTY.
KUN (SNIFF)
BASHA (SHOVE)
YOU REEK!!!
I'VE ASKED YOU BEFORE TO REFRAIN FROM DRINKING ON MILITARY DRILL DAYS...
...LIEUTENANT.
AN INSTRUCTOR WHO SMELLS LIKE A BAR SETS A BAD EXAMPLE FOR THE STUDENTS.
DON'T WORRY. I'M USED TO BEING DISRESPECTED.
...YOU'RE NOT.

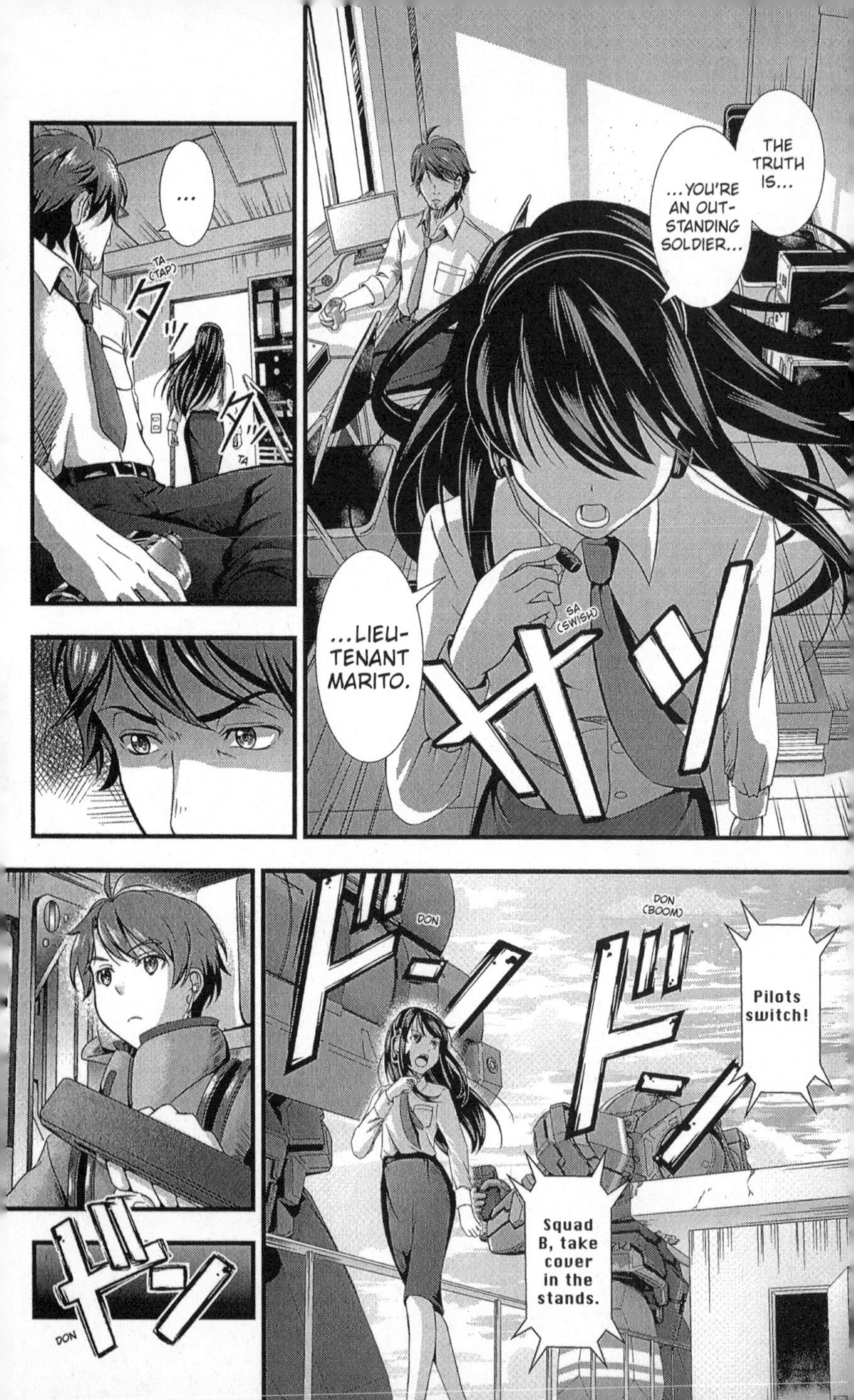
THE TRUTH IS...
...YOU'RE AN OUT-STANDING SOLDIER...
...LIEU-TENANT MARITO.
SA (SWISH)
...
TA (TAP)
TA
DON (BOOM)
DON
Pilots switch!
Squad B, take cover in the stands.
DON

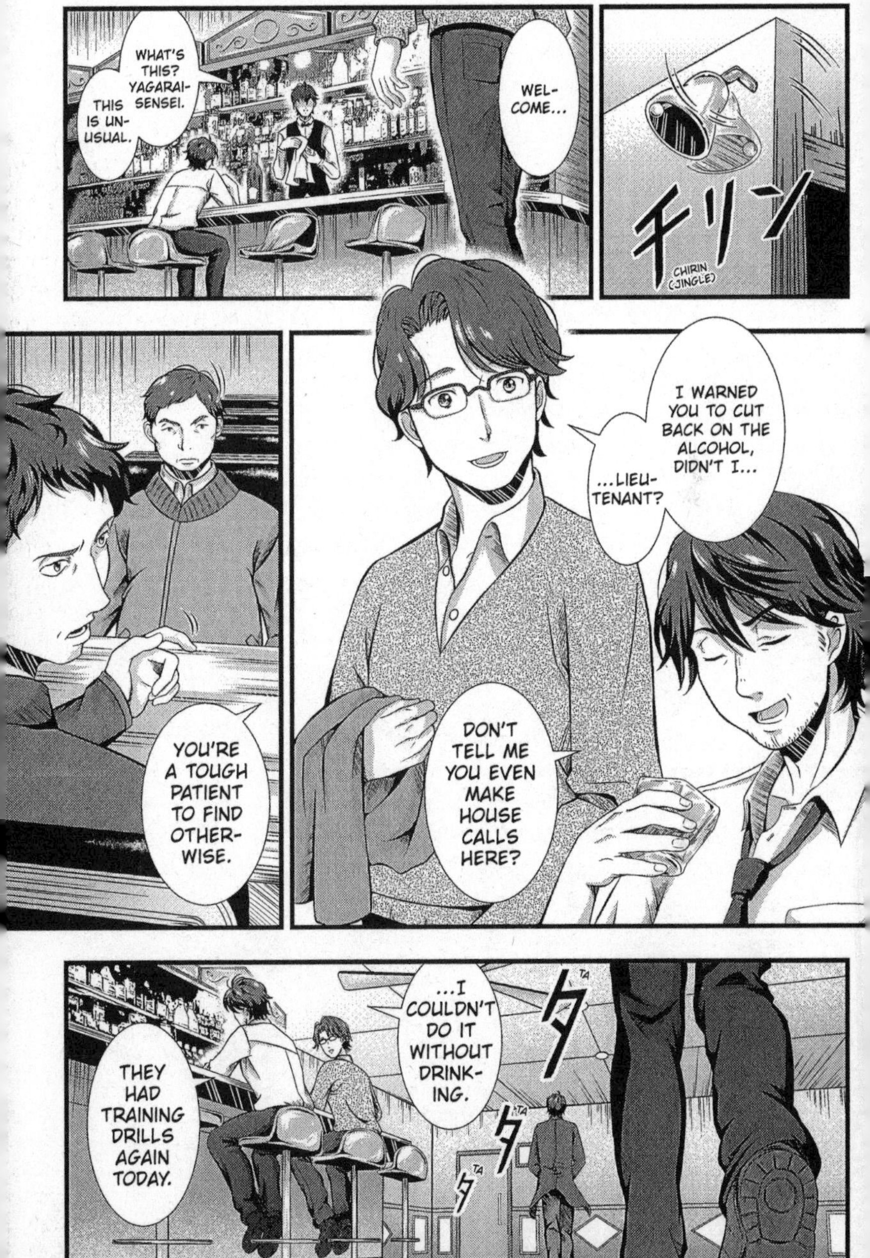

チリン
CHIRIN (JINGLE)
WEL-COME...
WHAT'S THIS? YAGARAI-SENSEI.
THIS IS UN-USUAL.
I WARNED YOU TO CUT BACK ON THE ALCOHOL, DIDN'T I...
...LIEU-TENANT?
DON'T TELL ME YOU EVEN MAKE HOUSE CALLS HERE?
YOU'RE A TOUGH PATIENT TO FIND OTHER-WISE.
タ TA
タ TA
タ TA
...I COULDN'T DO IT WITHOUT DRINK-ING.
THEY HAD TRAINING DRILLS AGAIN TODAY.

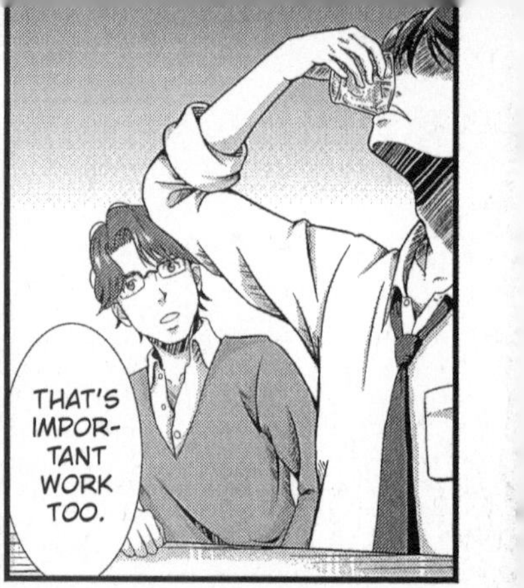
THAT'S IMPOR-TANT WORK TOO.

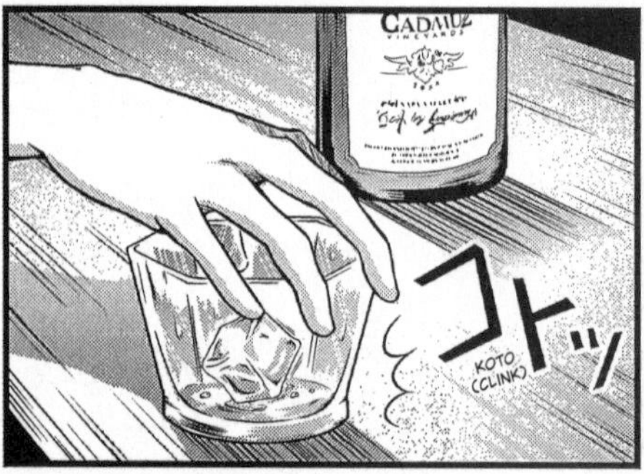
CADMUZ
コトッ
KOTO (CLINK)

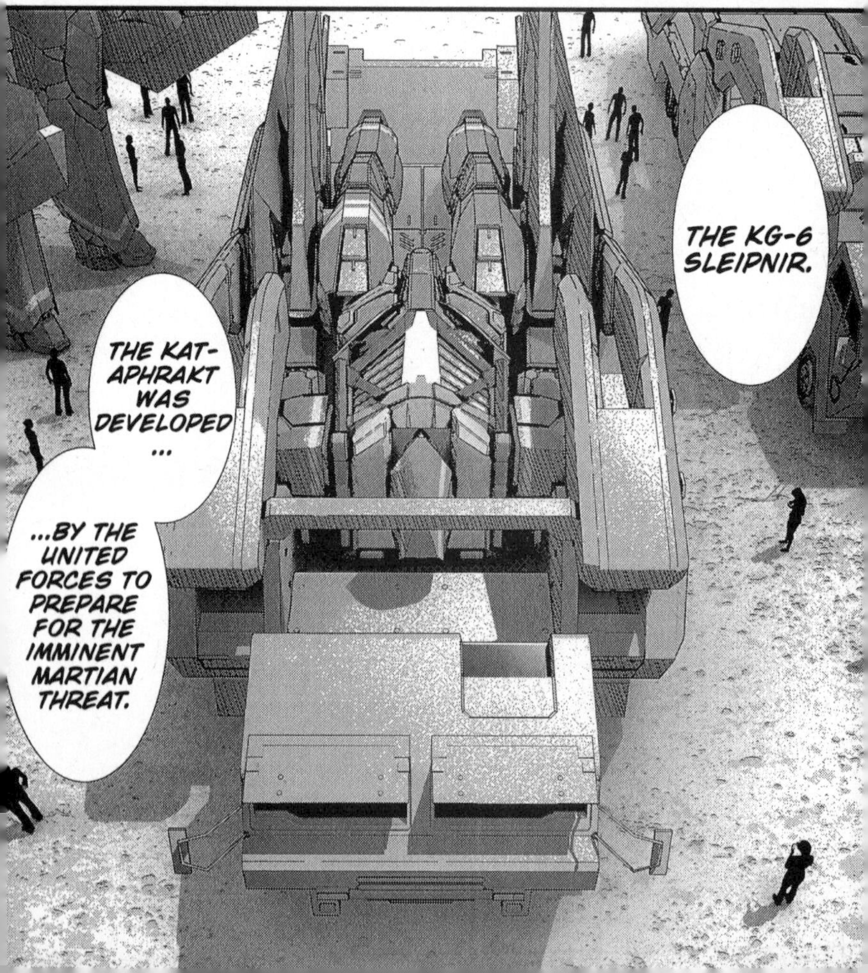
THE KG-6 SLEIPNIR.
THE KAT-APHRAKT WAS DEVELOPED...
...BY THE UNITED FORCES TO PREPARE FOR THE IMMINENT MARTIAN THREAT.

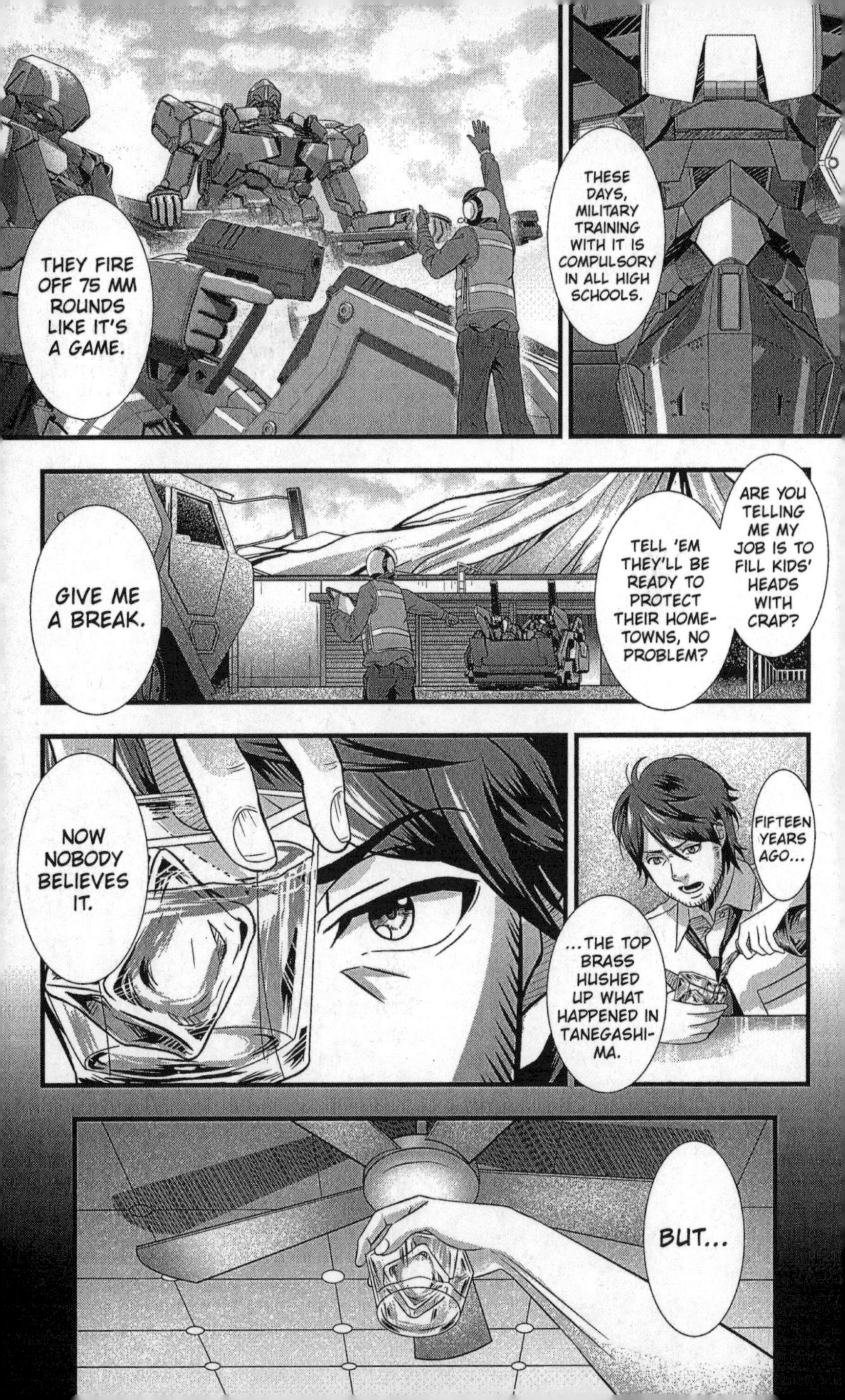
THESE DAYS, MILITARY TRAINING WITH IT IS COMPULSORY IN ALL HIGH SCHOOLS.
THEY FIRE OFF 75 MM ROUNDS LIKE IT'S A GAME.
ARE YOU TELLING ME MY JOB IS TO FILL KIDS' HEADS WITH CRAP?
TELL 'EM THEY'LL BE READY TO PROTECT THEIR HOME-TOWNS, NO PROBLEM?
GIVE ME A BREAK.
FIFTEEN YEARS AGO...
...THE TOP BRASS HUSHED UP WHAT HAPPENED IN TANEGASHI-MA.
NOW NOBODY BELIEVES IT.
BUT...

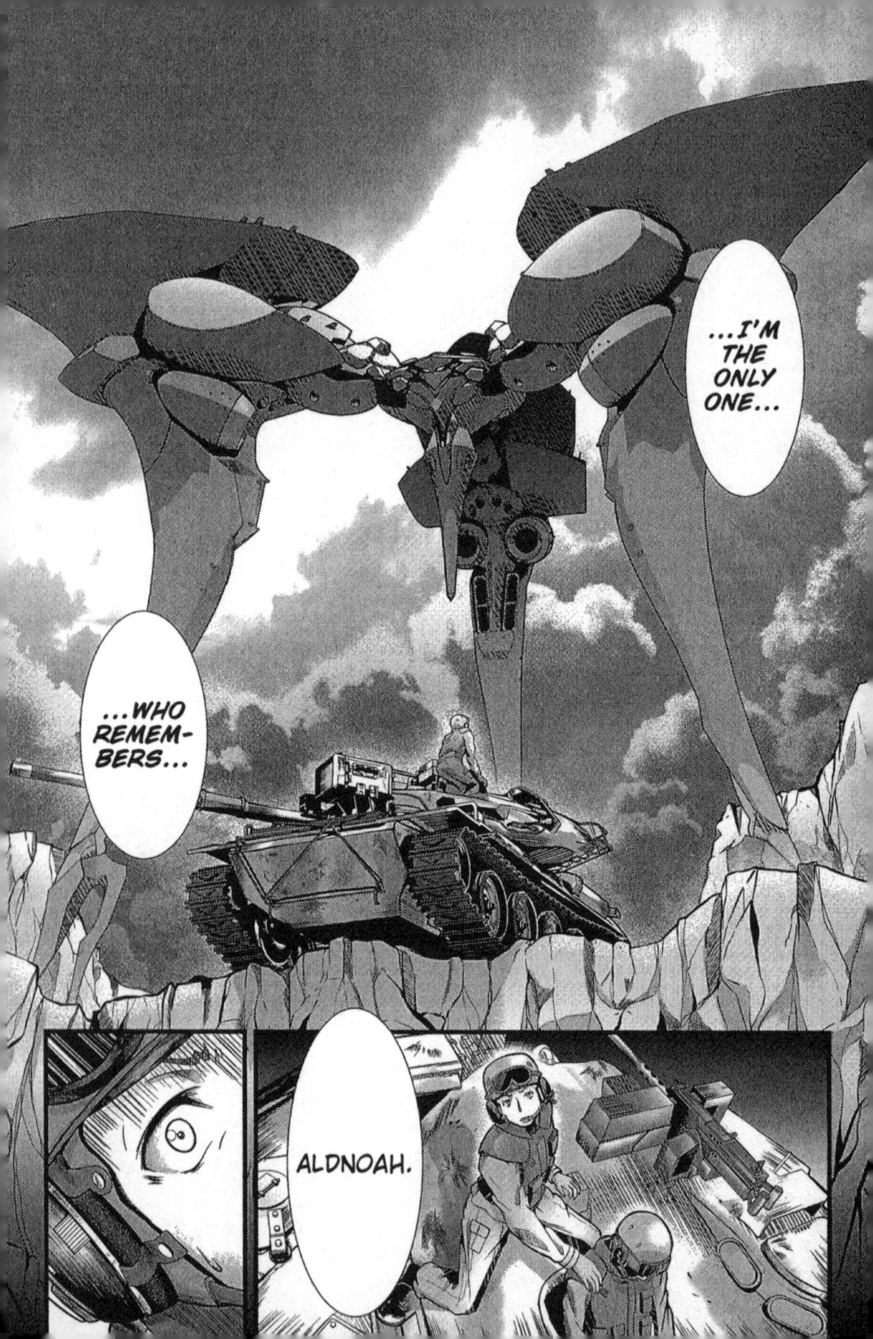
...I'M THE ONLY ONE...
...WHO REMEM-BERS...
ALDNOAH.

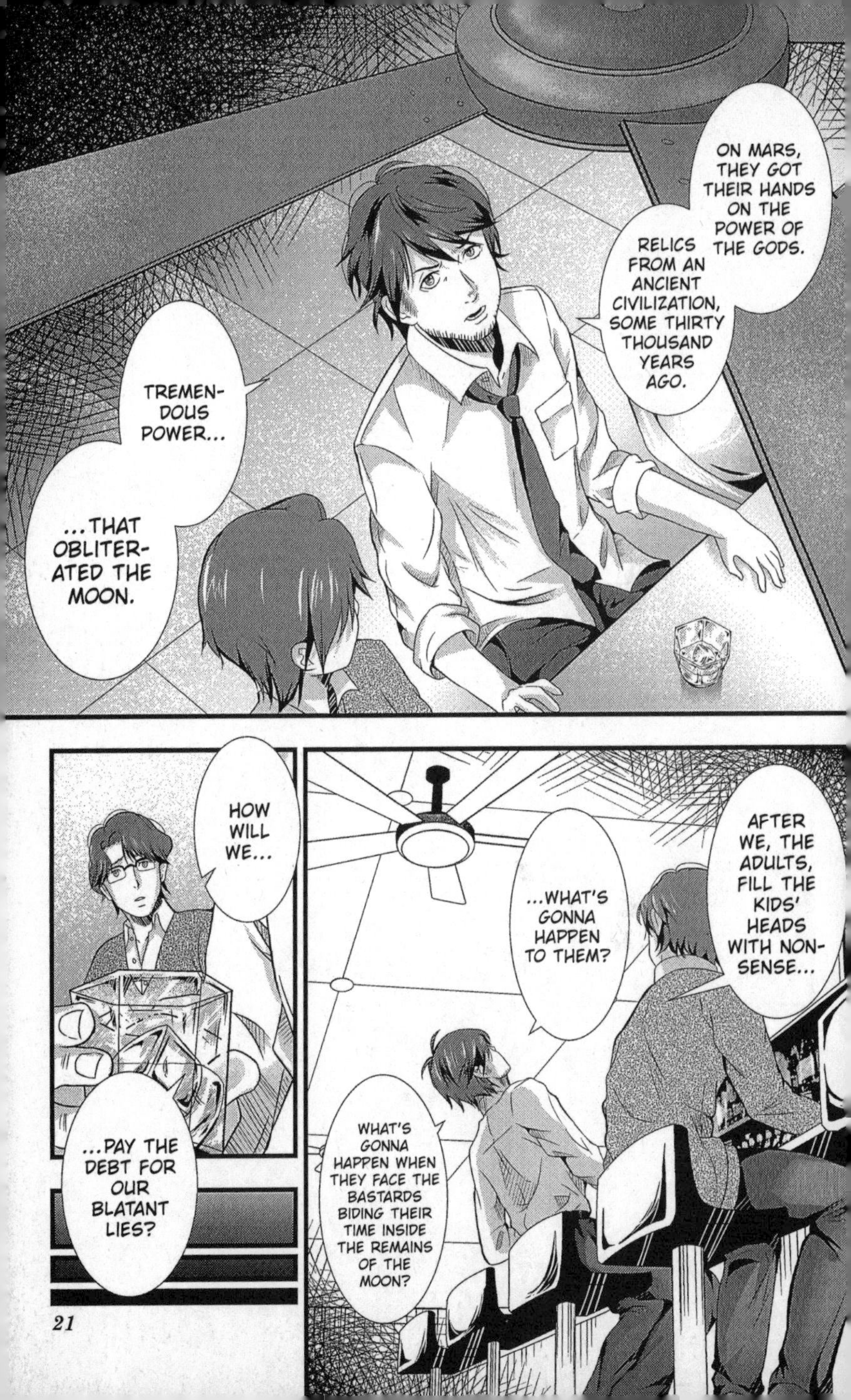
ON MARS, THEY GOT THEIR HANDS ON THE POWER OF THE GODS.
RELICS FROM AN ANCIENT CIVILIZATION, SOME THIRTY THOUSAND YEARS AGO.
TREMEN-DOUS POWER...
...THAT OBLITER-ATED THE MOON.
AFTER WE, THE ADULTS, FILL THE KIDS' HEADS WITH NON-SENSE...
...WHAT'S GONNA HAPPEN TO THEM?
WHAT'S GONNA HAPPEN WHEN THEY FACE THE BASTARDS BIDING THEIR TIME INSIDE THE REMAINS OF THE MOON?
HOW WILL WE...
...PAY THE DEBT FOR OUR BLATANT LIES?

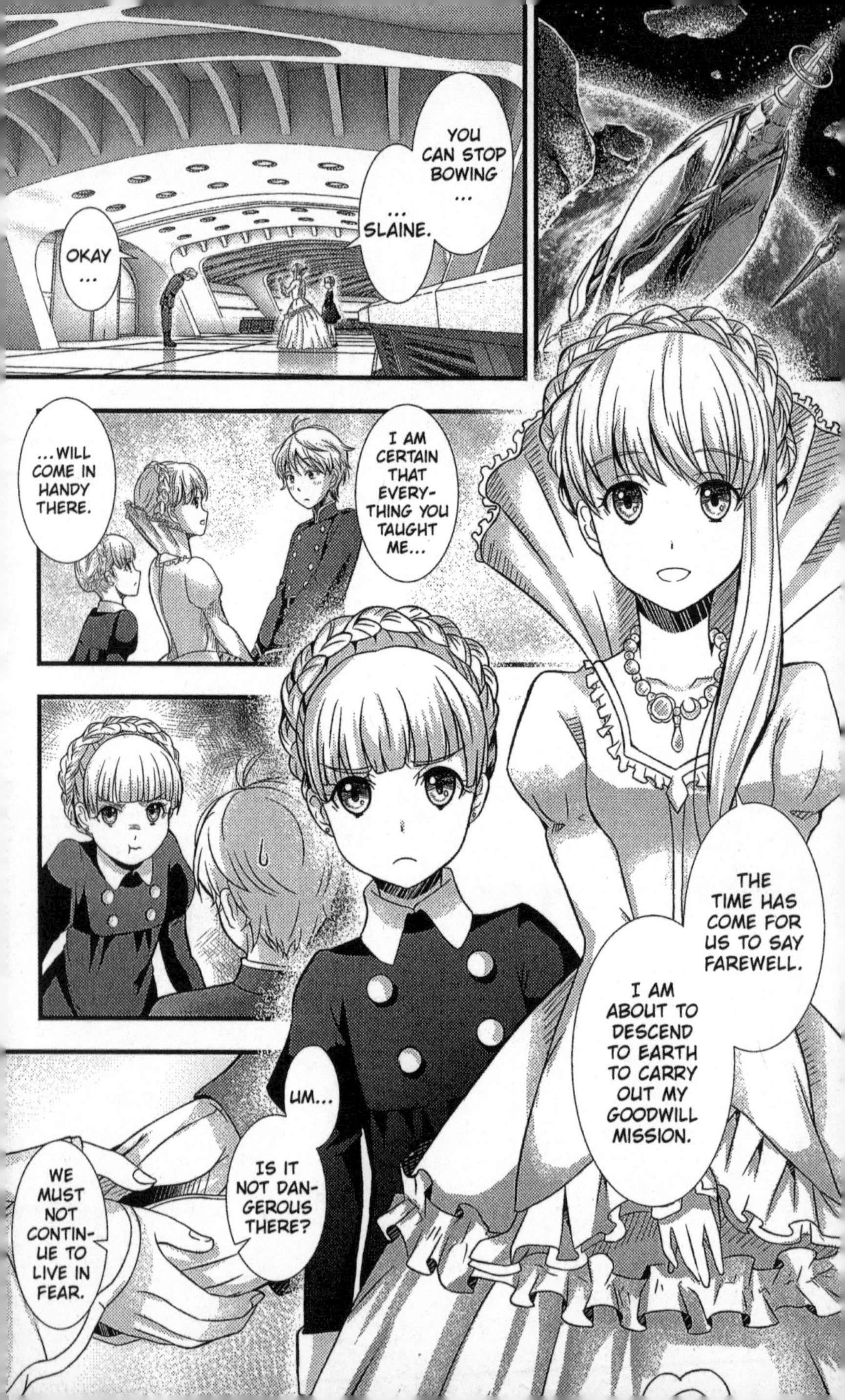
YOU CAN STOP BOWING ... ... SLAINE.
OKAY ...
THE TIME HAS COME FOR US TO SAY FAREWELL.
I AM ABOUT TO DESCEND TO EARTH TO CARRY OUT MY GOODWILL MISSION.
I AM CERTAIN THAT EVERY-THING YOU TAUGHT ME...
...WILL COME IN HANDY THERE.
UM...
IS IT NOT DAN-GEROUS THERE?
WE MUST NOT CONTIN-UE TO LIVE IN FEAR.

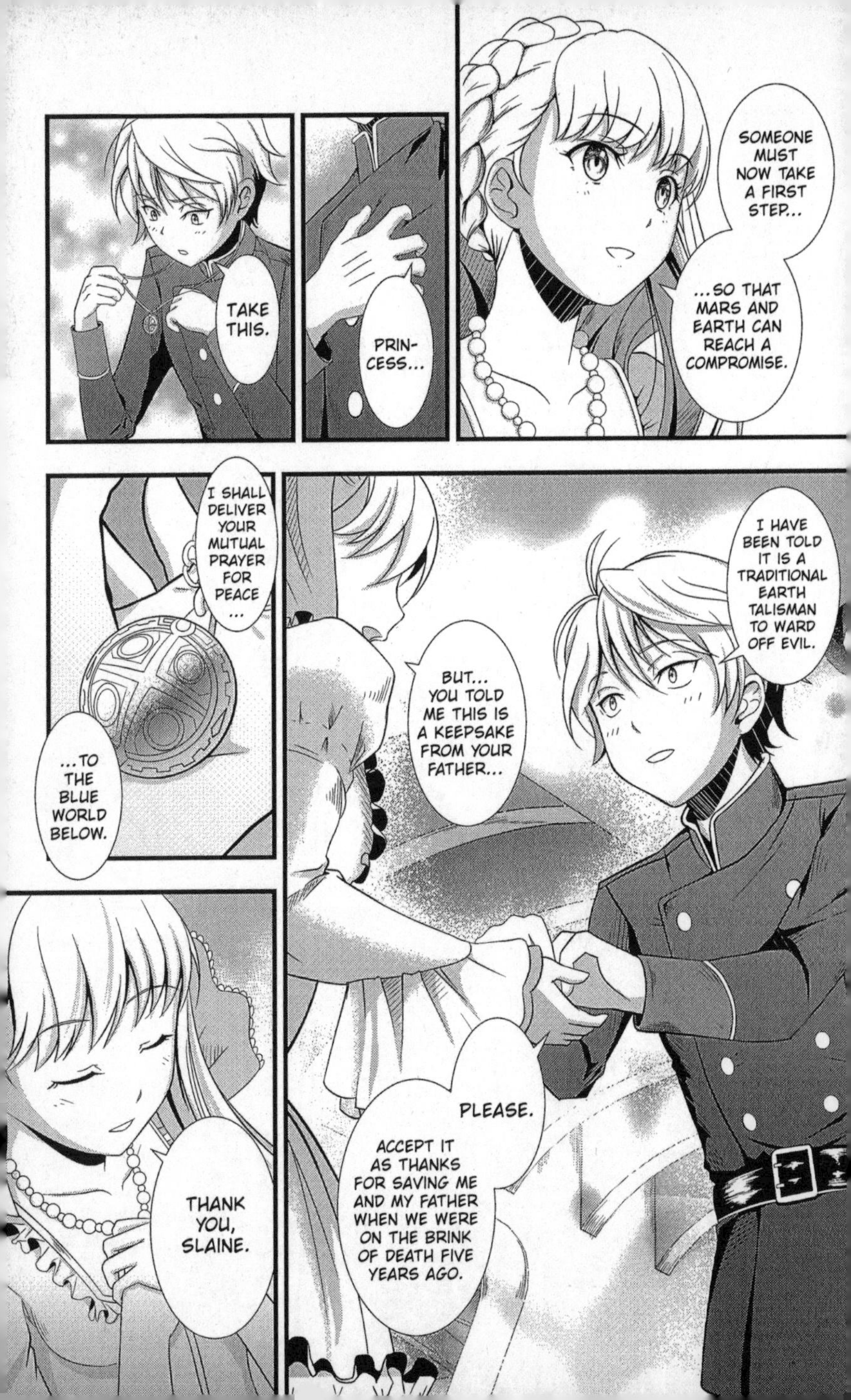
SOMEONE MUST NOW TAKE A FIRST STEP...
...SO THAT MARS AND EARTH CAN REACH A COMPROMISE.
PRIN-CESS...
TAKE THIS.
I HAVE BEEN TOLD IT IS A TRADITIONAL EARTH TALISMAN TO WARD OFF EVIL.
BUT... YOU TOLD ME THIS IS A KEEPSAKE FROM YOUR FATHER...
PLEASE.
ACCEPT IT AS THANKS FOR SAVING ME AND MY FATHER WHEN WE WERE ON THE BRINK OF DEATH FIVE YEARS AGO.
I SHALL DELIVER YOUR MUTUAL PRAYER FOR PEACE...
...TO THE BLUE WORLD BELOW.
THANK YOU, SLAINE.

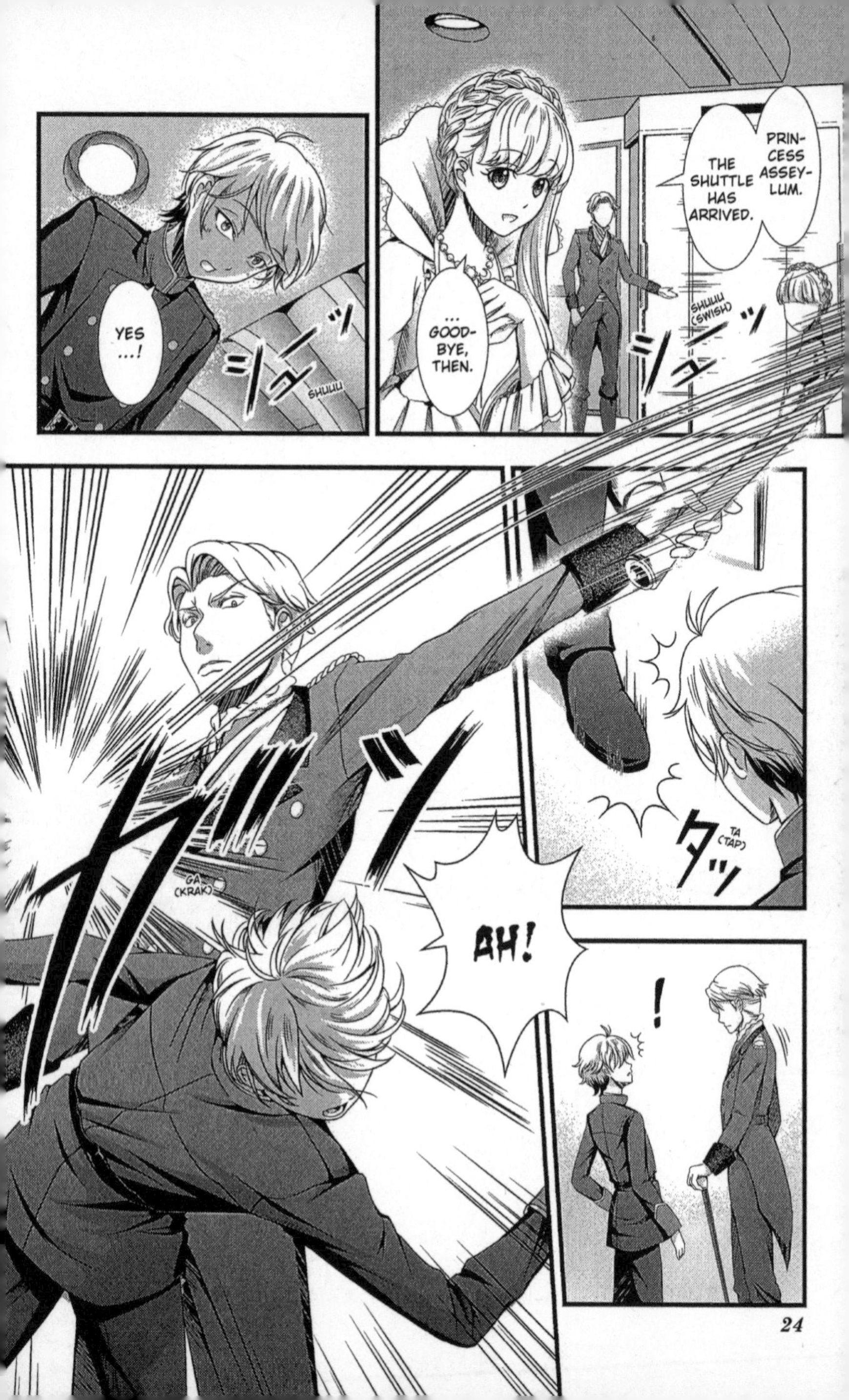
PRIN-CESS ASSEY-LUM.
THE SHUTTLE HAS ARRIVED.
... GOOD-BYE, THEN.
SHUUU (SWISH)
YES ...!
SHUUU
TA (TAP)
!
GA (KRAK)
AH!

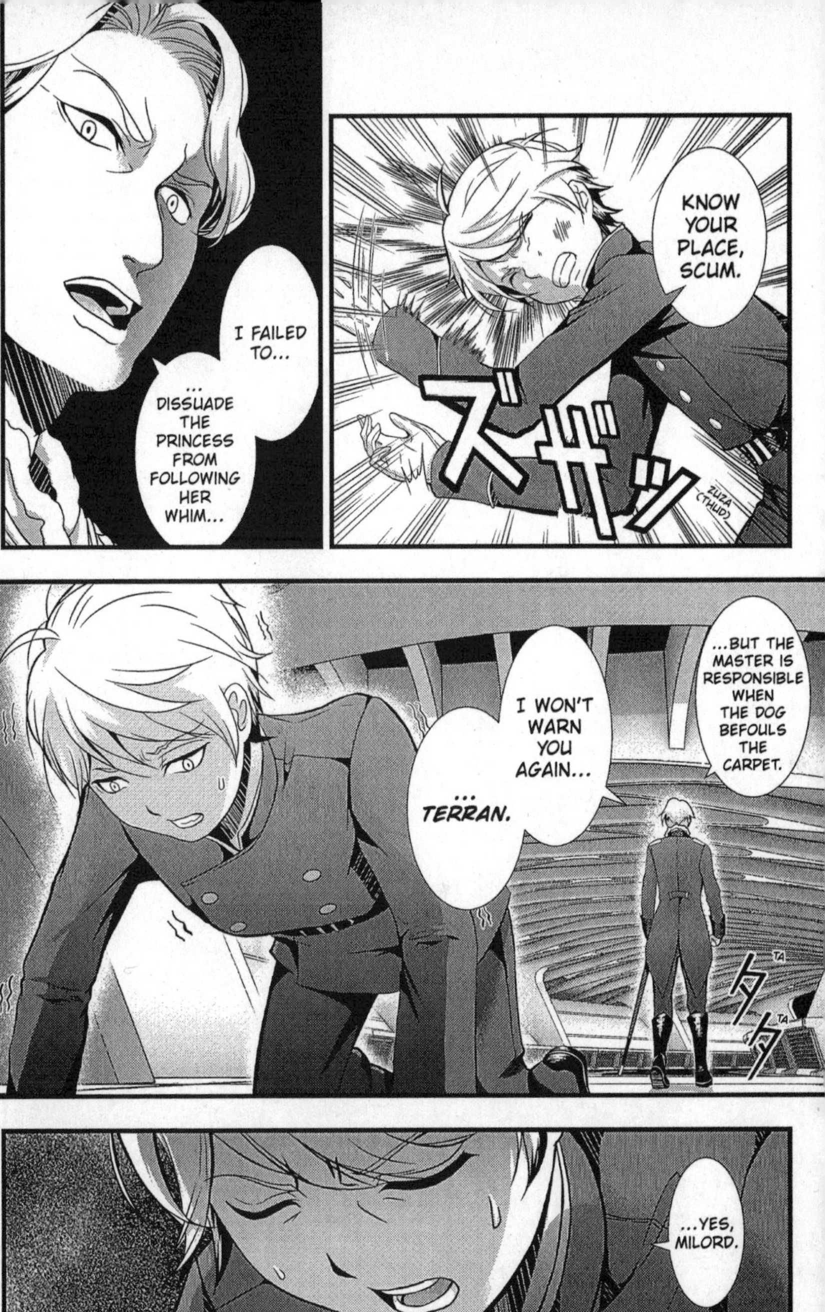
KNOW YOUR PLACE, SCUM.
ZUZA (THUD)
I FAILED TO...
...DISSUADE THE PRINCESS FROM FOLLOWING HER WHIM...
...BUT THE MASTER IS RESPONSIBLE WHEN THE DOG BEFOULS THE CARPET.
I WON'T WARN YOU AGAIN...
...TERRAN.
TA
TA
...YES, MILORD.

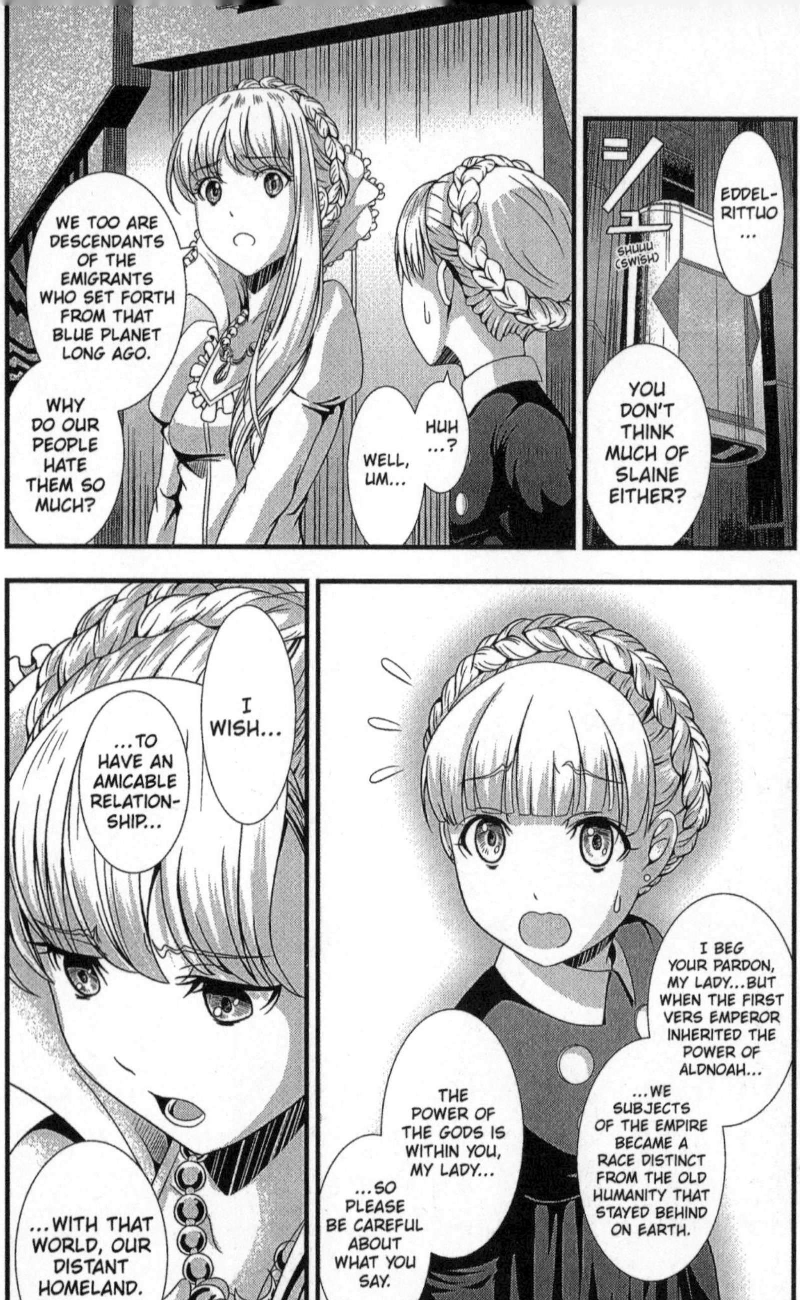
EDDEL-RITTUO...
SHUUU (SWISH)
YOU DON'T THINK MUCH OF SLAINE EITHER?
HUH...?
WELL, UM...
WE TOO ARE DESCENDANTS OF THE EMIGRANTS WHO SET FORTH FROM THAT BLUE PLANET LONG AGO.
WHY DO OUR PEOPLE HATE THEM SO MUCH?
I BEG YOUR PARDON, MY LADY...BUT WHEN THE FIRST VERS EMPEROR INHERITED THE POWER OF ALDNOAH...
...WE SUBJECTS OF THE EMPIRE BECAME A RACE DISTINCT FROM THE OLD HUMANITY THAT STAYED BEHIND ON EARTH.
THE POWER OF THE GODS IS WITHIN YOU, MY LADY...
...SO PLEASE BE CAREFUL ABOUT WHAT YOU SAY.
I WISH...
...TO HAVE AN AMICABLE RELATION-SHIP...
...WITH THAT WORLD, OUR DISTANT HOMELAND.

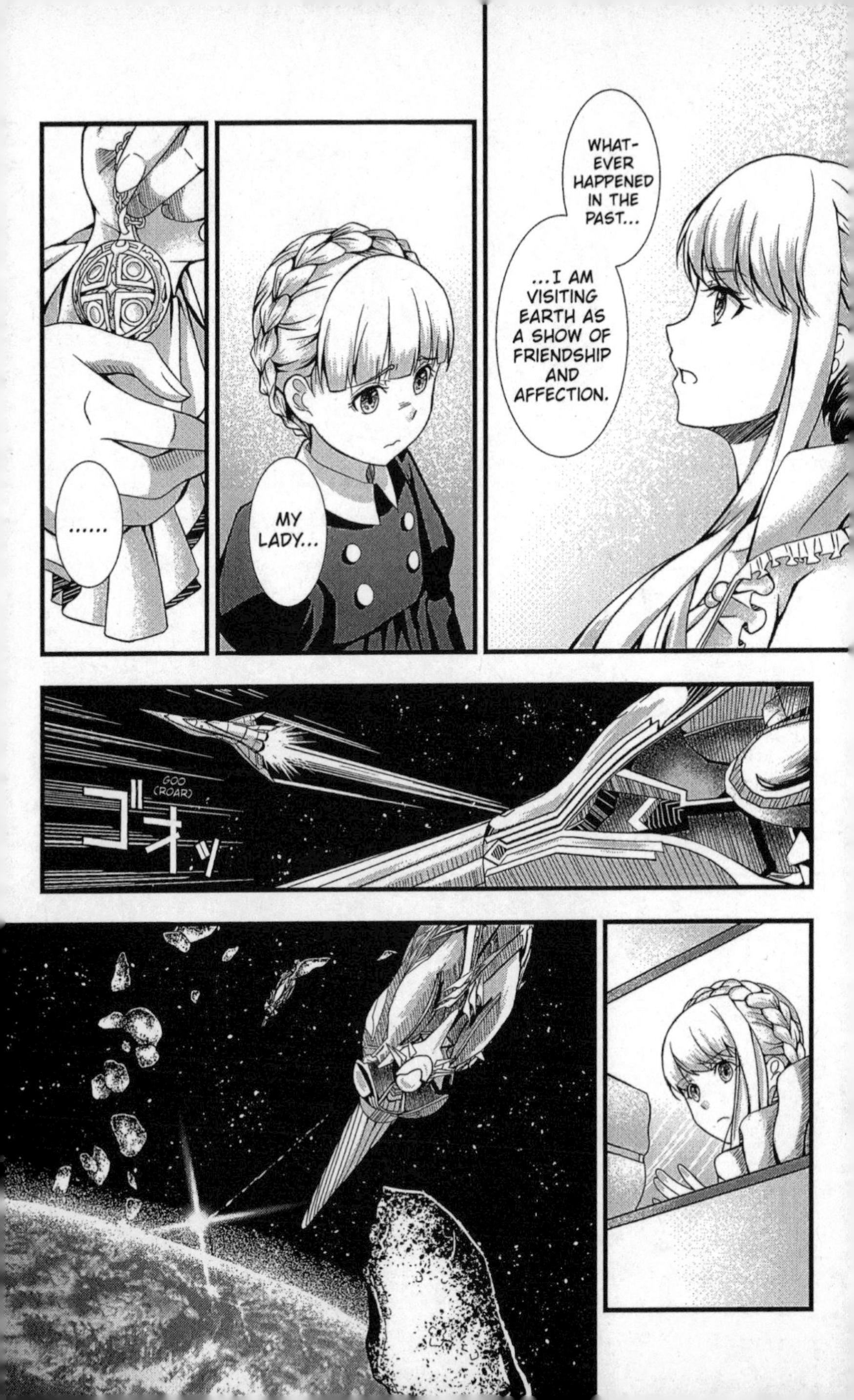
WHAT-EVER HAPPENED IN THE PAST...
...I AM VISITING EARTH AS A SHOW OF FRIENDSHIP AND AFFECTION.
MY LADY...
......
GOO (ROAR)
ゴオッ

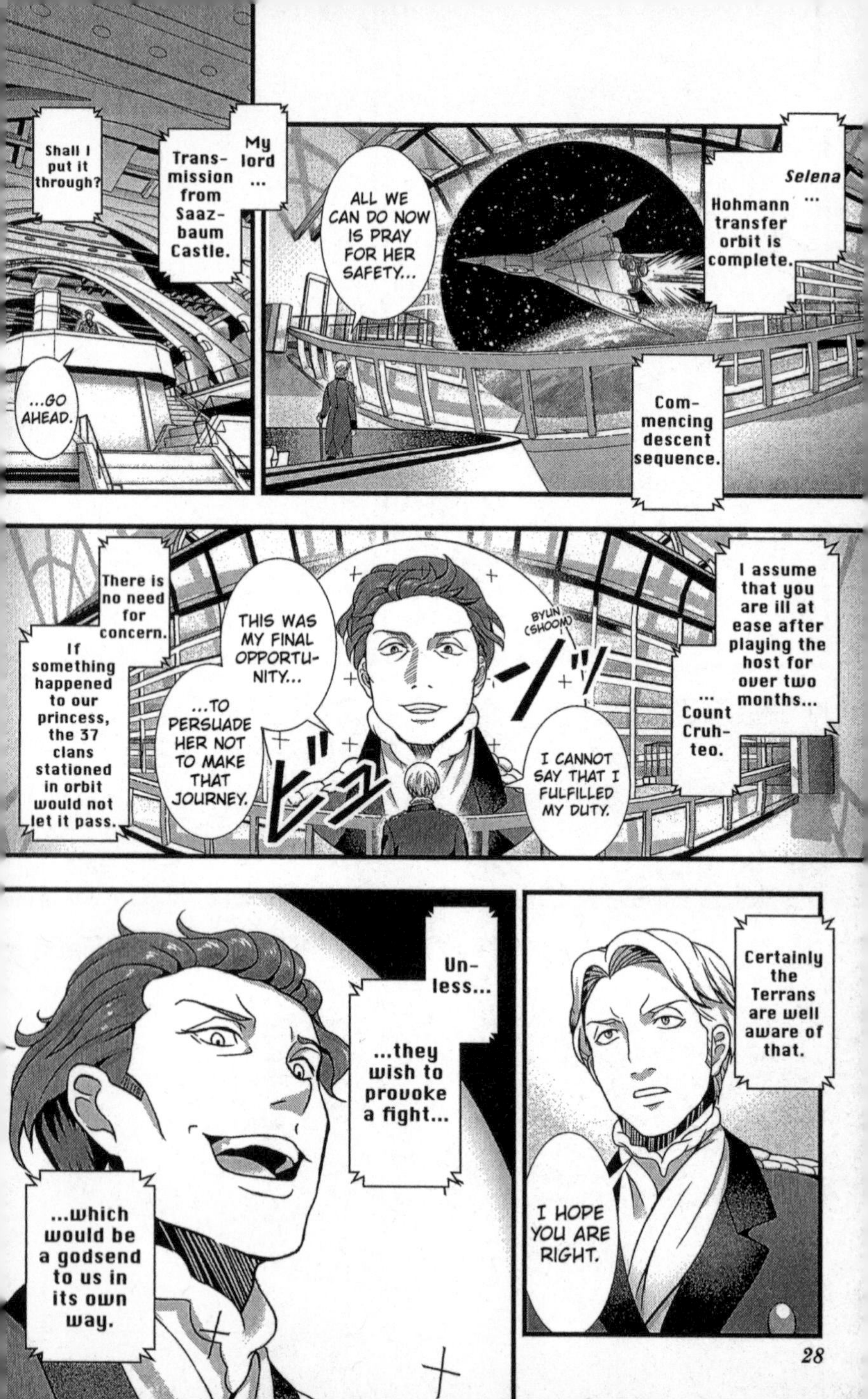
Selena ... Hohmann transfer orbit is complete.
Commencing descent sequence.
ALL WE CAN DO NOW IS PRAY FOR HER SAFETY...
My lord ...
Transmission from Saazbaum Castle.
Shall I put it through?
...GO AHEAD.
I assume that you are ill at ease after playing the host for over two months...
... Count Cruhteo.
I CANNOT SAY THAT I FULFILLED MY DUTY.
BYUN (SHOOM)
THIS WAS MY FINAL OPPORTUNITY...
...TO PERSUADE HER NOT TO MAKE THAT JOURNEY.
There is no need for concern.
If something happened to our princess, the 37 clans stationed in orbit would not let it pass.
Certainly the Terrans are well aware of that.
I HOPE YOU ARE RIGHT.
Unless...
...they wish to provoke a fight...
...which would be a godsend to us in its own way.

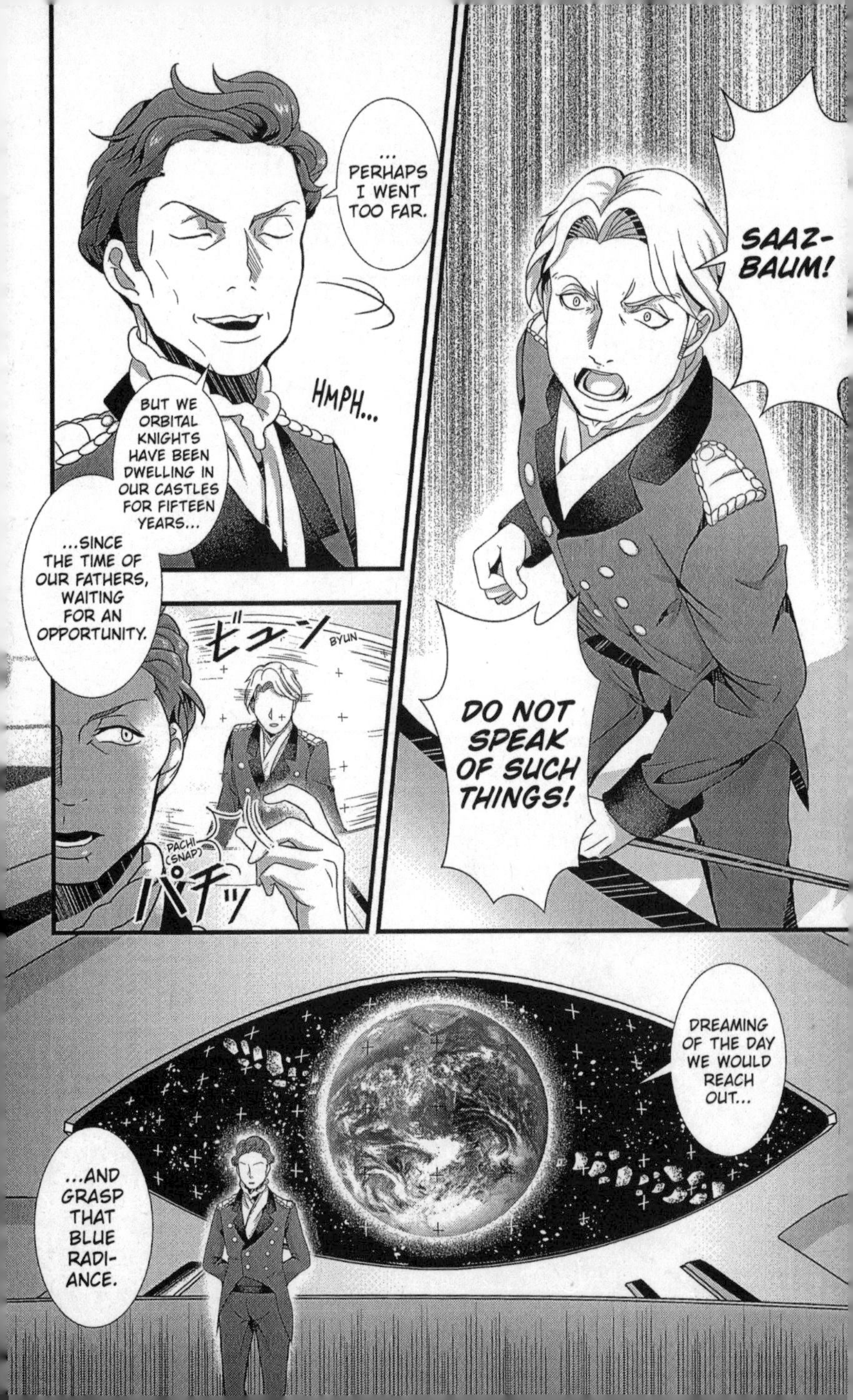
SAAZ-BAUM!
DO NOT SPEAK OF SUCH THINGS!
... PERHAPS I WENT TOO FAR.
HMPH...
BUT WE ORBITAL KNIGHTS HAVE BEEN DWELLING IN OUR CASTLES FOR FIFTEEN YEARS...
...SINCE THE TIME OF OUR FATHERS, WAITING FOR AN OPPORTUNITY.
ビュン
BYUN
PACHI (SNAP)
パチッ
DREAMING OF THE DAY WE WOULD REACH OUT...
...AND GRASP THAT BLUE RADI-ANCE.

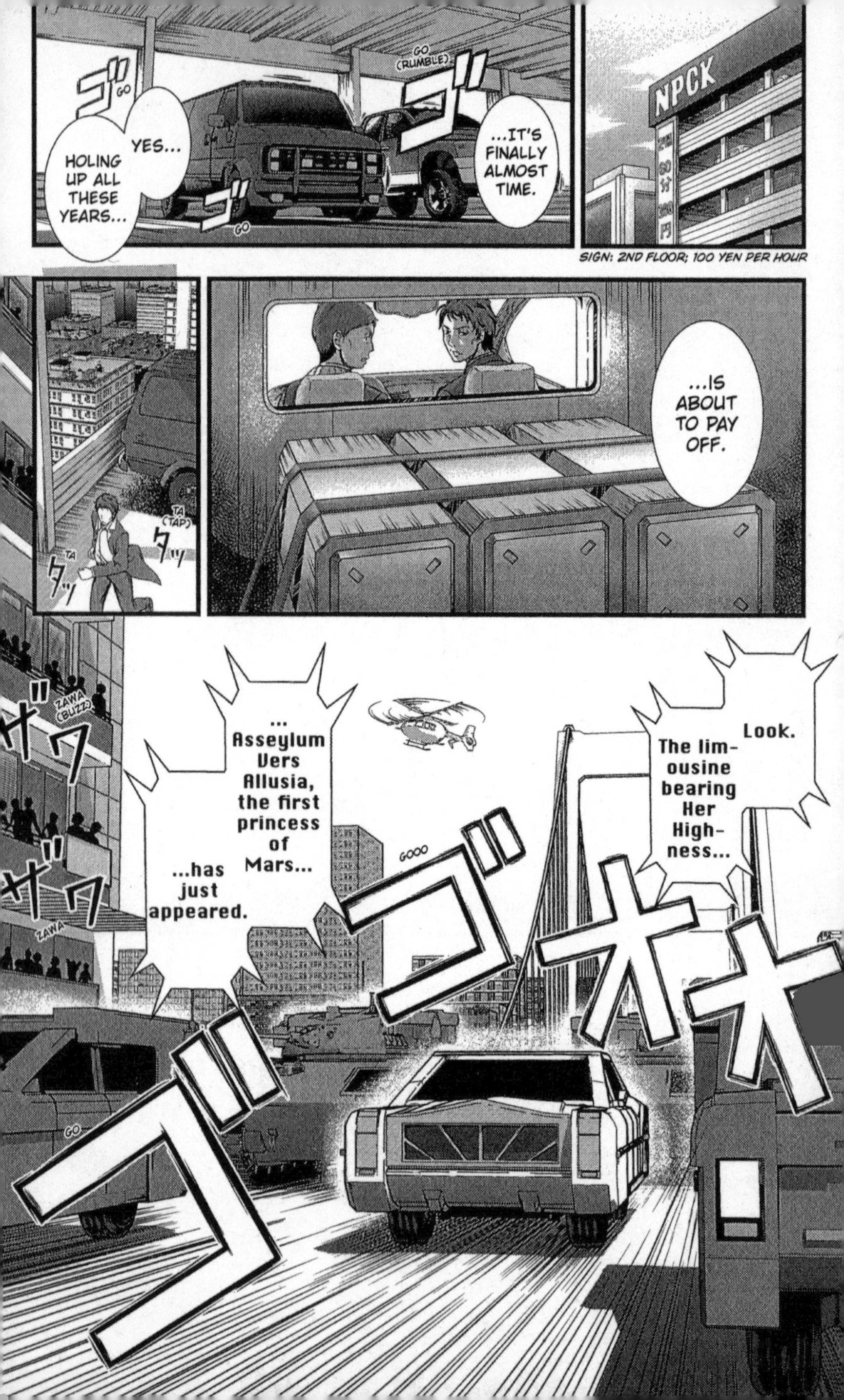
NPCK
SIGN: 2ND FLOOR; 100 YEN PER HOUR
GO (RUMBLE)
...IT'S FINALLY ALMOST TIME.
YES...
HOLING UP ALL THESE YEARS...
GO
GO
...IS ABOUT TO PAY OFF.
TA (TAP)
TA
Look. The limousine bearing Her Highness...
...Asseylum Vers Allusia, the first princess of Mars...
...has just appeared.
GOOO
ZAWA (BUZZ)
ZAWA
GO

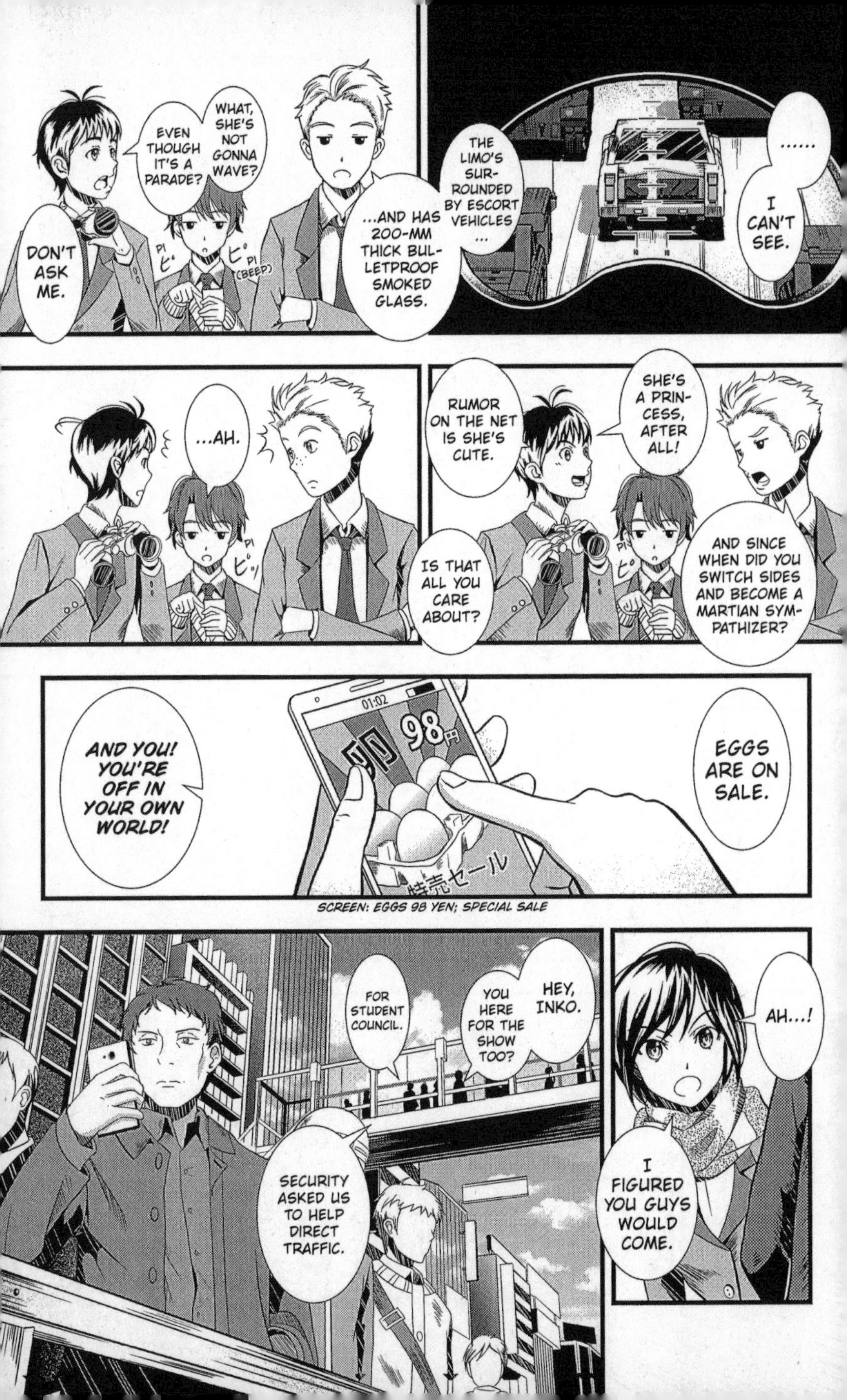
......
I CAN'T SEE.
THE LIMO'S SURROUNDED BY ESCORT VEHICLES ...
...AND HAS 200-MM THICK BULLETPROOF SMOKED GLASS.
WHAT, SHE'S NOT GONNA WAVE?
EVEN THOUGH IT'S A PARADE?
PI ピ
PI ピ (BEEP)
DON'T ASK ME.
SHE'S A PRINCESS, AFTER ALL!
RUMOR ON THE NET IS SHE'S CUTE.
AND SINCE WHEN DID YOU SWITCH SIDES AND BECOME A MARTIAN SYMPATHIZER?
IS THAT ALL YOU CARE ABOUT?
PI ピ
...AH.
PI ピ
01:02
卵 98円
特売セール
EGGS ARE ON SALE.
AND YOU! YOU'RE OFF IN YOUR OWN WORLD!
SCREEN: EGGS 98 YEN; SPECIAL SALE
AH...!
I FIGURED YOU GUYS WOULD COME.
HEY, INKO.
YOU HERE FOR THE SHOW TOO?
FOR STUDENT COUNCIL.
SECURITY ASKED US TO HELP DIRECT TRAFFIC.

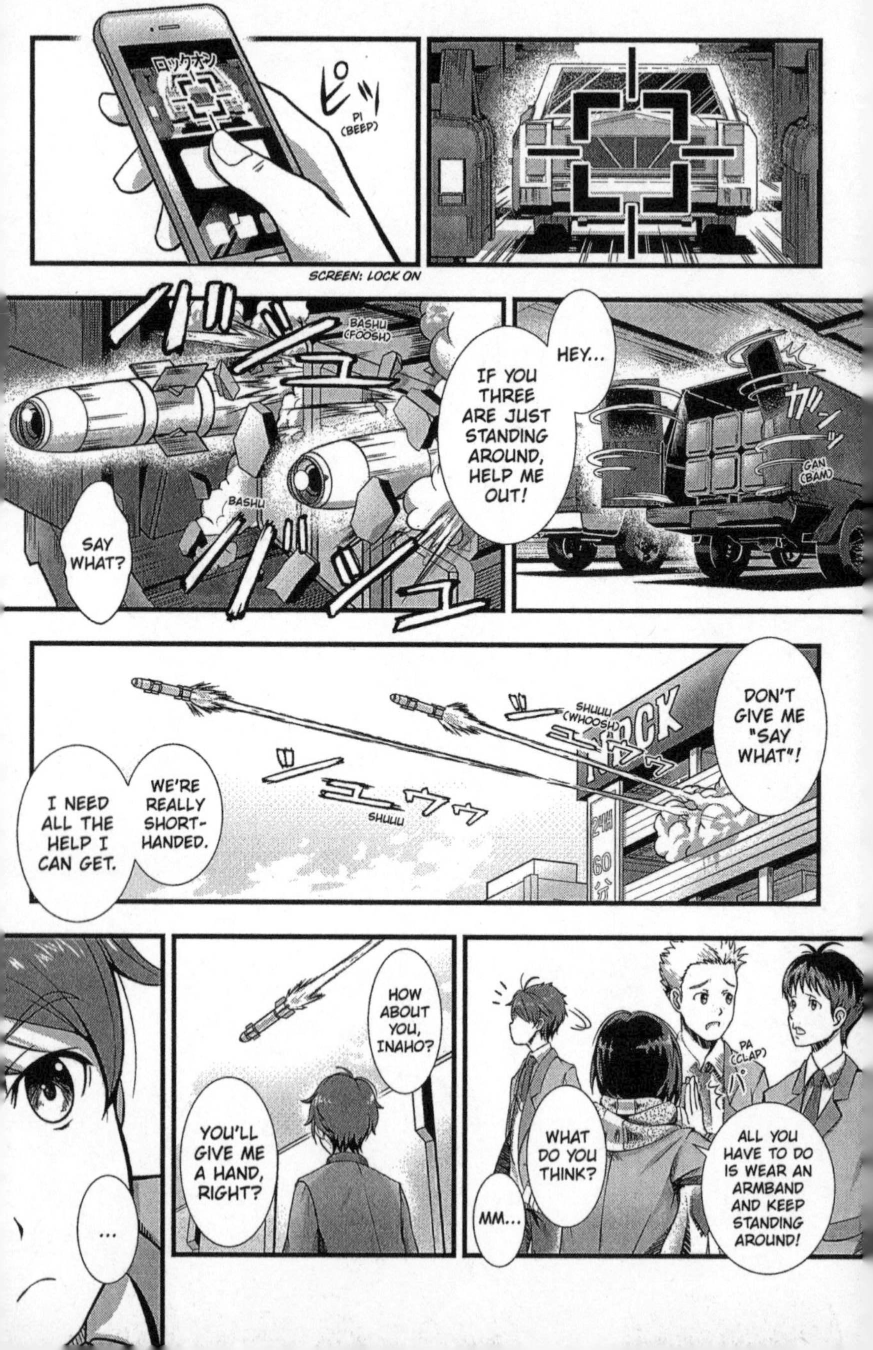
ロックオン
PI (BEEP)
SCREEN: LOCK ON
HEY...
IF YOU THREE ARE JUST STANDING AROUND, HELP ME OUT!
GAN (BAM)
BASHU (FOOSH)
BASHU
SAY WHAT?
DON'T GIVE ME "SAY WHAT"!
SHUUU (WHOOSH)
SHUUU
WE'RE REALLY SHORT-HANDED.
I NEED ALL THE HELP I CAN GET.
ALL YOU HAVE TO DO IS WEAR AN ARMBAND AND KEEP STANDING AROUND!
PA (CLAP)
WHAT DO YOU THINK?
MM...
HOW ABOUT YOU, INAHO?
YOU'LL GIVE ME A HAND, RIGHT?
...

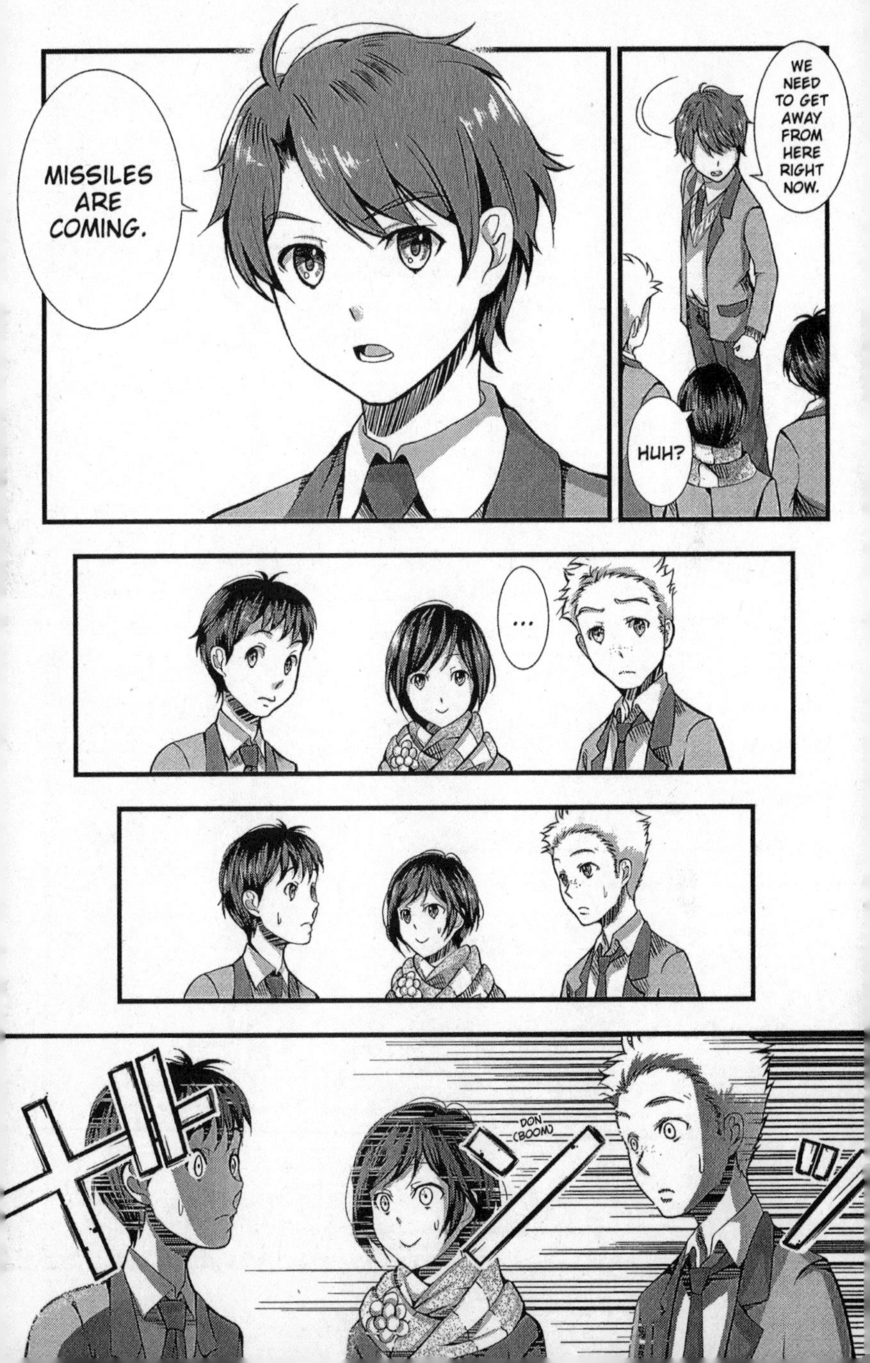
MISSILES ARE COMING.
WE NEED TO GET AWAY FROM HERE RIGHT NOW.
HUH?
...
DON (BOOM)

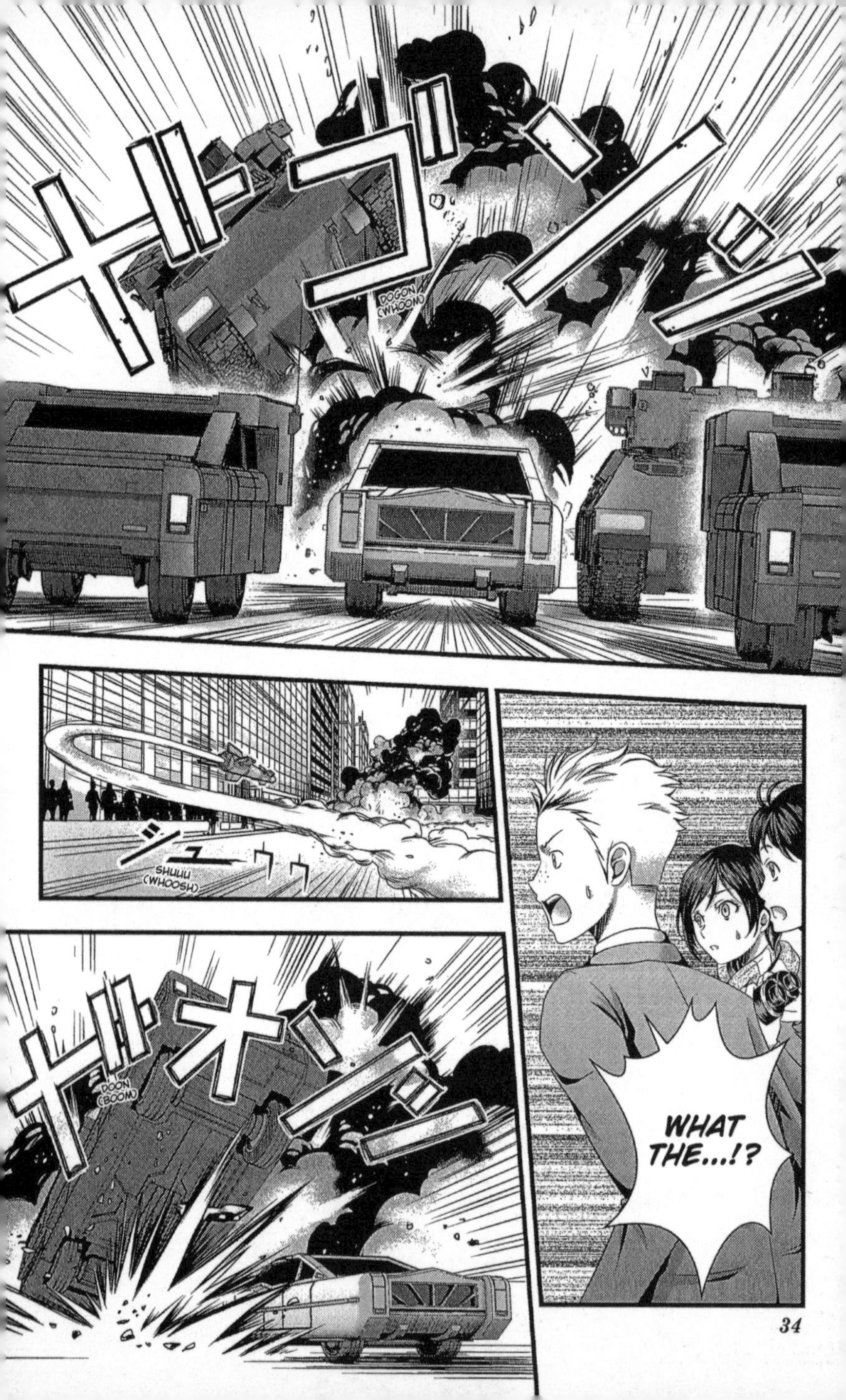
DOGON (WHOOM)
WHAT THE...!?
SHUUU (WHOOSH)
DOON (BOOM)

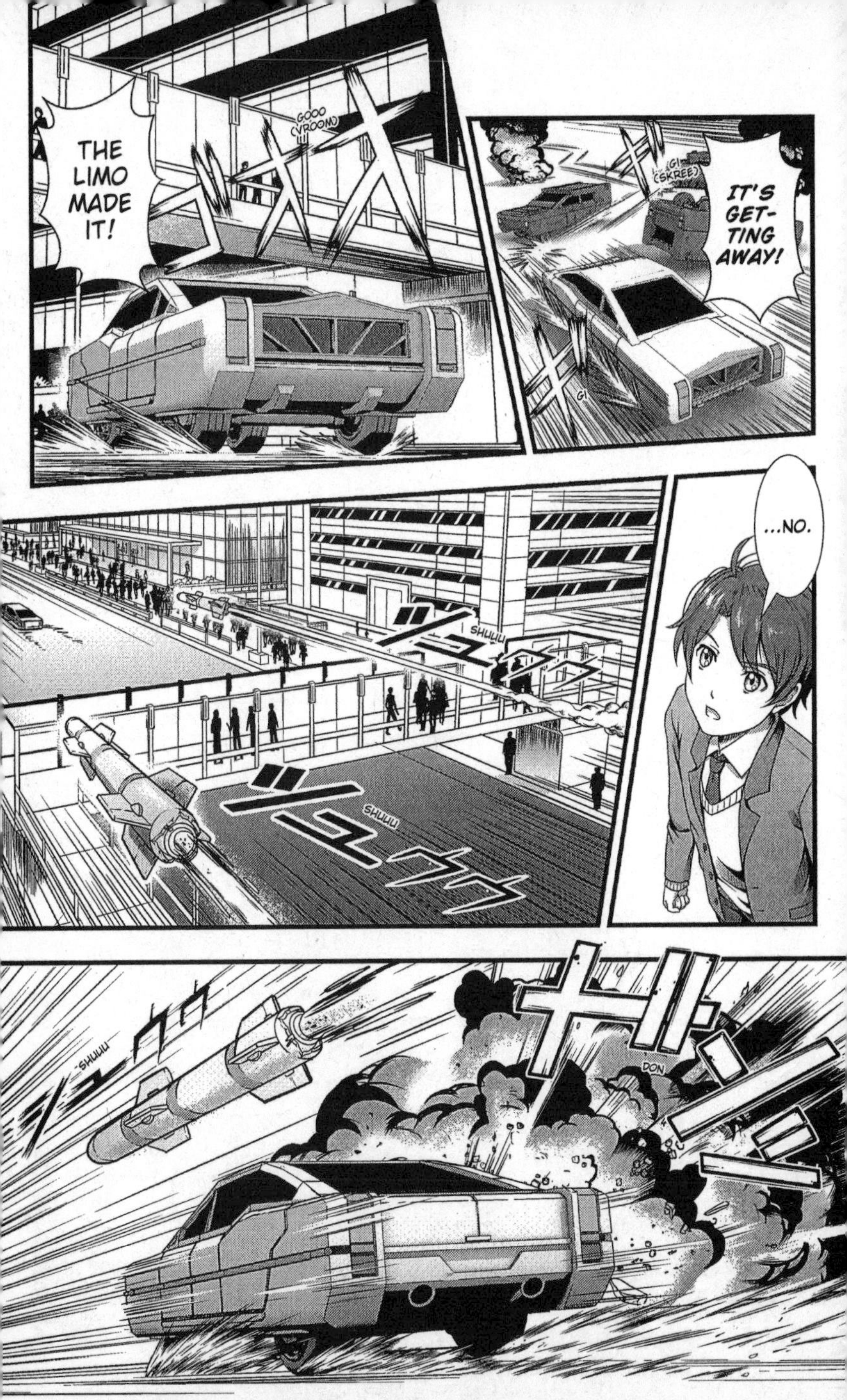
IT'S GET-TING AWAY!
GI (SKREE)
GI
THE LIMO MADE IT!
GOOO (VROOM)
...NO.
SHUUU
SHUUU
SHUUU
DON

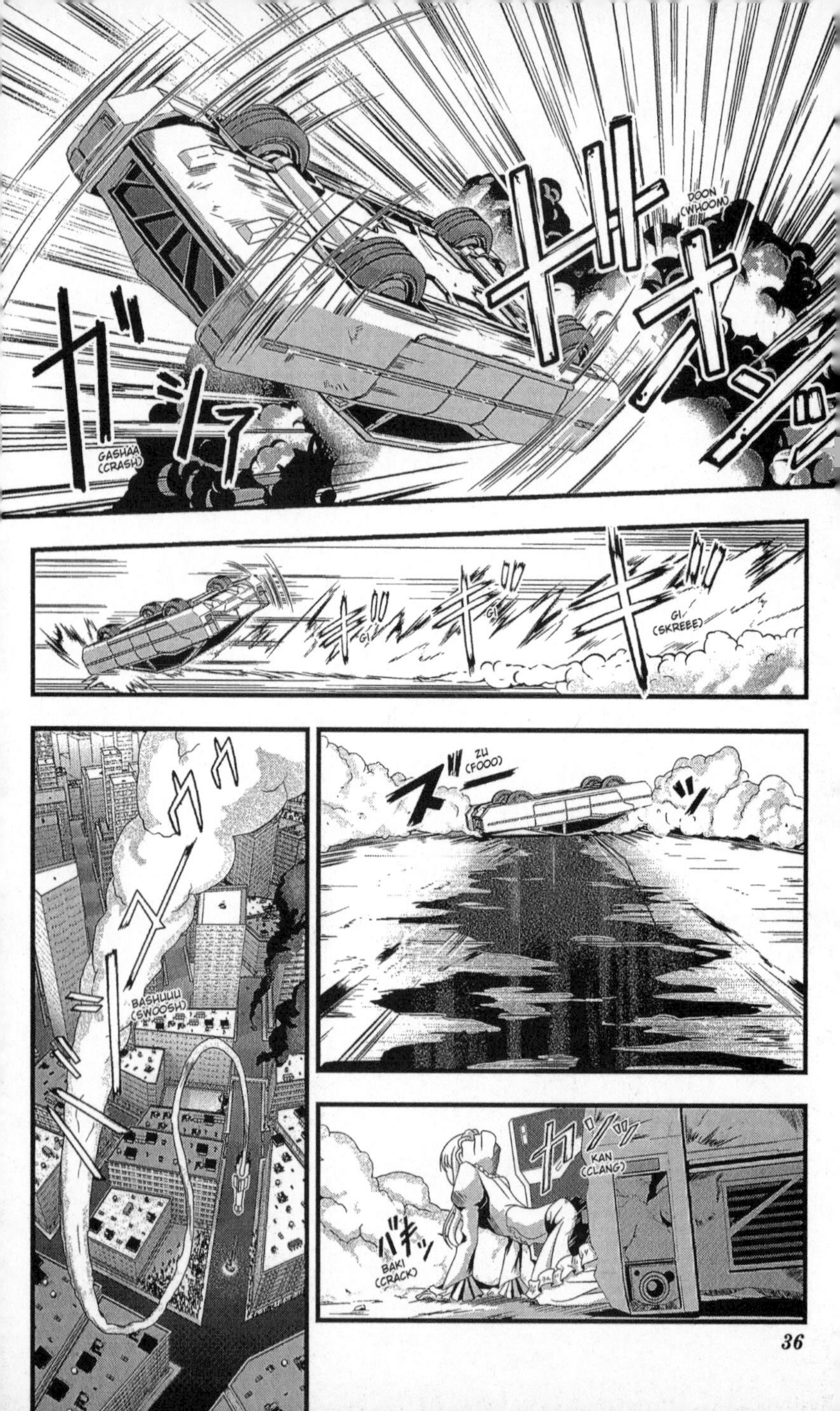
DOON (WHOOM)
GASHAA (CRASH)
GI (SKREEE)
GI
GI
ZU (FOOO)
KAN (CLANG)
BAKI (CRACK)
BASHUUU (SWOOSH)

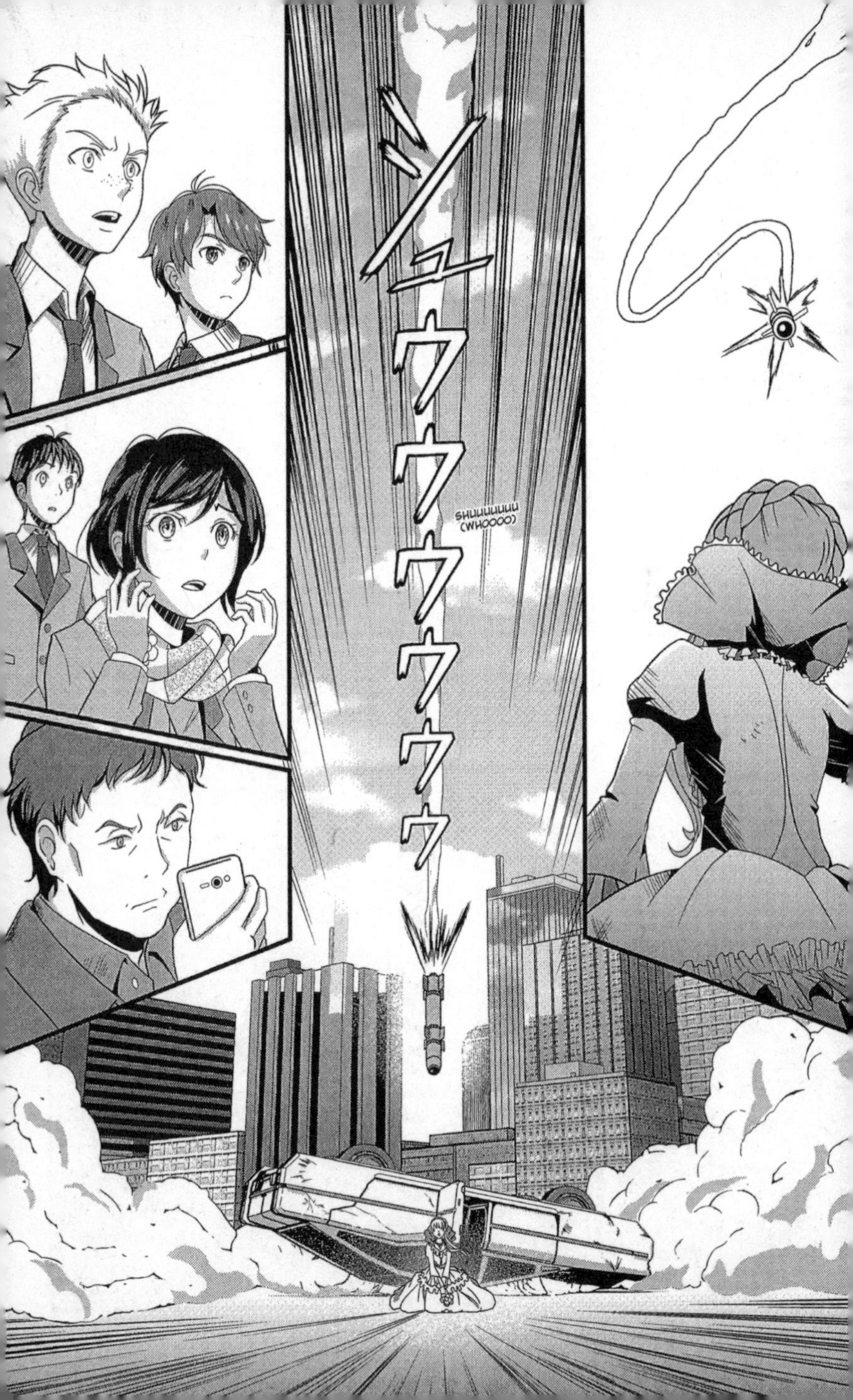
シュウウウウウウ
SHUUUUUUUU
(WHOOOO)

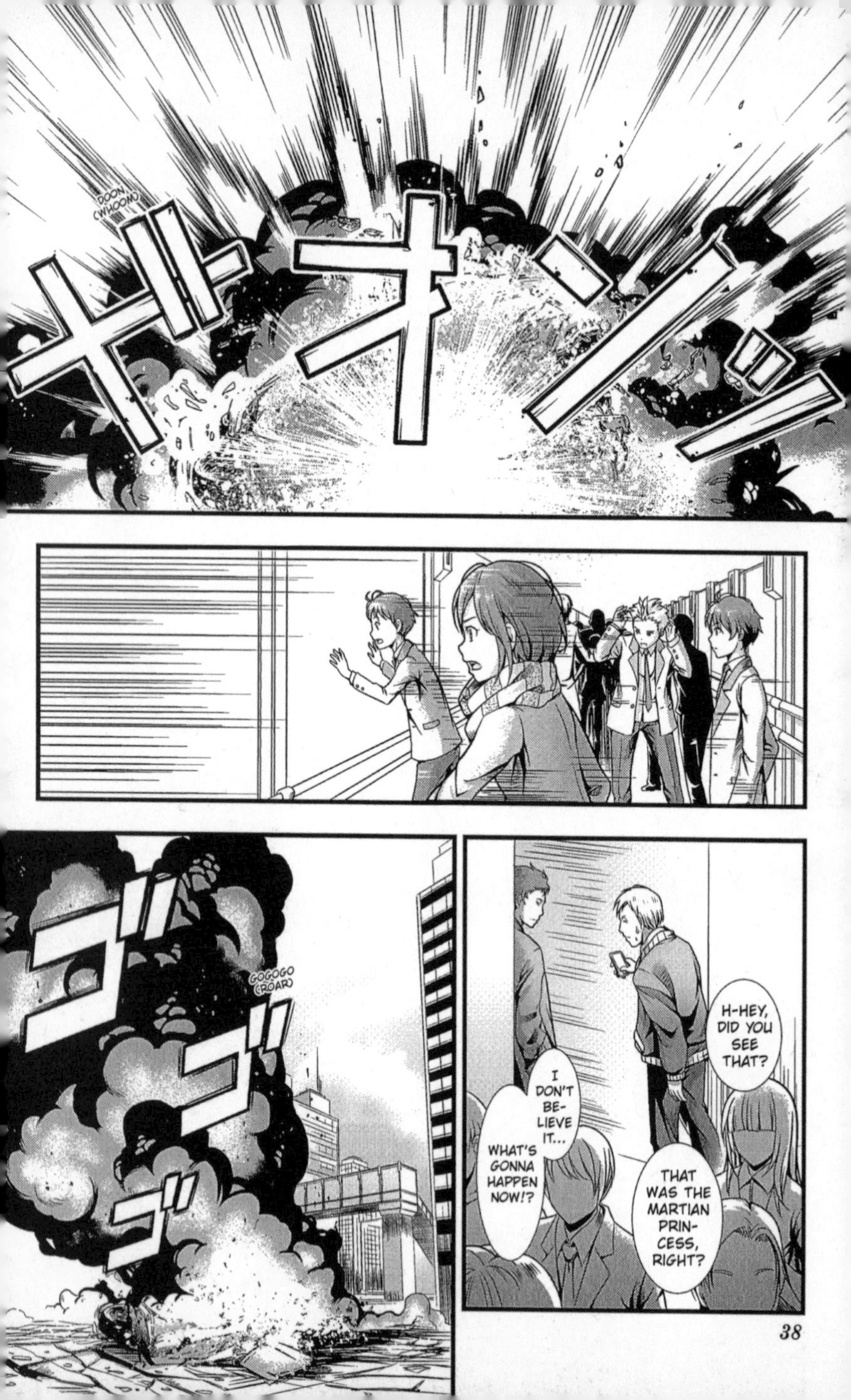
DOON (WHOOM)
H-HEY, DID YOU SEE THAT?
I DON'T BE-LIEVE IT...
THAT WAS THE MARTIAN PRIN-CESS, RIGHT?
WHAT'S GONNA HAPPEN NOW!?
GOGOGO (ROAR)

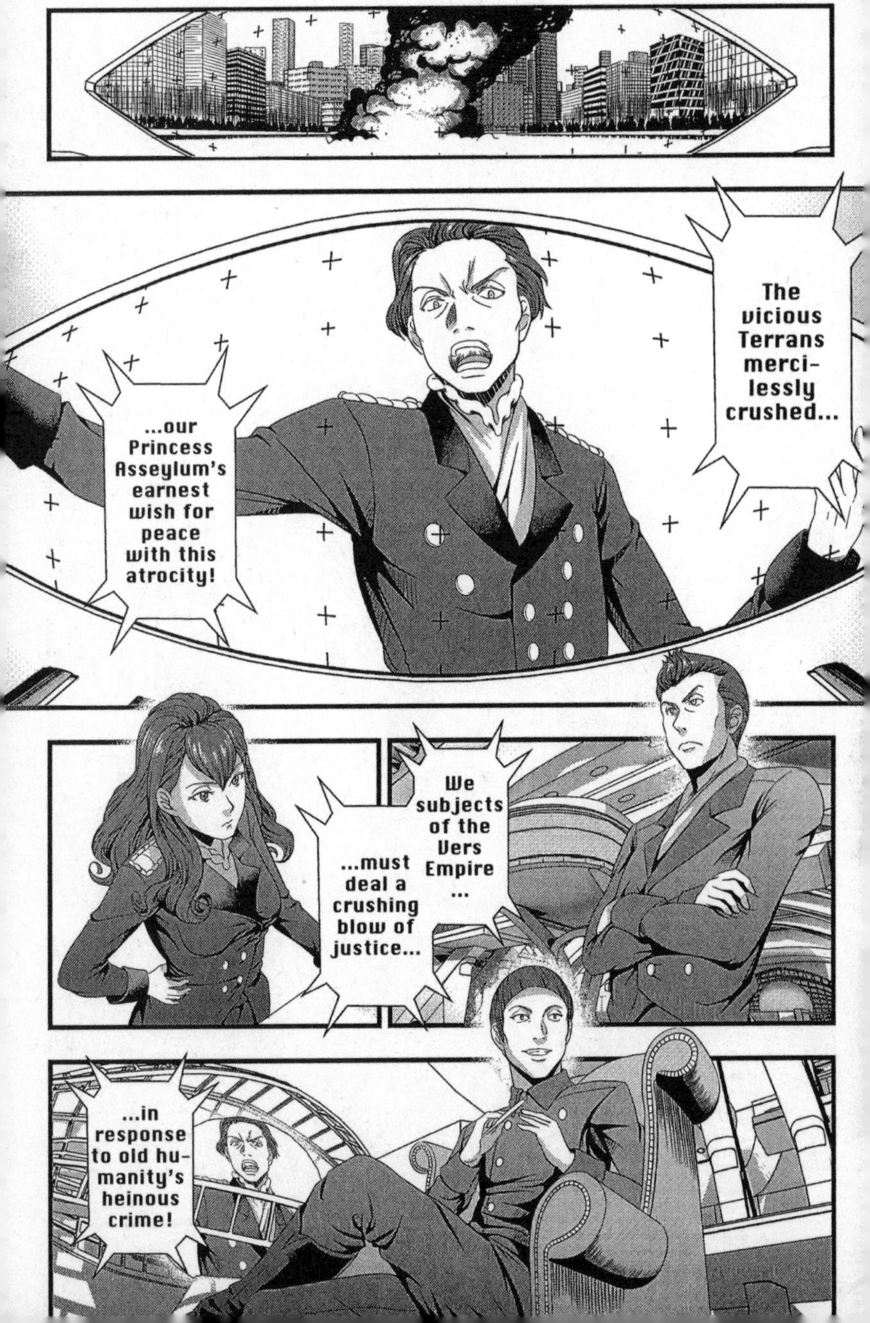
The vicious Terrans merci-lessly crushed...
...our Princess Asseylum's earnest wish for peace with this atrocity!
We subjects of the Vers Empire ...
...must deal a crushing blow of justice...
...in response to old hu-manity's heinous crime!

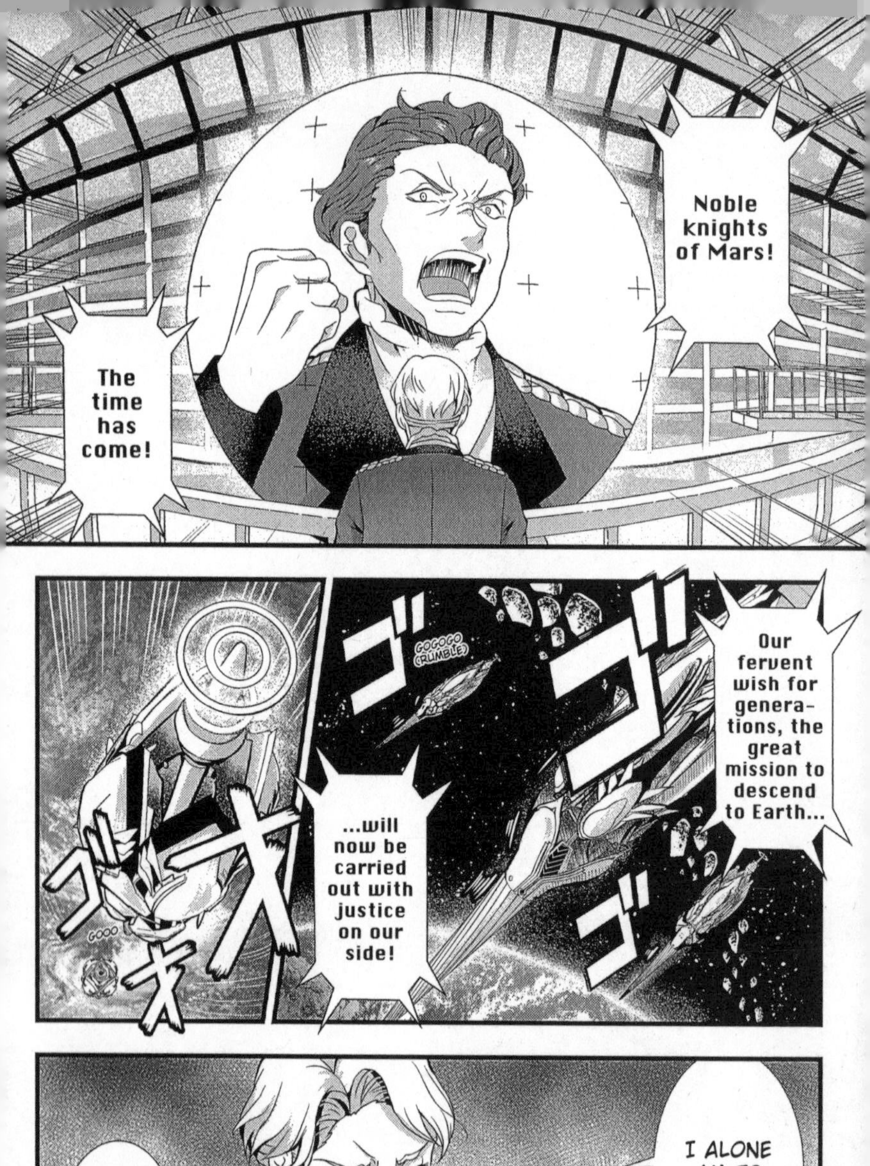
Noble knights of Mars!
The time has come!
Our fervent wish for generations, the great mission to descend to Earth...
GOGOGO (RUMBLE)
...will now be carried out with justice on our side!
GOOO
I ALONE AM TO BLAME...
...FOR NOT BEING ABLE TO DISSUADE THE PRINCESS FROM GOING TO EARTH.

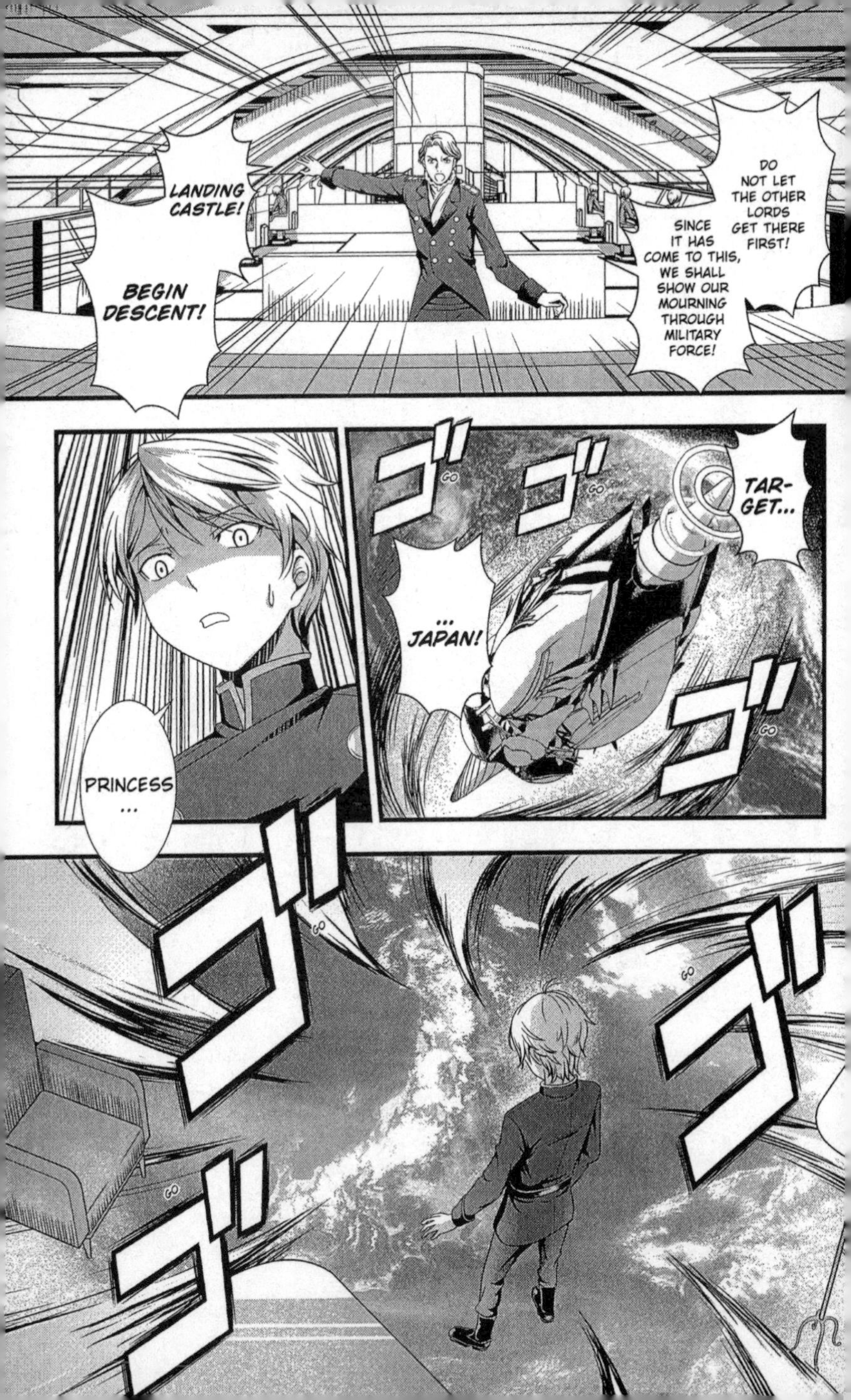
DO NOT LET THE OTHER LORDS GET THERE FIRST!
SINCE IT HAS COME TO THIS, WE SHALL SHOW OUR MOURNING THROUGH MILITARY FORCE!
LANDING CASTLE!
BEGIN DESCENT!
GO
GO
TAR-GET...
...JAPAN!
GO
PRINCESS...
GO
GO
GO

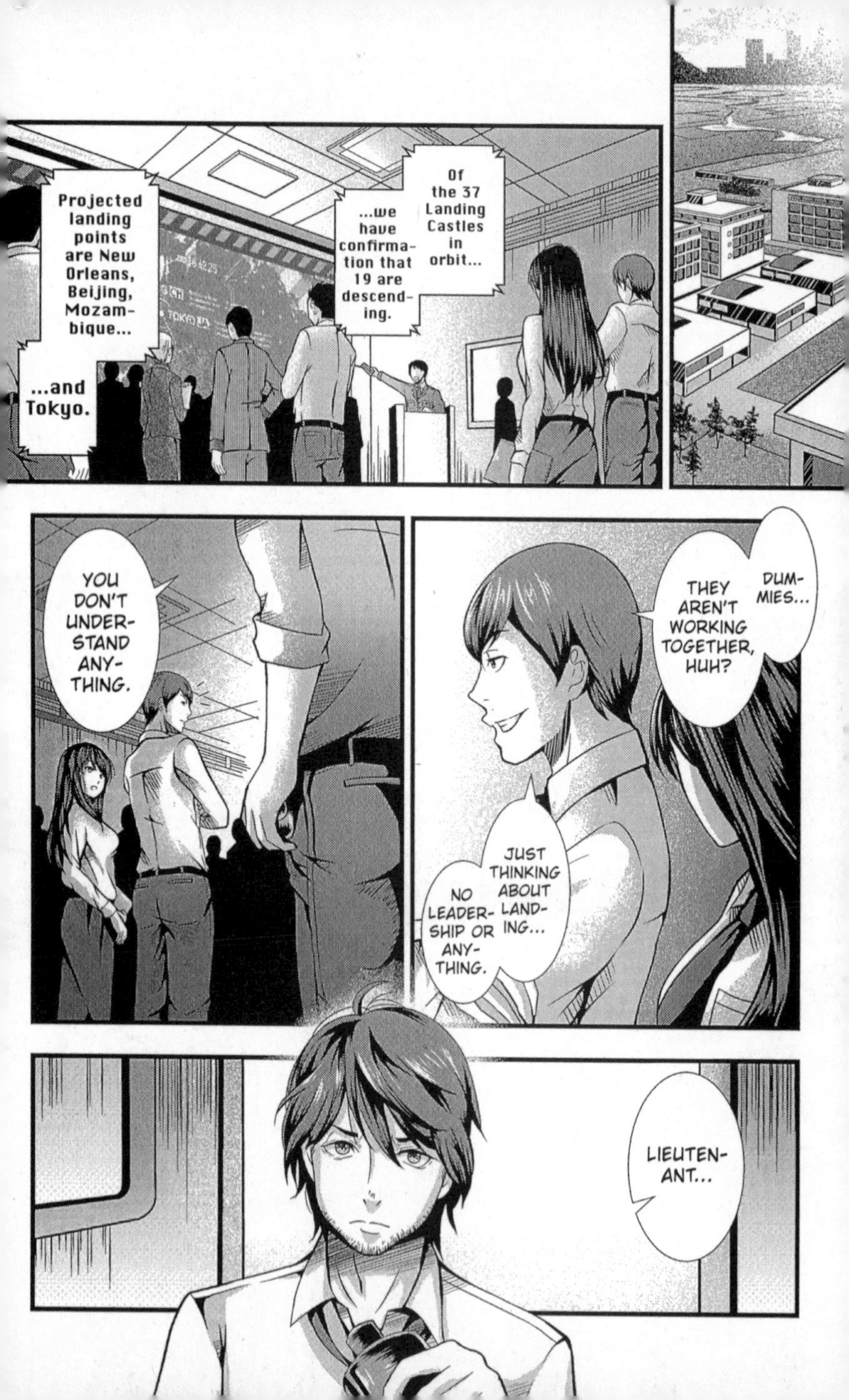

Of the 37 Landing Castles in orbit...
...we have confirmation that 19 are descending.
Projected landing points are New Orleans, Beijing, Mozambique...
...and Tokyo.
DUMMIES...
THEY AREN'T WORKING TOGETHER, HUH?
JUST THINKING ABOUT LANDING...
NO LEADERSHIP OR ANYTHING.
YOU DON'T UNDERSTAND ANYTHING.
LIEUTENANT...

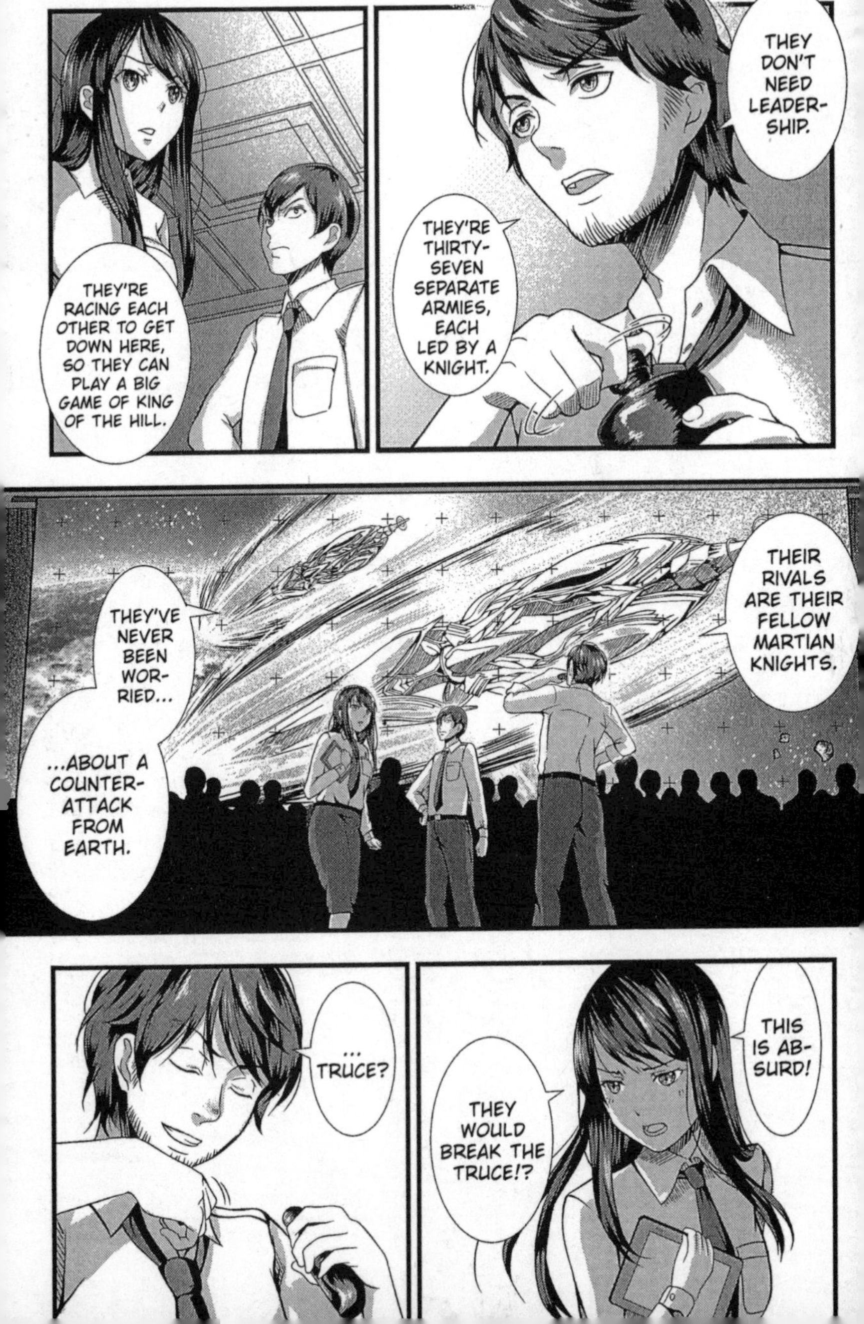
THEY DON'T NEED LEADER-SHIP.
THEY'RE THIRTY-SEVEN SEPARATE ARMIES, EACH LED BY A KNIGHT.
THEY'RE RACING EACH OTHER TO GET DOWN HERE, SO THEY CAN PLAY A BIG GAME OF KING OF THE HILL.
THEIR RIVALS ARE THEIR FELLOW MARTIAN KNIGHTS.
THEY'VE NEVER BEEN WOR-RIED...
...ABOUT A COUNTER-ATTACK FROM EARTH.
THIS IS AB-SURD!
THEY WOULD BREAK THE TRUCE!?
... TRUCE?

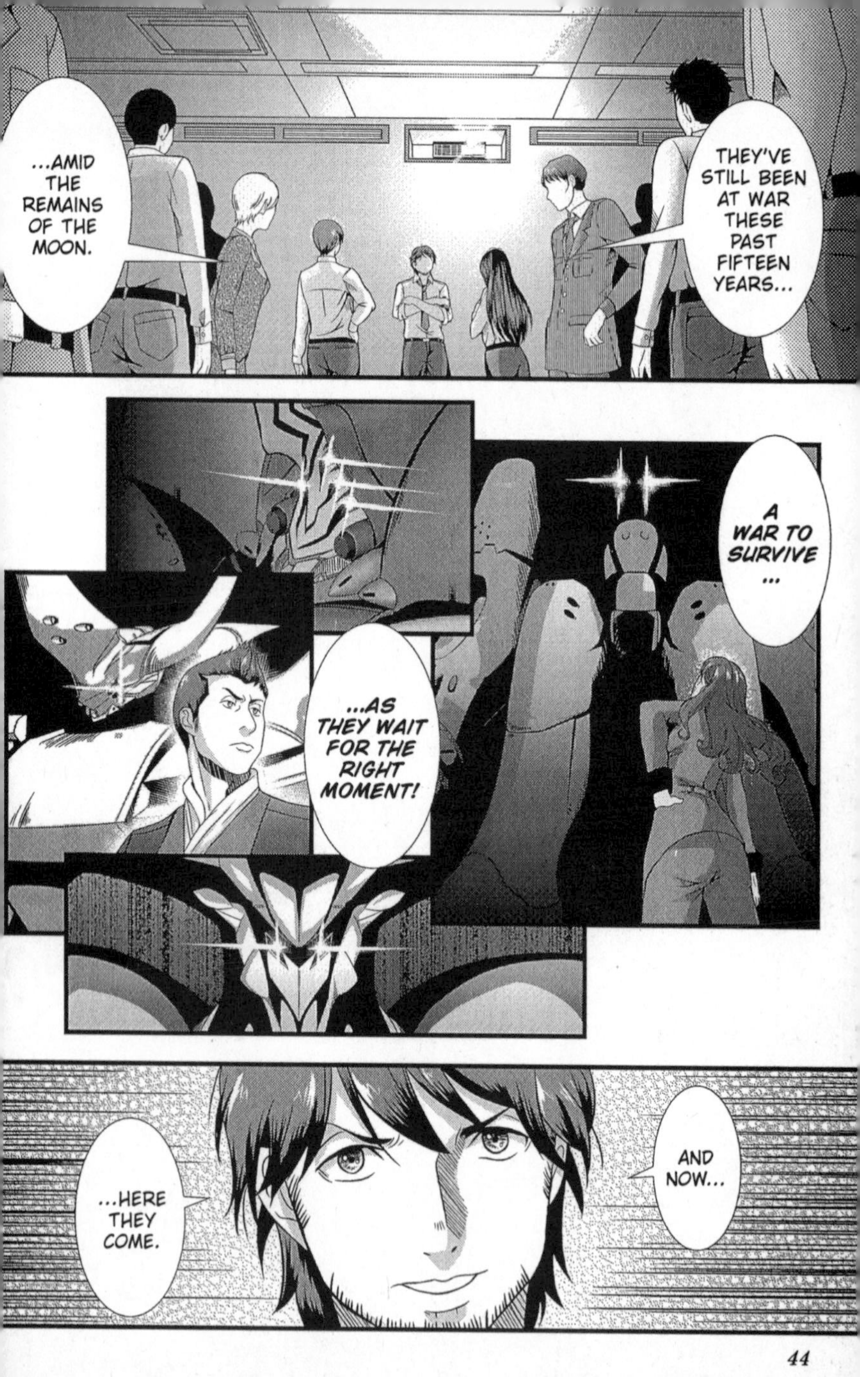
THEY'VE STILL BEEN AT WAR THESE PAST FIFTEEN YEARS...
...AMID THE REMAINS OF THE MOON.
A WAR TO SURVIVE ...
...AS THEY WAIT FOR THE RIGHT MOMENT!
AND NOW...
...HERE THEY COME.

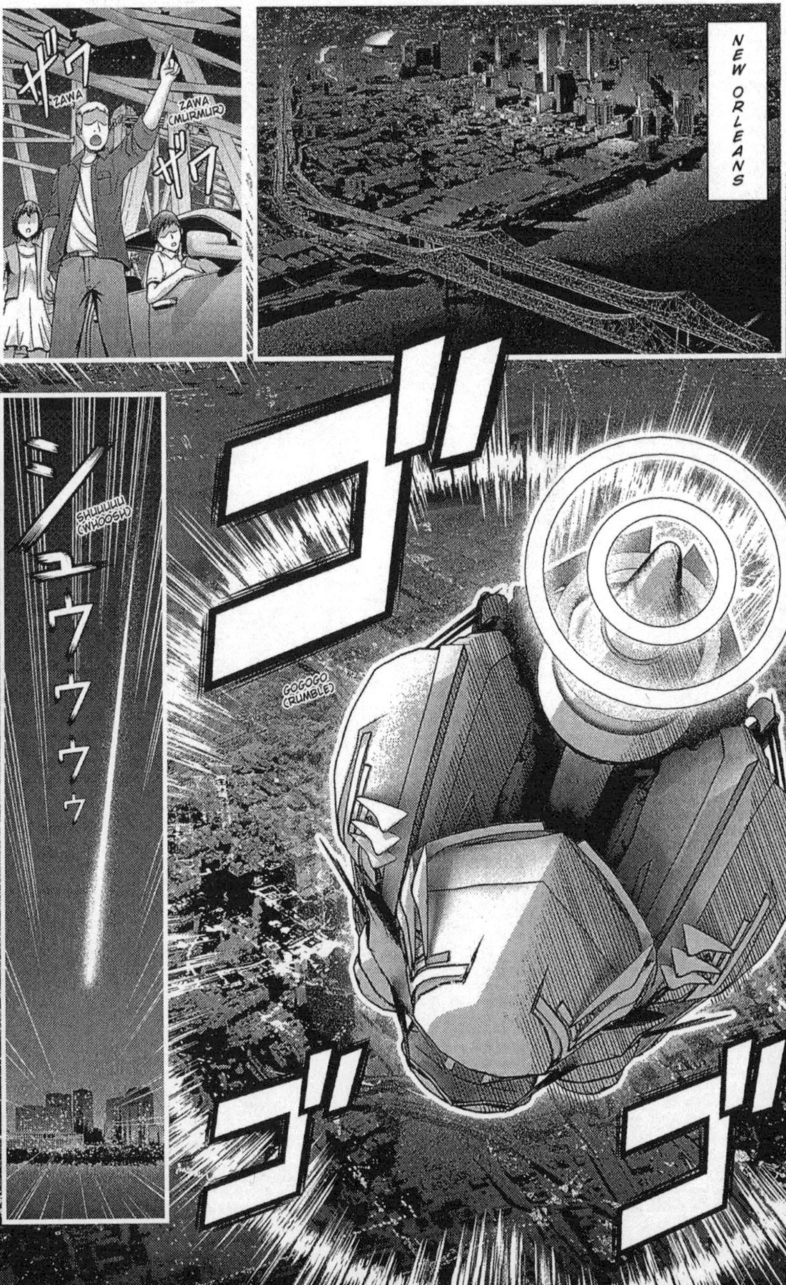
NEW ORLEANS
ZAWA
ZAWA (MURMUR)
GOGOGO (RUMBLE)
SHUUUUUU (WHOOSH)

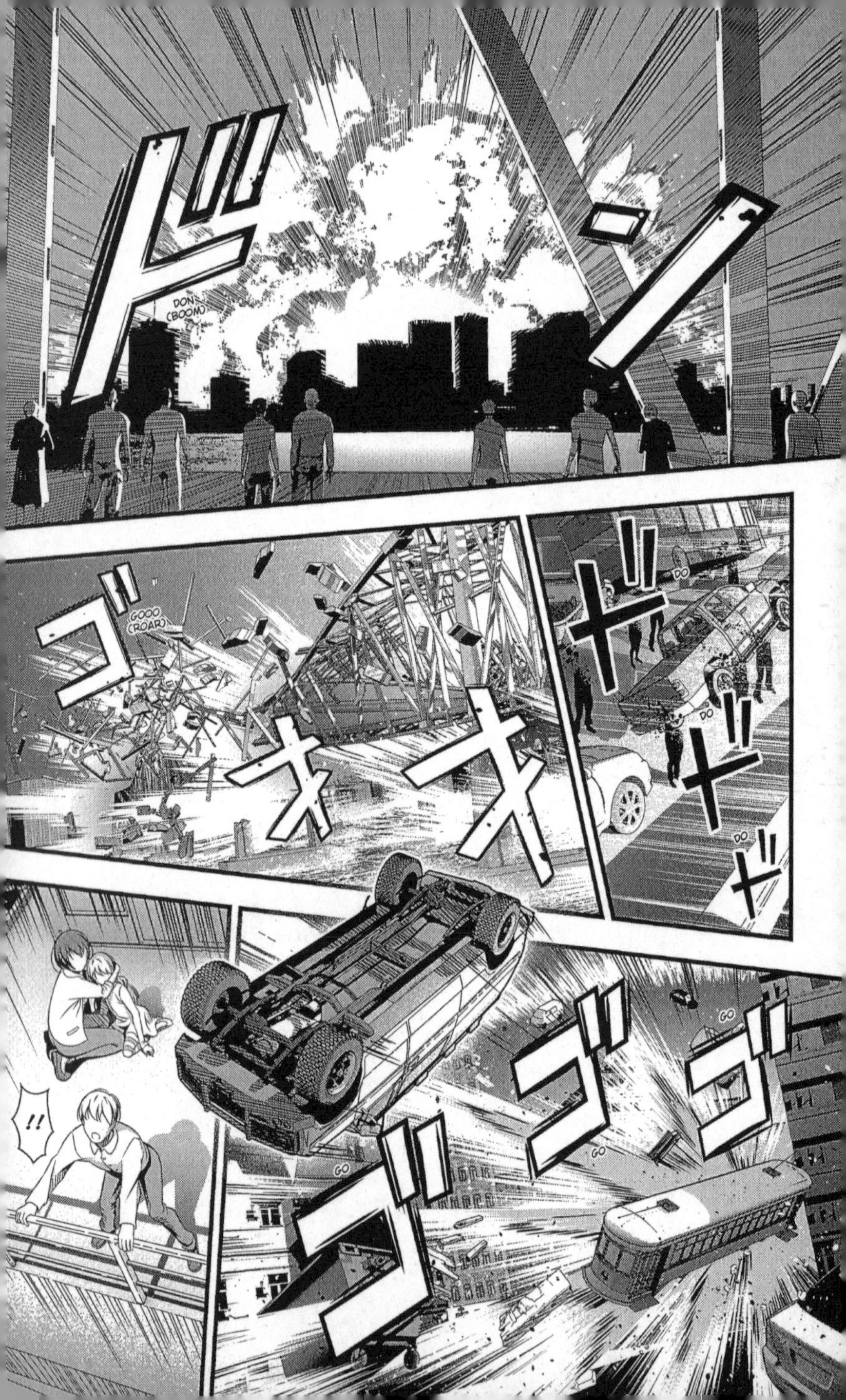
ドーン
DON (BOOM)
ドドド
DO
DO
DO
ゴオオ
GOOO (ROAR)
ゴゴゴ
GO
GO
GO
!!

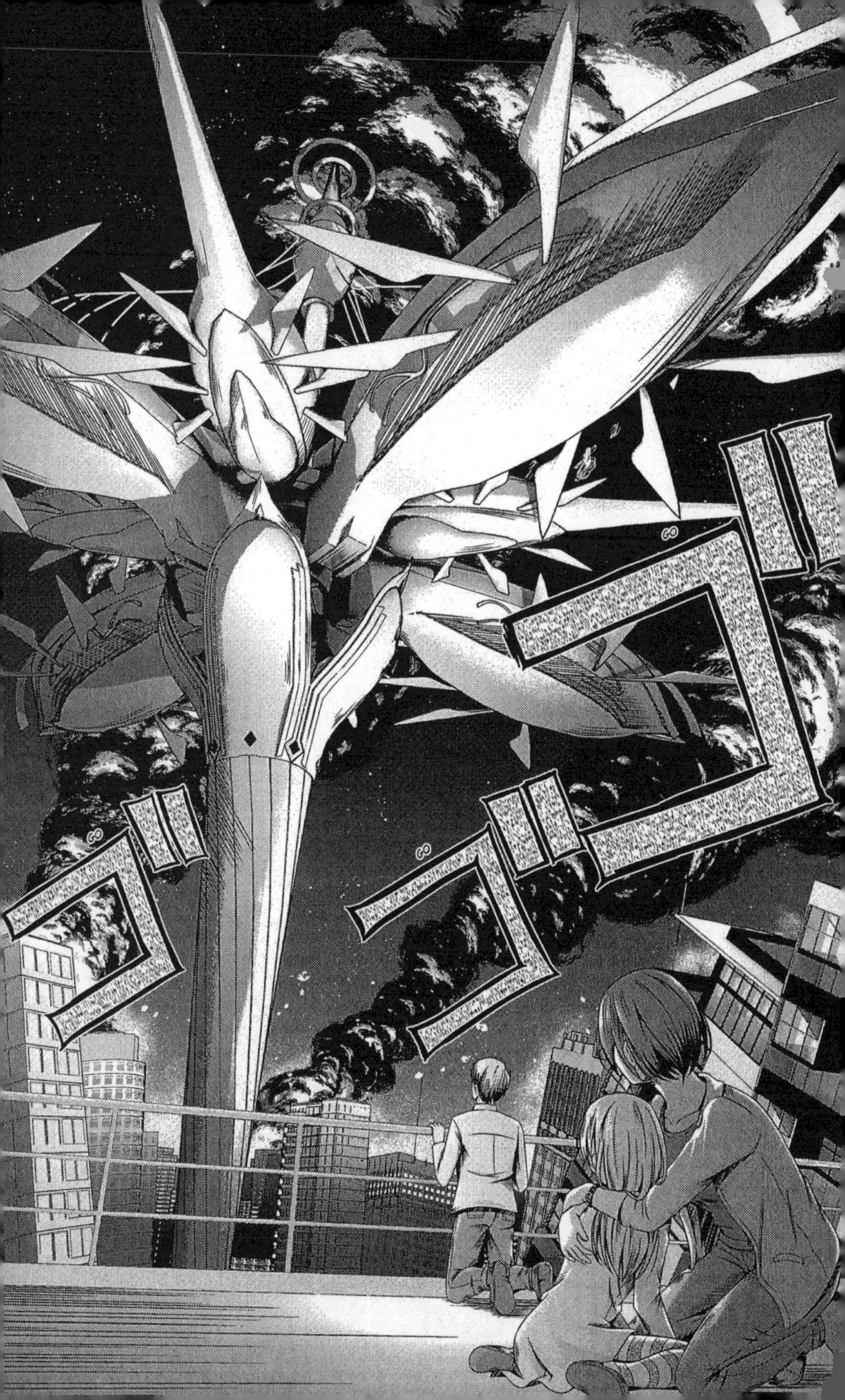
ゴゴゴ
GO GO GO

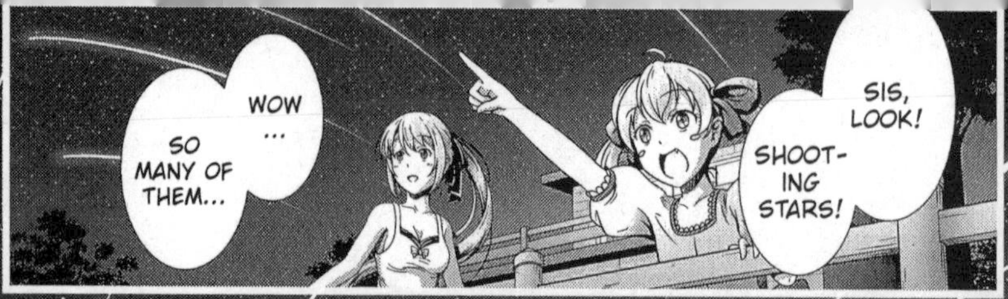
SIS, LOOK!
SHOOT-ING STARS!
WOW...
SO MANY OF THEM...

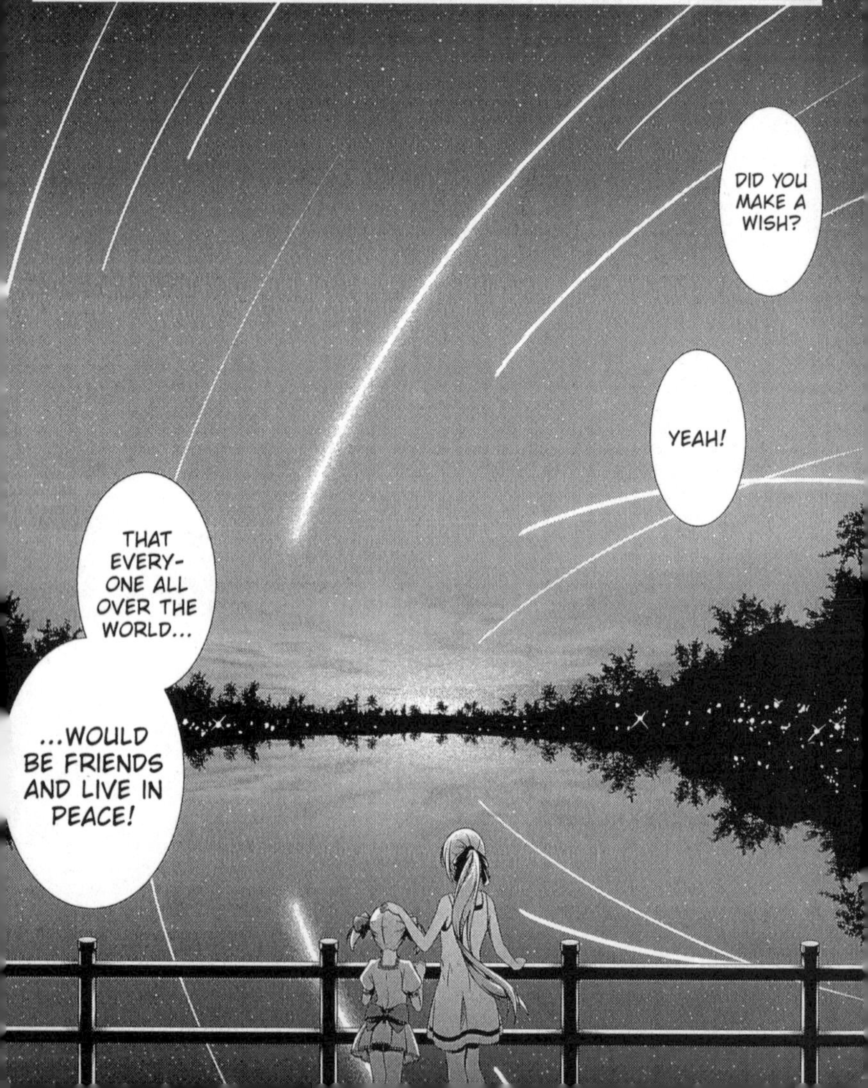
DID YOU MAKE A WISH?
YEAH!
THAT EVERY-ONE ALL OVER THE WORLD...
...WOULD BE FRIENDS AND LIVE IN PEACE!

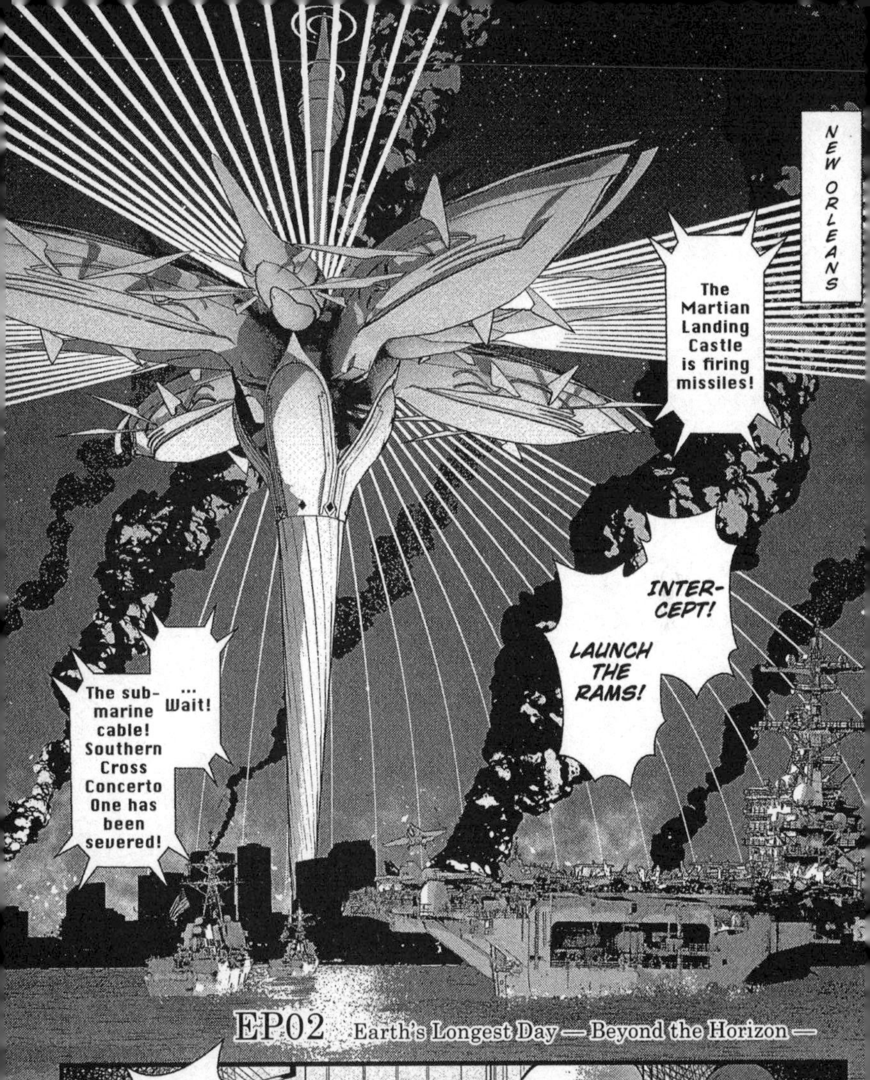
NEW ORLEANS
The Martian Landing Castle is firing missiles!
INTERCEPT!
LAUNCH THE RAMS!
...Wait!
The submarine cable! Southern Cross Concerto One has been severed!

EP02 Earth's Longest Day — Beyond the Horizon —

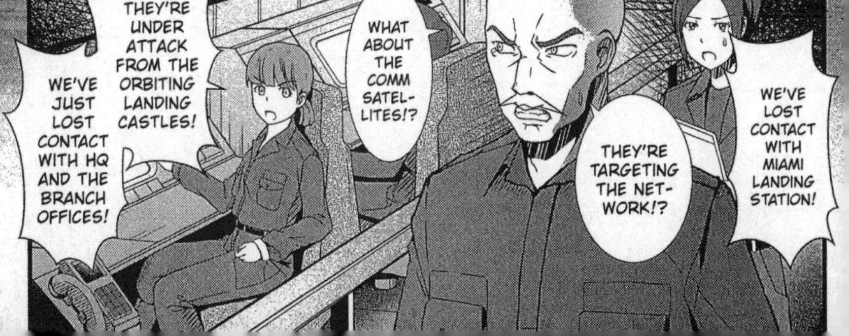
WE'VE LOST CONTACT WITH MIAMI LANDING STATION!
THEY'RE TARGETING THE NETWORK!?
WHAT ABOUT THE COMM SATELLITES!?
THEY'RE UNDER ATTACK FROM THE ORBITING LANDING CASTLES!
WE'VE JUST LOST CONTACT WITH HQ AND THE BRANCH OFFICES!

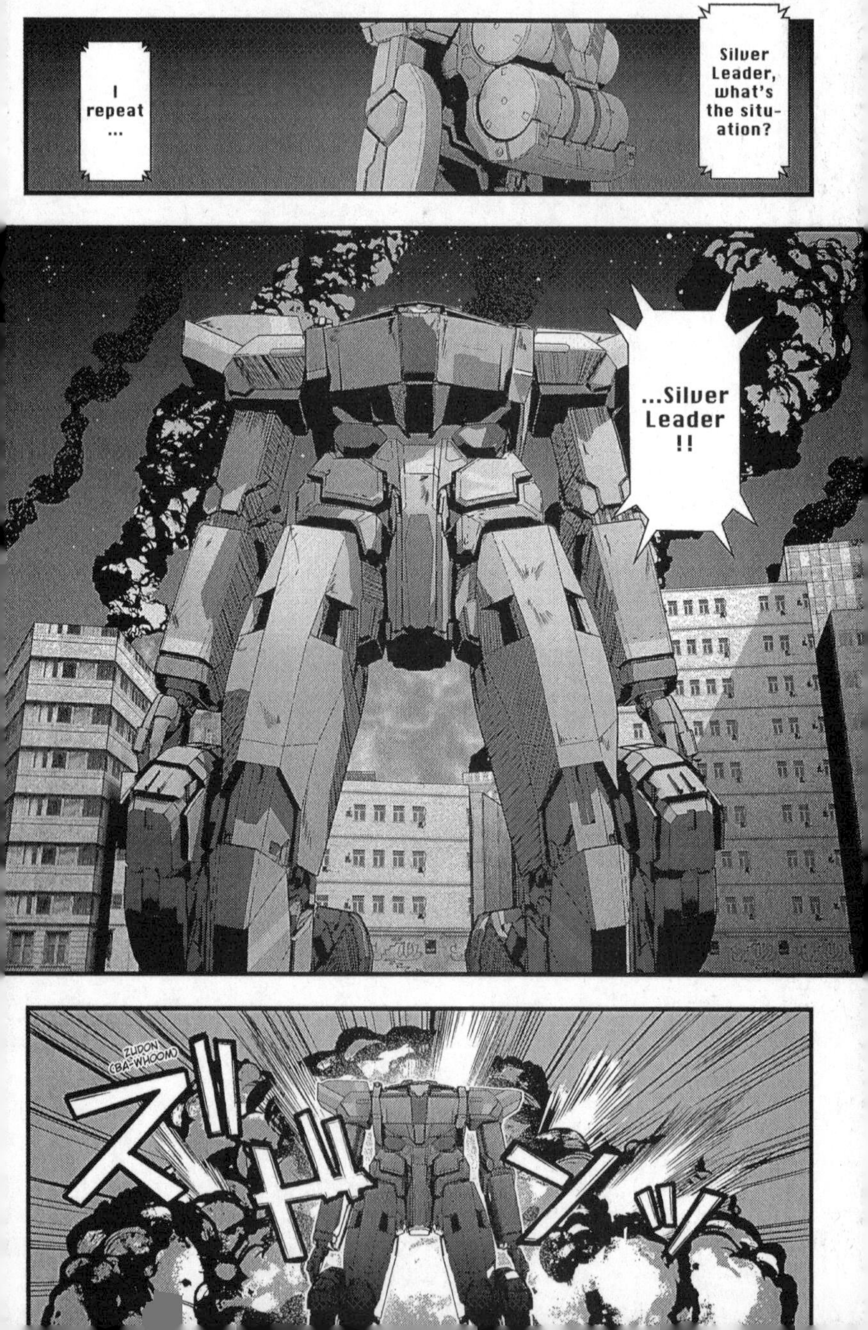
Silver Leader, what's the situation?
I repeat ...
...Silver Leader !!
ZUDON (BA-WHOOM)

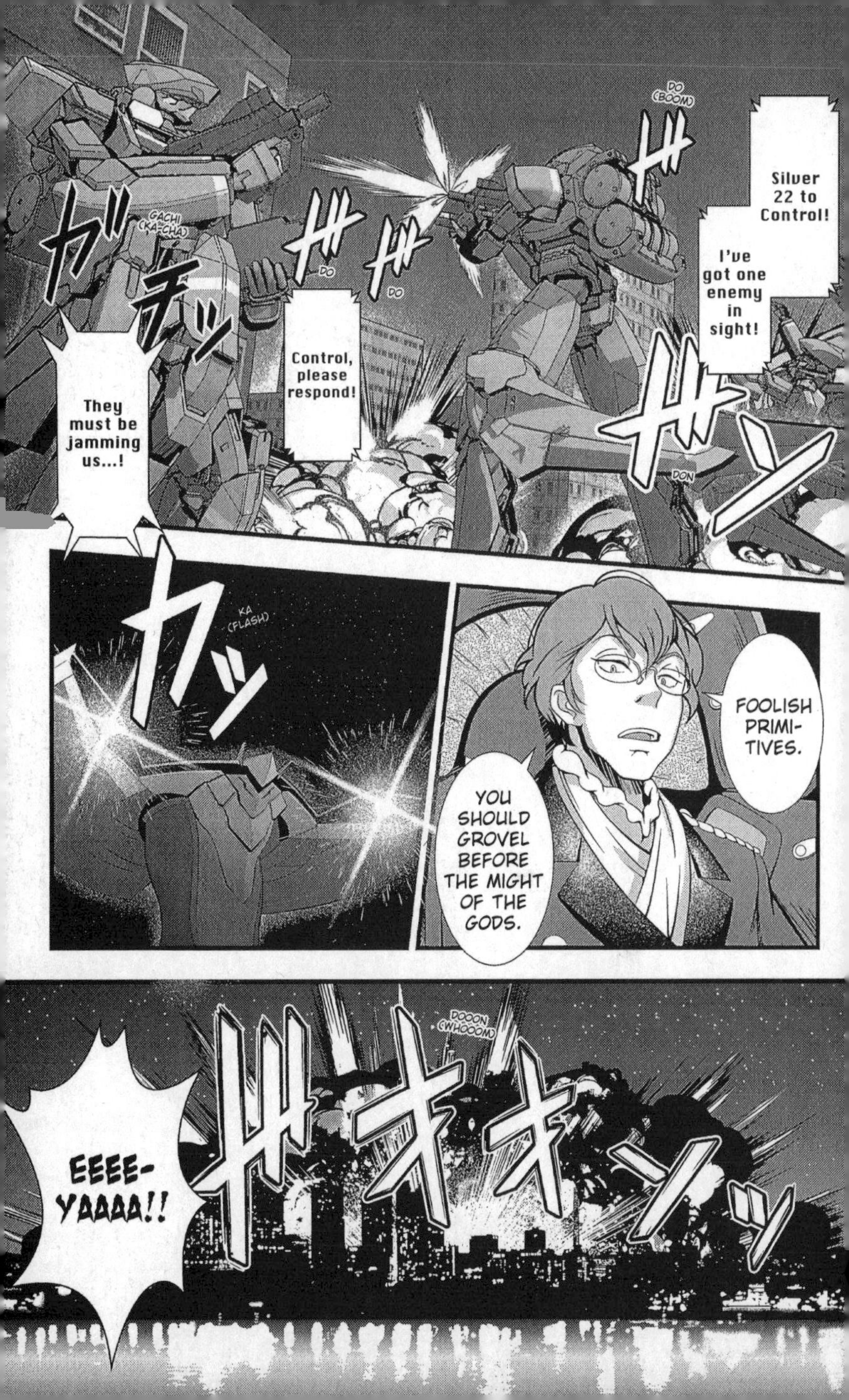
Silver 22 to Control!
I've got one enemy in sight!
DO (BOOM)
DON
DO
DO
Control, please respond!
GACHI (KA-CHA)
They must be jamming us...!
FOOLISH PRIMI-TIVES.
YOU SHOULD GROVEL BEFORE THE MIGHT OF THE GODS.
KA (FLASH)
DOOON (WHOOOM)
EEEE-YAAAA!!

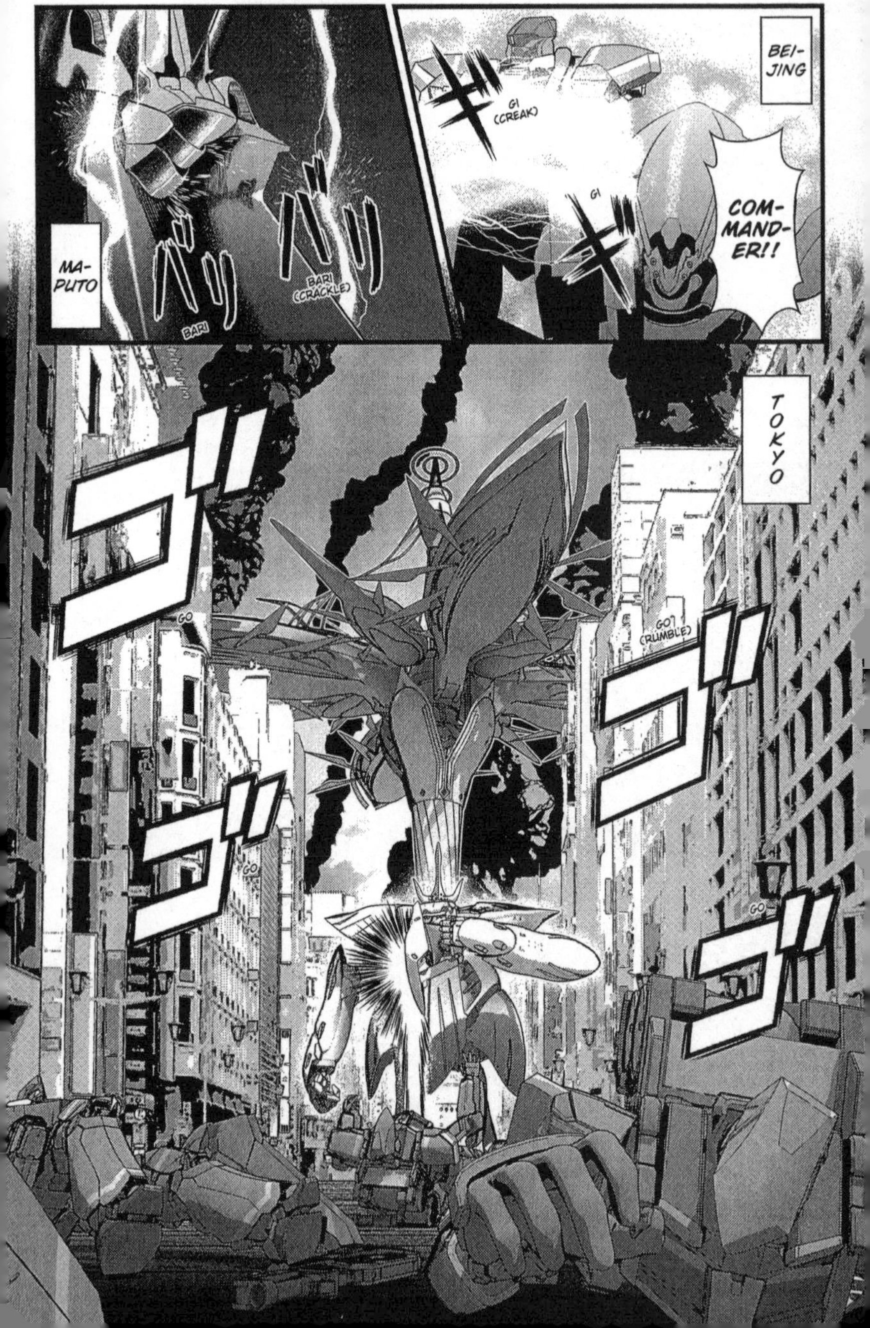
BEI-JING
COM-MAND-ER!!
GI (CREAK)
GI
BARI (CRACKLE)
MA-PUTO
BARI
TOKYO
GO (RUMBLE)
GO
GO
GO

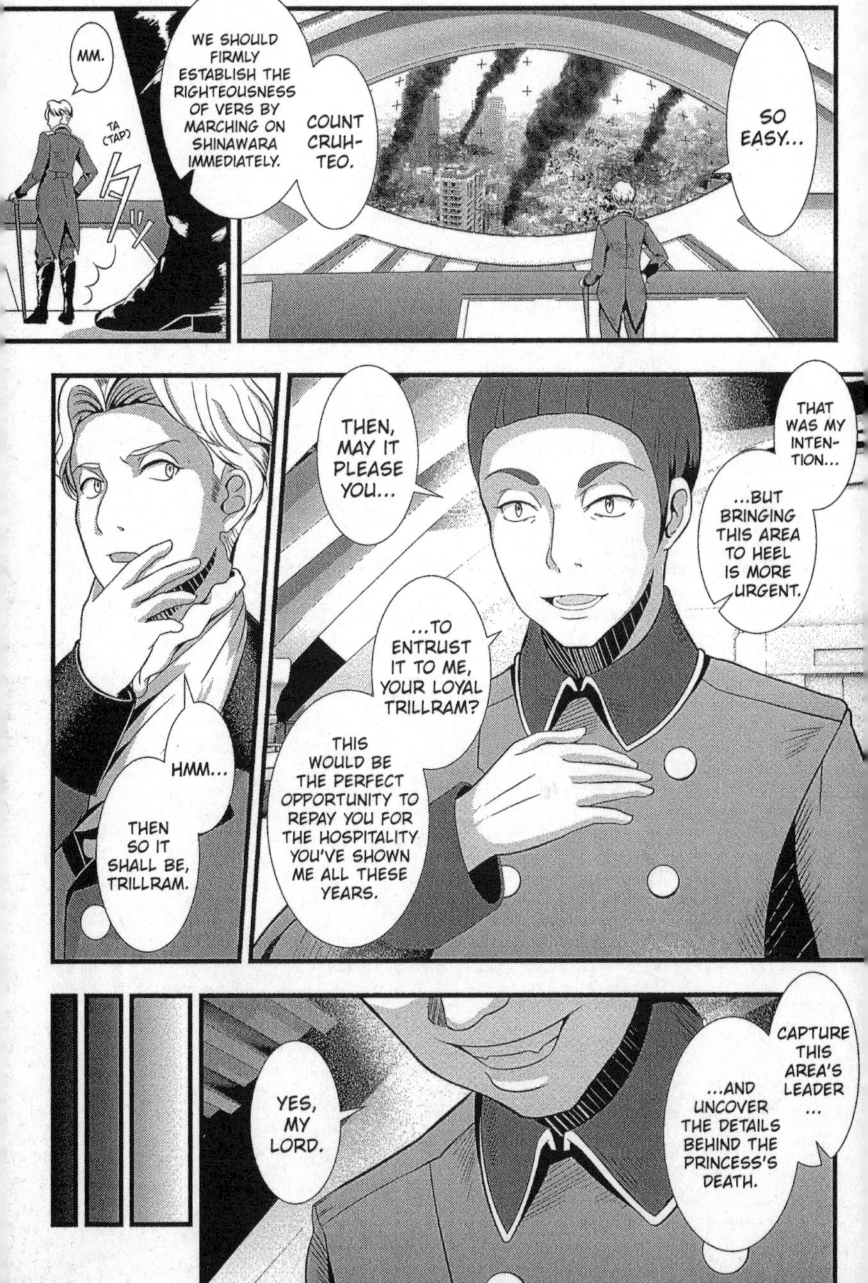
SO EASY...
COUNT CRUHTEO.
WE SHOULD FIRMLY ESTABLISH THE RIGHTEOUSNESS OF VERS BY MARCHING ON SHINAWARA IMMEDIATELY.
TA (TAP)
MM.
THAT WAS MY INTENTION...
...BUT BRINGING THIS AREA TO HEEL IS MORE URGENT.
THEN, MAY IT PLEASE YOU...
...TO ENTRUST IT TO ME, YOUR LOYAL TRILLRAM?
THIS WOULD BE THE PERFECT OPPORTUNITY TO REPAY YOU FOR THE HOSPITALITY YOU'VE SHOWN ME ALL THESE YEARS.
HMM...
THEN SO IT SHALL BE, TRILLRAM.
CAPTURE THIS AREA'S LEADER...
...AND UNCOVER THE DETAILS BEHIND THE PRINCESS'S DEATH.
YES, MY LORD.

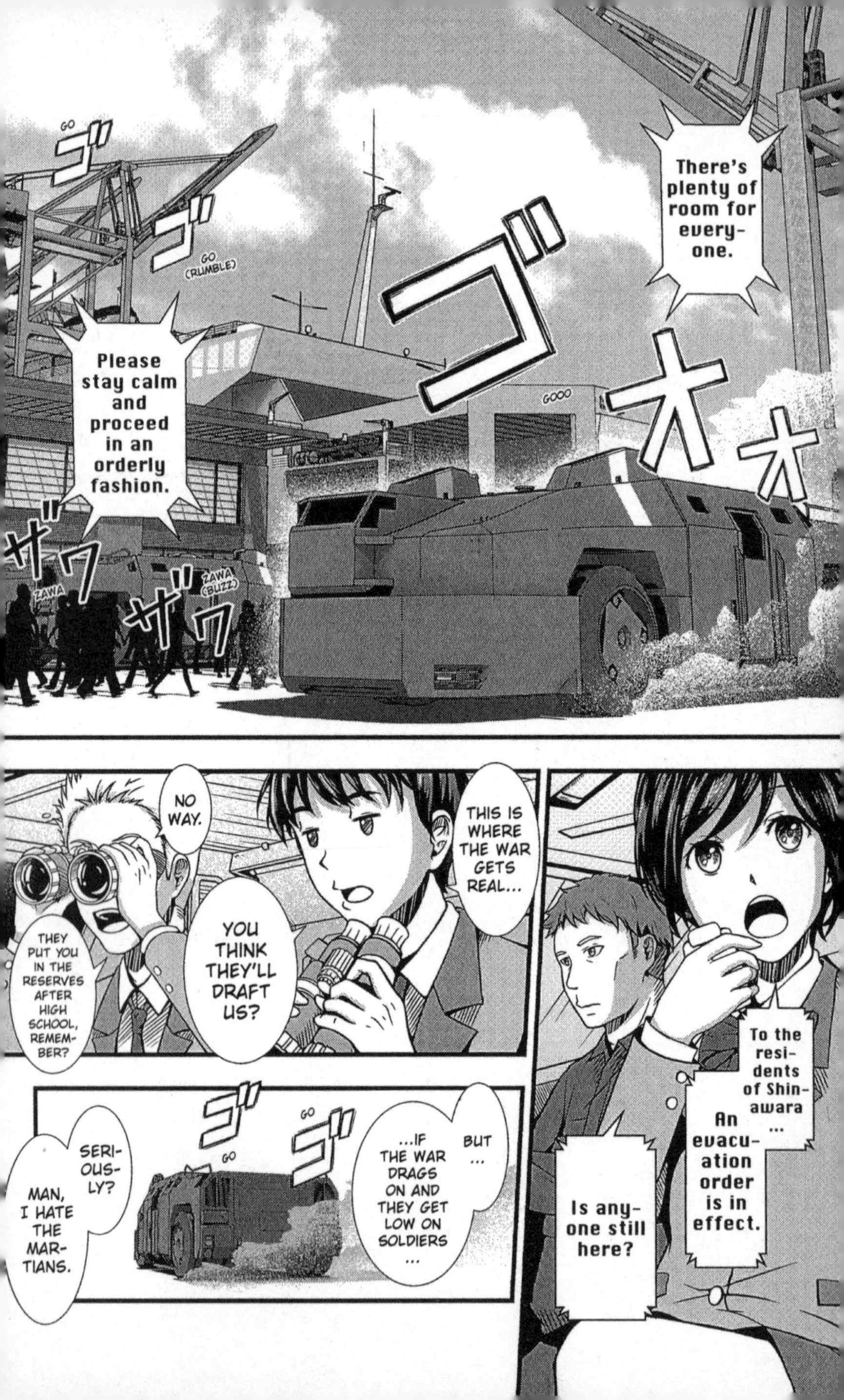
There's plenty of room for every-one.
GOOO
GO
GO (RUMBLE)
Please stay calm and proceed in an orderly fashion.
ZAWA (BUZZ)
ZAWA
To the resi-dents of Shin-awara ...
An evacu-ation order is in effect.
Is any-one still here?
THIS IS WHERE THE WAR GETS REAL...
NO WAY.
YOU THINK THEY'LL DRAFT US?
THEY PUT YOU IN THE RESERVES AFTER HIGH SCHOOL, REMEM-BER?
BUT ...
...IF THE WAR DRAGS ON AND THEY GET LOW ON SOLDIERS ...
GO
GO
SERI-OUS-LY?
MAN, I HATE THE MAR-TIANS.

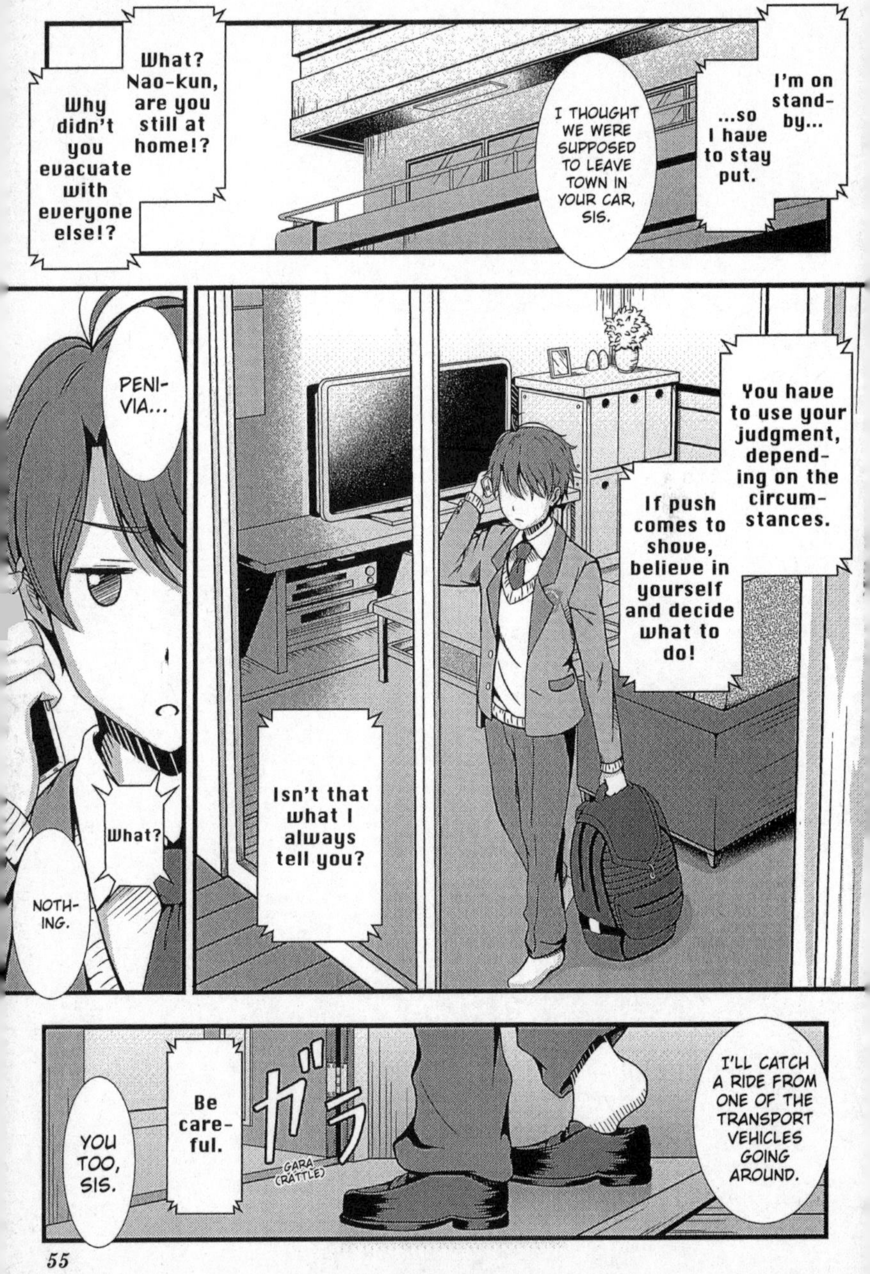
I'm on stand-by...
...so I have to stay put.
I THOUGHT WE WERE SUPPOSED TO LEAVE TOWN IN YOUR CAR, SIS.
What? Nao-kun, are you still at home!?
Why didn't you evacuate with everyone else!?
You have to use your judgment, depending on the circumstances.
If push comes to shove, believe in yourself and decide what to do!
Isn't that what I always tell you?
PENI-VIA...
What?
NOTH-ING.
I'LL CATCH A RIDE FROM ONE OF THE TRANSPORT VEHICLES GOING AROUND.
ガラ
GARA (RATTLE)
Be care-ful.
YOU TOO, SIS.

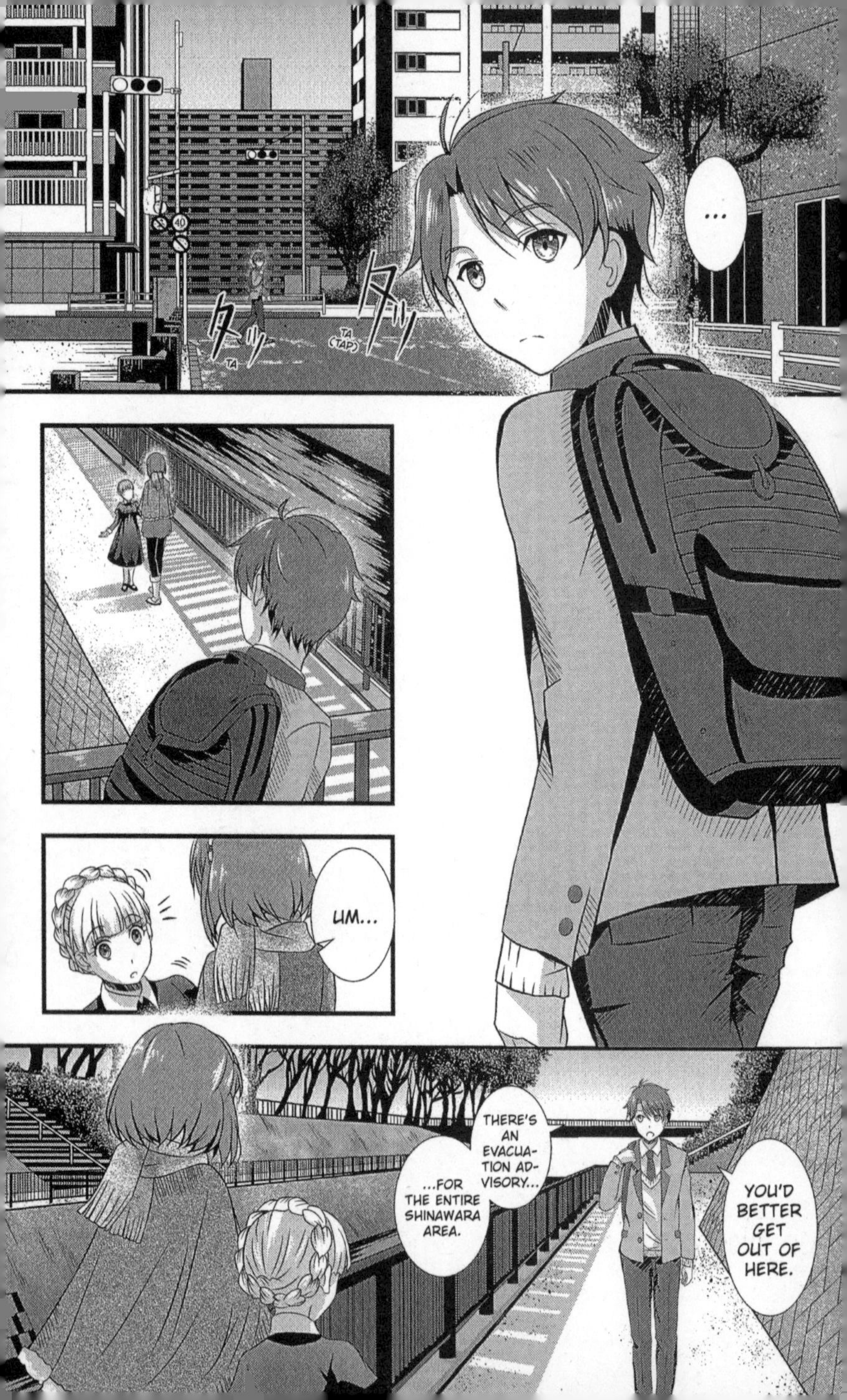

TA (TAP)
TA
...
UM...
YOU'D BETTER GET OUT OF HERE.
THERE'S AN EVACUATION ADVISORY...
...FOR THE ENTIRE SHINAWARA AREA.

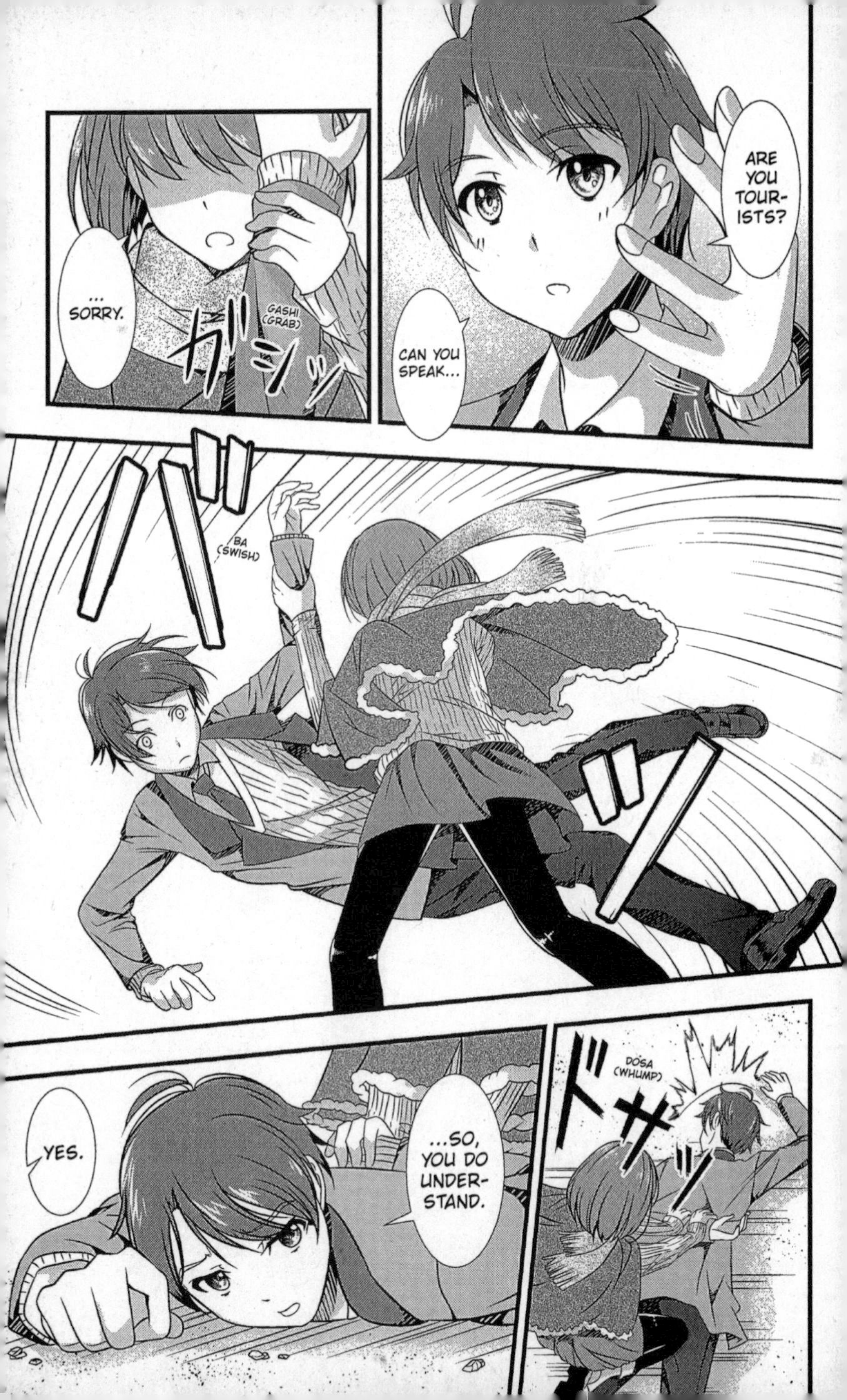
ARE YOU TOUR-ISTS?
CAN YOU SPEAK...
GASHI (GRAB)
... SORRY.
BA (SWISH)
DOSA (WHUMP)
...SO, YOU DO UNDER-STAND.
YES.

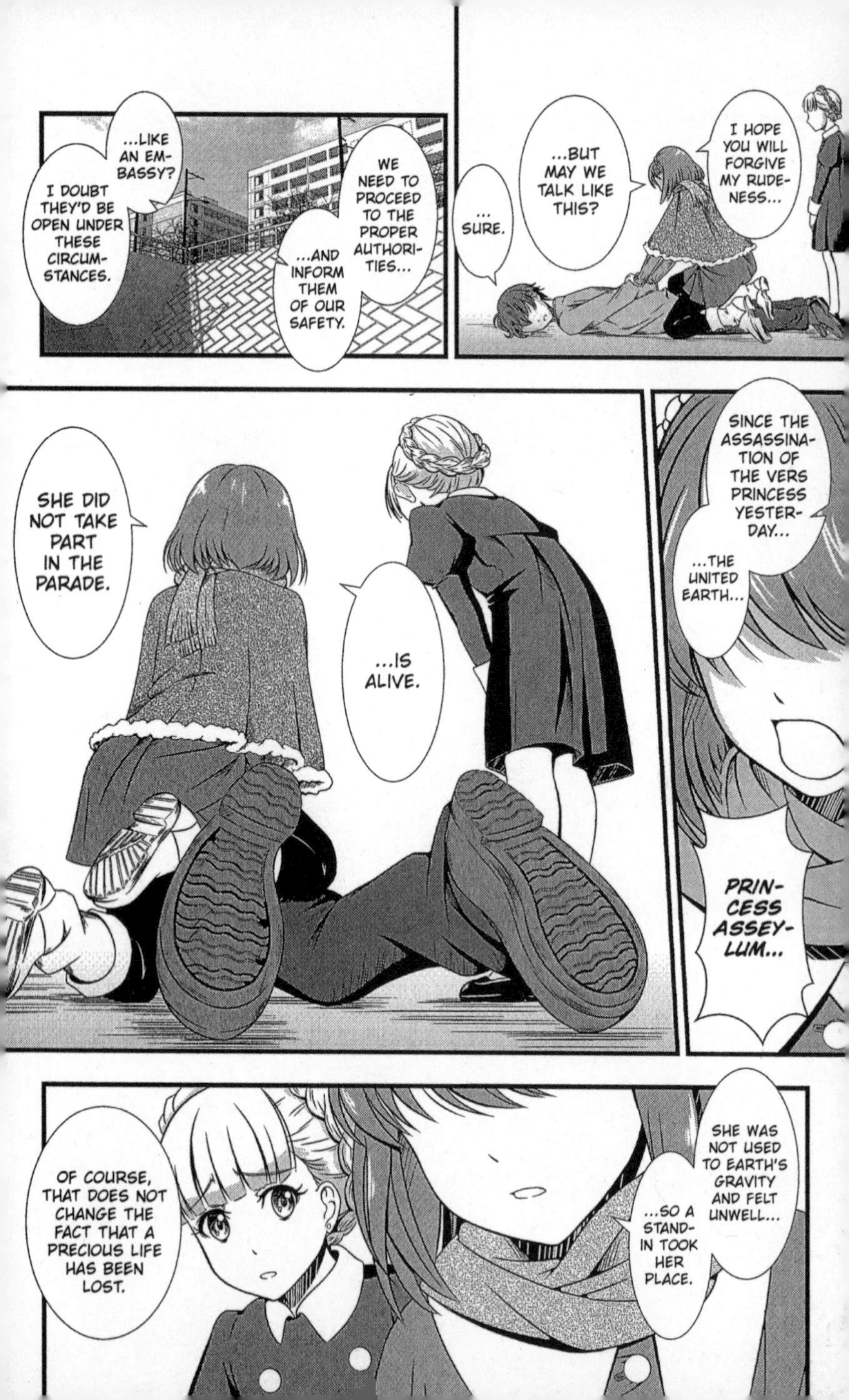
I HOPE YOU WILL FORGIVE MY RUDENESS...
...BUT MAY WE TALK LIKE THIS?
... SURE.
WE NEED TO PROCEED TO THE PROPER AUTHORITIES...
...AND INFORM THEM OF OUR SAFETY.
...LIKE AN EMBASSY?
I DOUBT THEY'D BE OPEN UNDER THESE CIRCUMSTANCES.
SINCE THE ASSASSINATION OF THE VERS PRINCESS YESTERDAY...
...THE UNITED EARTH...
PRINCESS ASSEYLUM...
...IS ALIVE.
SHE DID NOT TAKE PART IN THE PARADE.
SHE WAS NOT USED TO EARTH'S GRAVITY AND FELT UNWELL...
...SO A STAND-IN TOOK HER PLACE.
OF COURSE, THAT DOES NOT CHANGE THE FACT THAT A PRECIOUS LIFE HAS BEEN LOST.

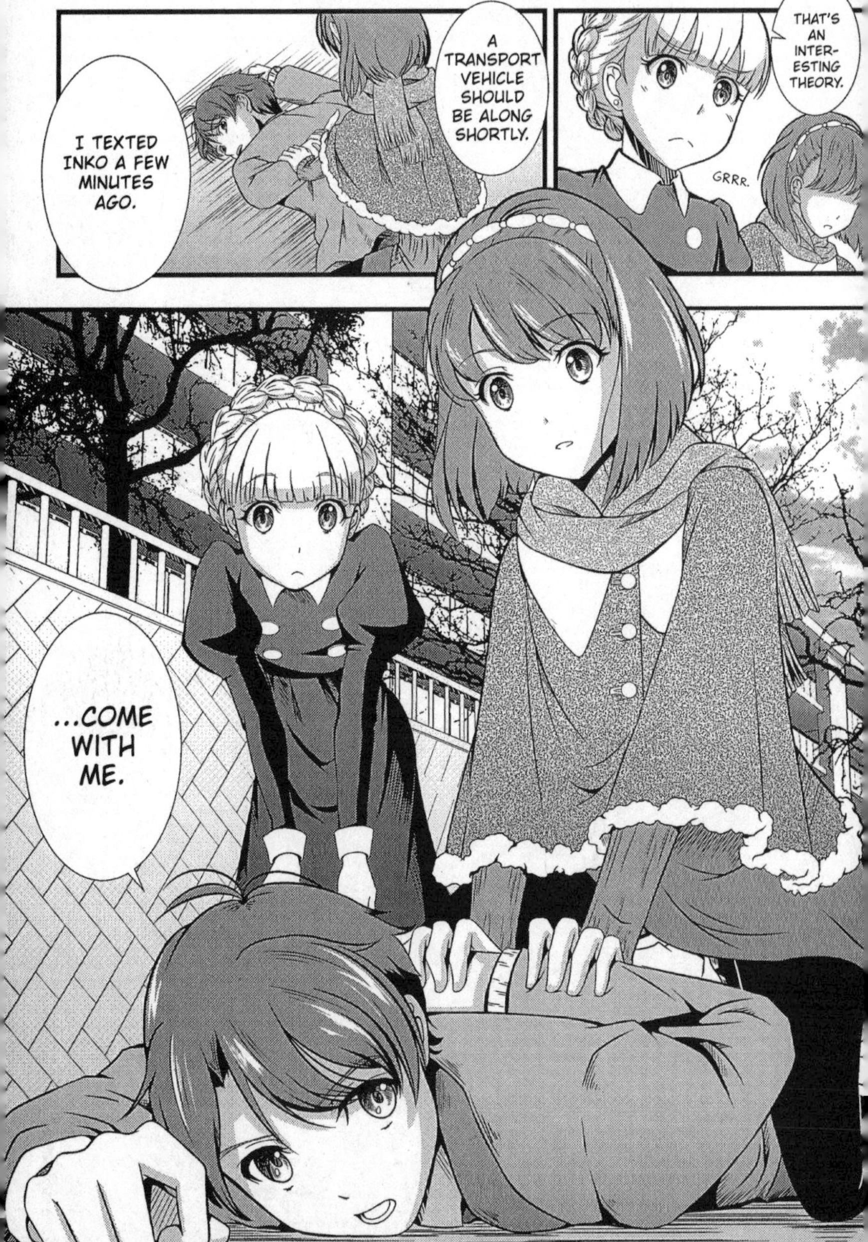
THAT'S AN INTER-ESTING THEORY.
GRRR.
A TRANSPORT VEHICLE SHOULD BE ALONG SHORTLY.
I TEXTED INKO A FEW MINUTES AGO.
...COME WITH ME.

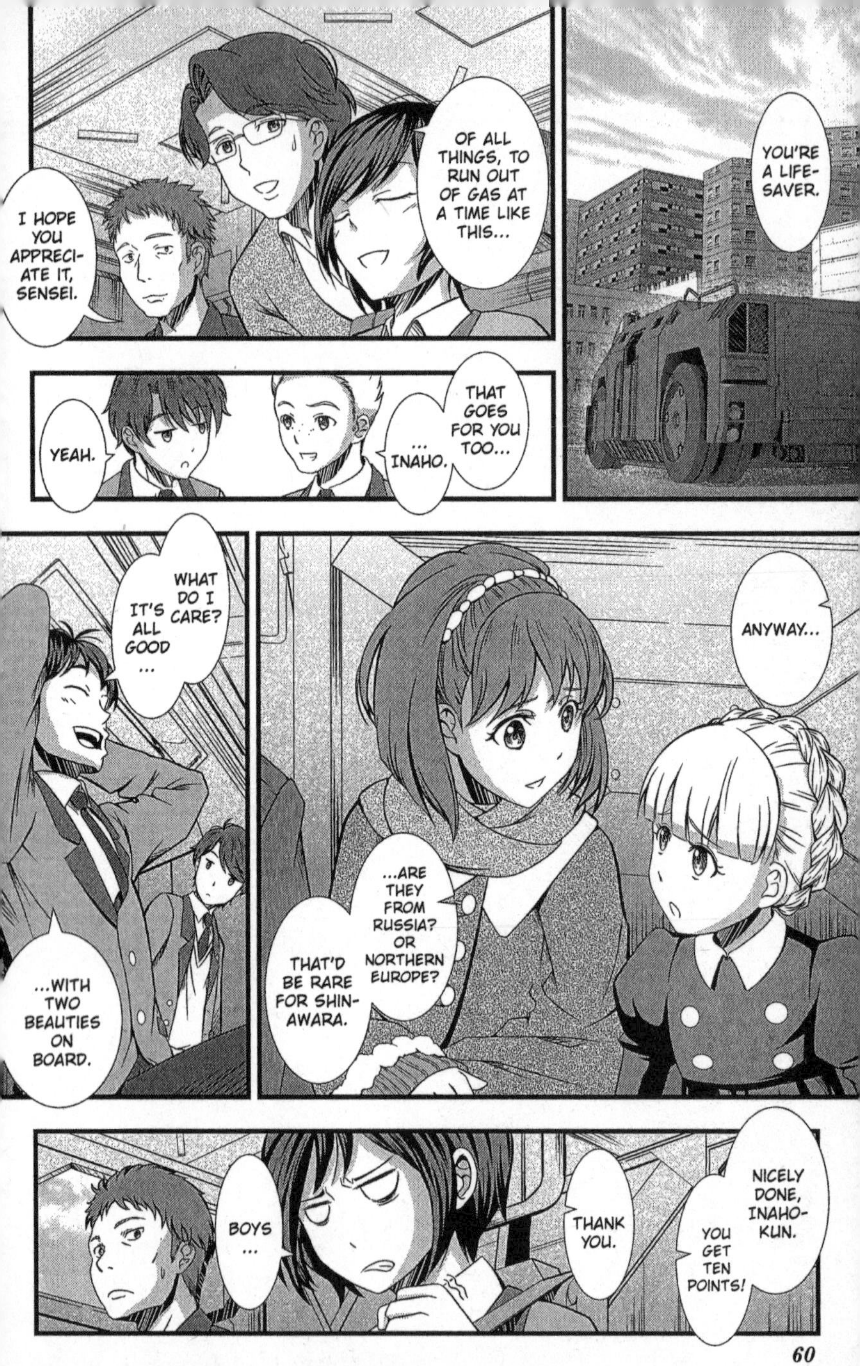
YOU'RE A LIFE-SAVER.
OF ALL THINGS, TO RUN OUT OF GAS AT A TIME LIKE THIS...
I HOPE YOU APPRECI-ATE IT, SENSEI.
THAT GOES FOR YOU TOO...
...INAHO.
YEAH.
ANYWAY...
...ARE THEY FROM RUSSIA? OR NORTHERN EUROPE?
THAT'D BE RARE FOR SHIN-AWARA.
WHAT DO I CARE?
IT'S ALL GOOD...
...WITH TWO BEAUTIES ON BOARD.
NICELY DONE, INAHO-KUN.
YOU GET TEN POINTS!
THANK YOU.
BOYS...

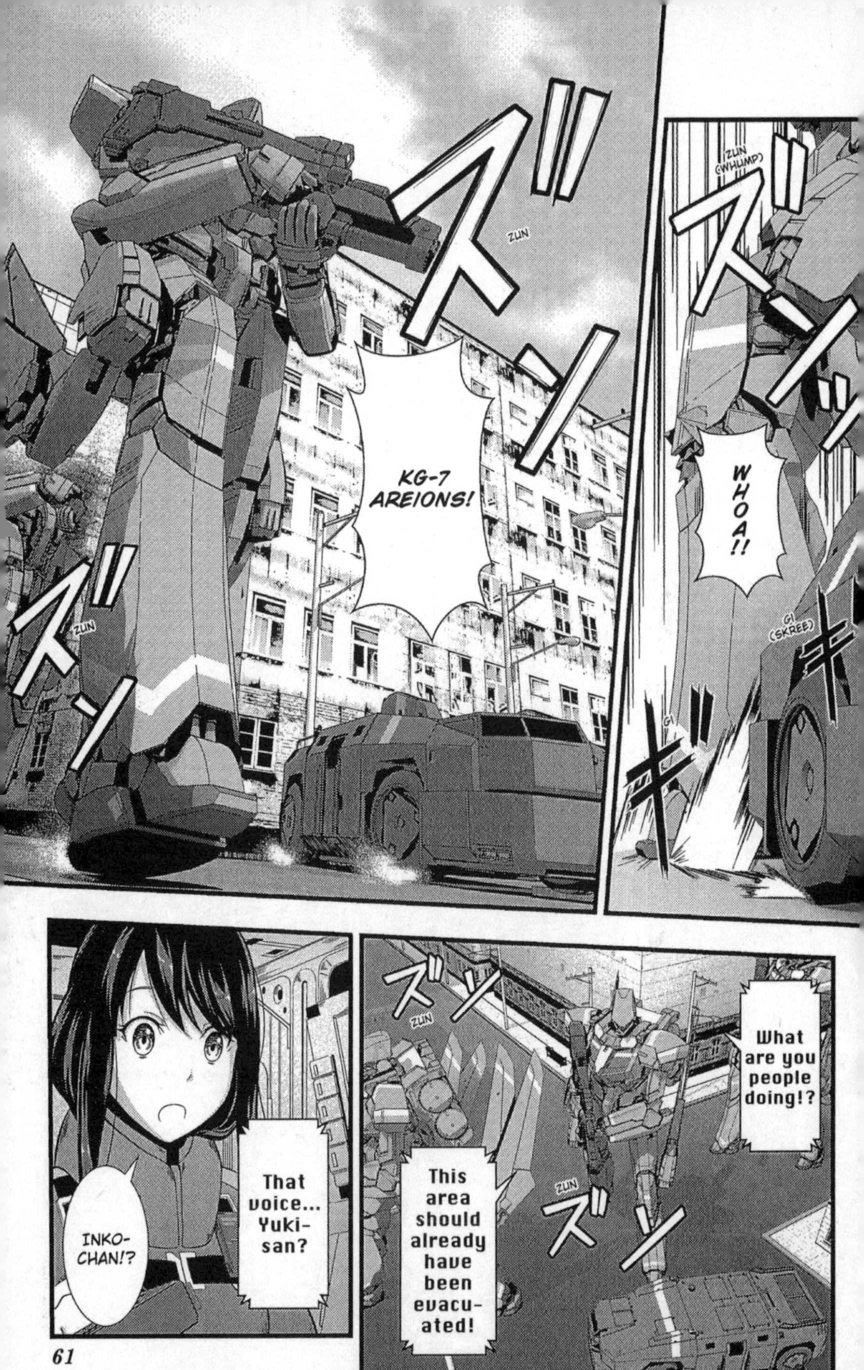
ZUN (WHUMP)
WHOA!!
GI (SKREE)
GI
ZUN
KG-7 AREIONS!
ZUN
What are you people doing!?
ZUN
This area should already have been evacuated!
ZUN
That voice... Yuki-san?
INKO-CHAN!?

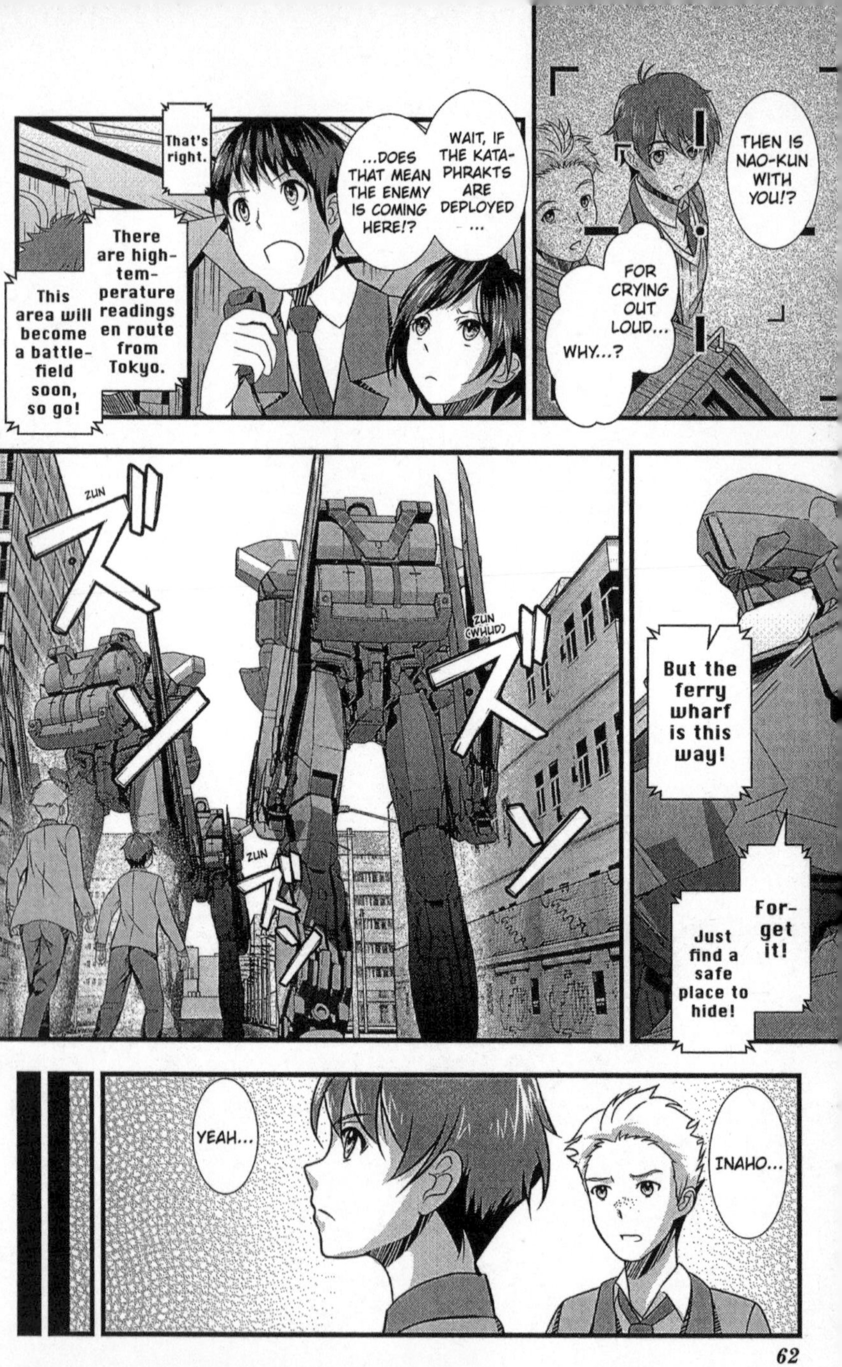
THEN IS NAO-KUN WITH YOU!?
FOR CRYING OUT LOUD... WHY...?
WAIT, IF THE KATAPHRAKTS ARE DEPLOYED...
...DOES THAT MEAN THE ENEMY IS COMING HERE!?
That's right.
There are high-temperature readings en route from Tokyo.
This area will become a battlefield soon, so go!
But the ferry wharf is this way!
Forget it!
Just find a safe place to hide!
ZUN (WHUD)
ZUN
ZUN
INAHO...
YEAH...

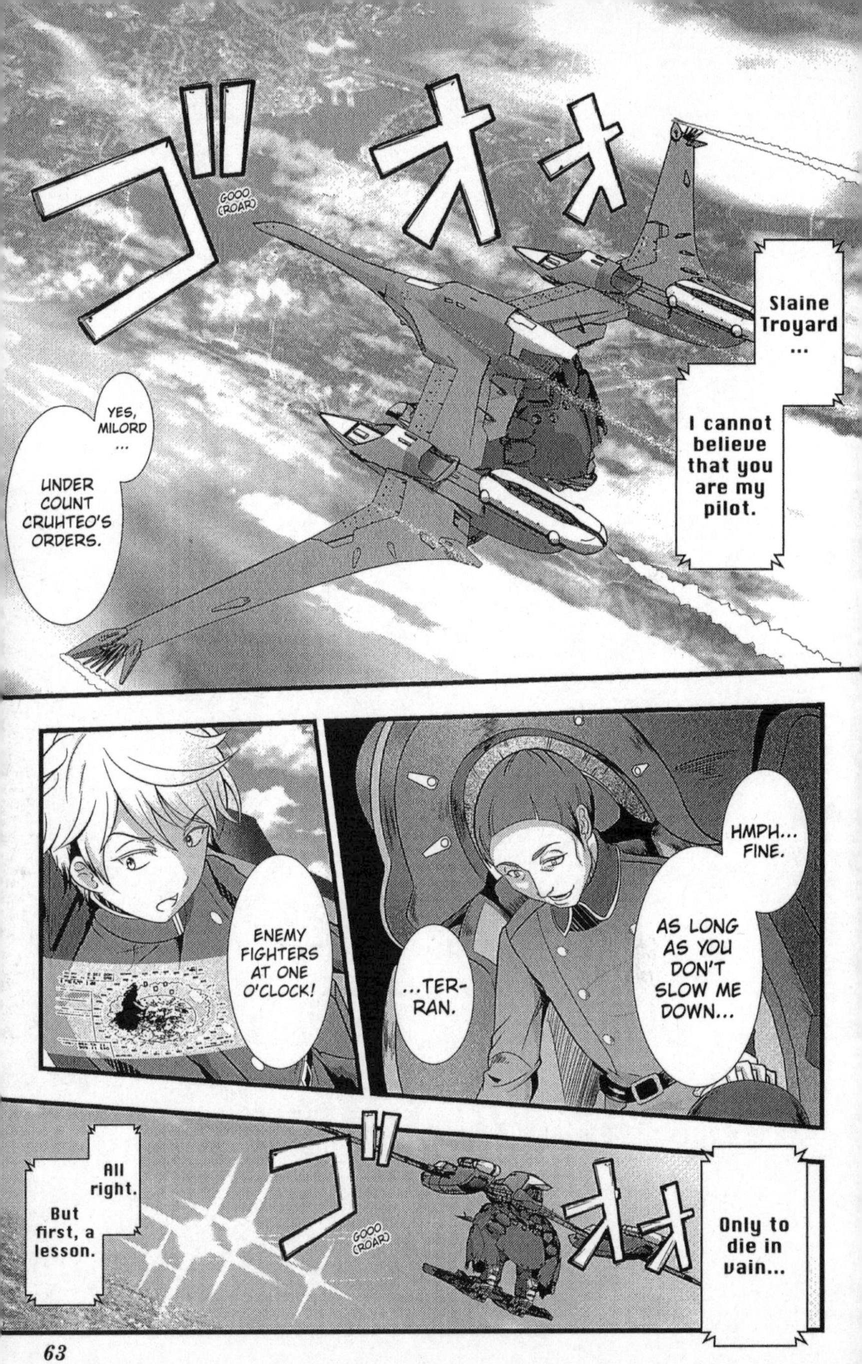
ゴオォ
GOOO (ROAR)
Slaine Troyard ...
I cannot believe that you are my pilot.
YES, MILORD ...
UNDER COUNT CRUHTEO'S ORDERS.
HMPH... FINE.
AS LONG AS YOU DON'T SLOW ME DOWN...
...TER-RAN.
ENEMY FIGHTERS AT ONE O'CLOCK!
Only to die in vain...
ゴオ
GOOO (ROAR)
All right.
But first, a lesson.

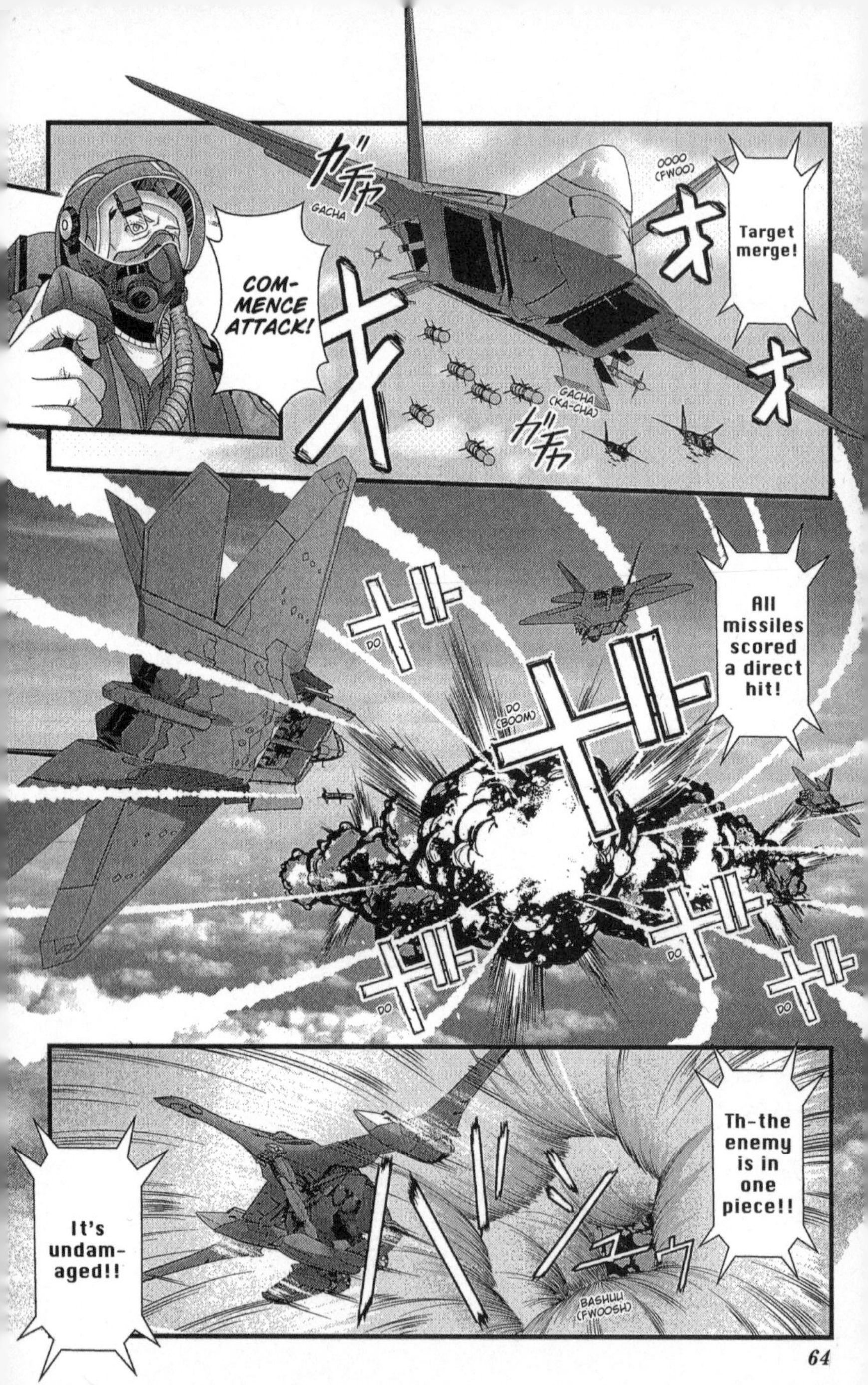
Target merge!
OOOO (FWOO)
GACHA (KA-CHA)
GACHA
COM-MENCE ATTACK!
All missiles scored a direct hit!
DO (BOOM)
DO
DO
DO
DO
Th-the enemy is in one piece!!
BASHUU (FWOOSH)
It's undam-aged!!

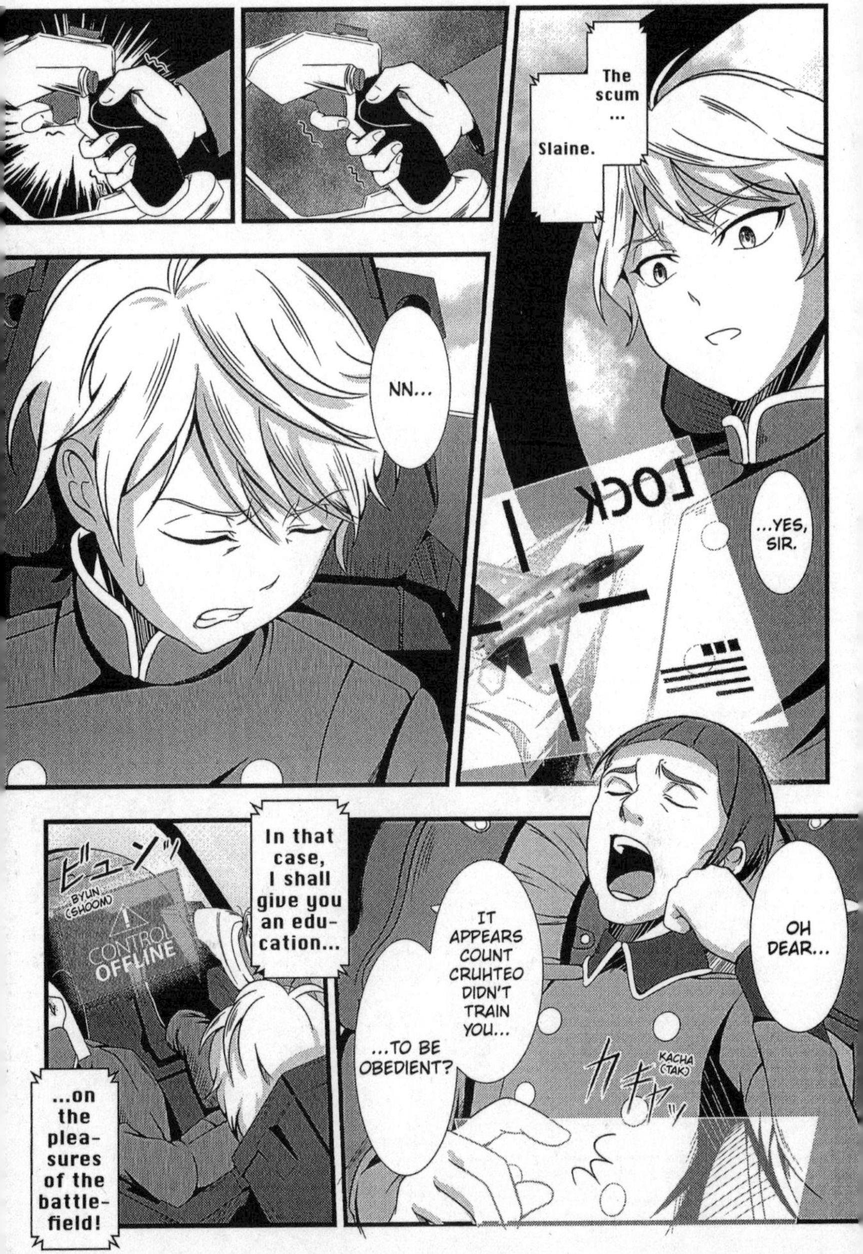
The scum ... Slaine.
LOCK
...YES, SIR.
NN...
OH DEAR...
IT APPEARS COUNT CRUHTEO DIDN'T TRAIN YOU...
...TO BE OBEDIENT?
カチャッ
KACHA (TAK)
In that case, I shall give you an edu-cation...
ビュンッ
BYUN (SHOOM)
CONTROL OFFLINE
...on the plea-sures of the battle-field!

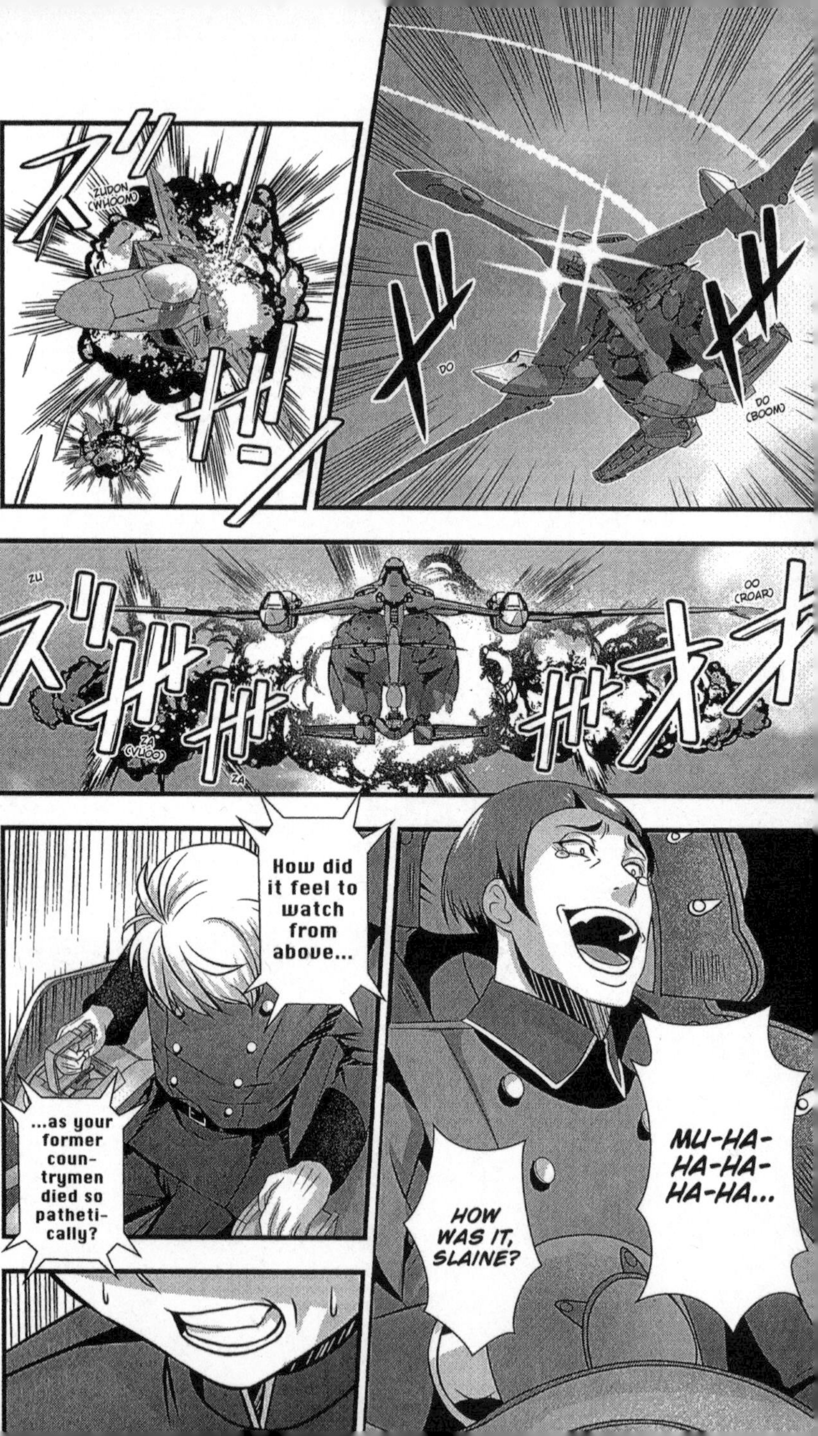
DO
DO (BOOM)
ZUDON (WHOOM)
OO (ROAR)
ZA
ZA (VUOO)
ZA
ZU
MU-HA-HA-HA-HA-HA...
HOW WAS IT, SLAINE?
How did it feel to watch from above...
...as your former coun-trymen died so patheti-cally?

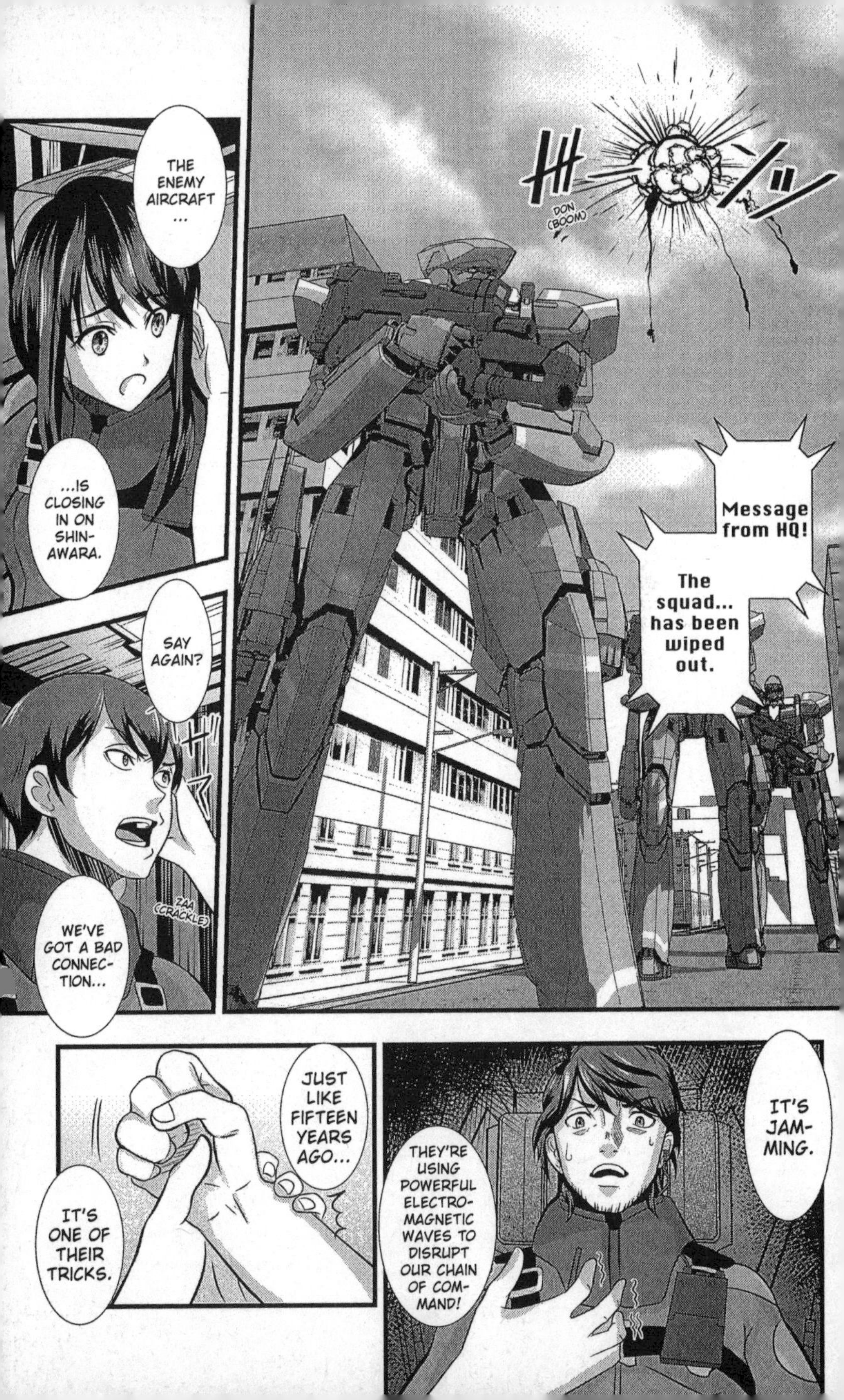
DON (BOOM)
Message from HQ!
The squad... has been wiped out.
THE ENEMY AIRCRAFT ...
...IS CLOSING IN ON SHIN-AWARA.
SAY AGAIN?
ZAA (CRACKLE)
WE'VE GOT A BAD CONNEC-TION...
IT'S JAM-MING.
THEY'RE USING POWERFUL ELECTRO-MAGNETIC WAVES TO DISRUPT OUR CHAIN OF COM-MAND!
JUST LIKE FIFTEEN YEARS AGO...
IT'S ONE OF THEIR TRICKS.

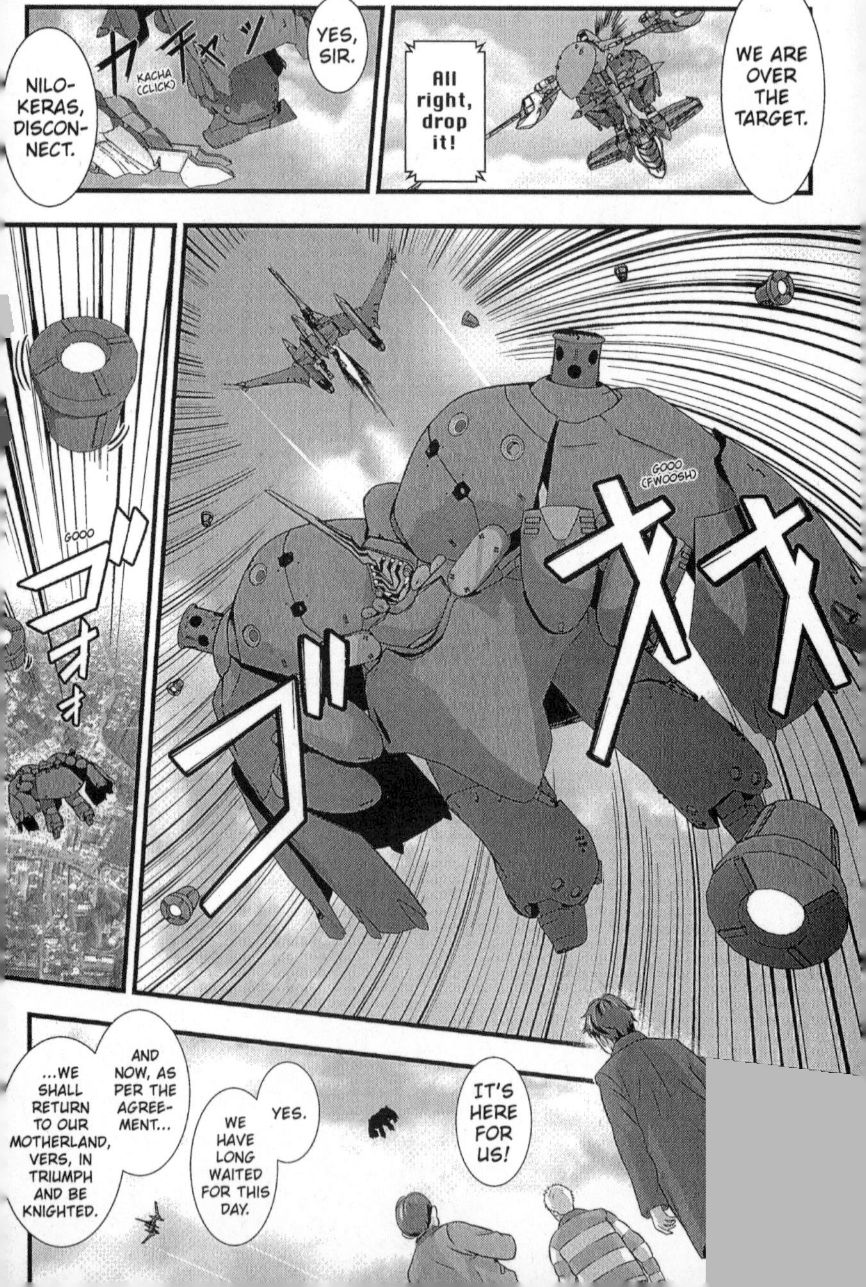
WE ARE OVER THE TARGET.
All right, drop it!
YES, SIR.
KACHA (CLICK)
NILO-KERAS, DISCONNECT.
GOOO (FWOOSH)
GOOO
IT'S HERE FOR US!
YES.
WE HAVE LONG WAITED FOR THIS DAY.
AND NOW, AS PER THE AGREEMENT...
...WE SHALL RETURN TO OUR MOTHERLAND, VERS, IN TRIUMPH AND BE KNIGHTED.

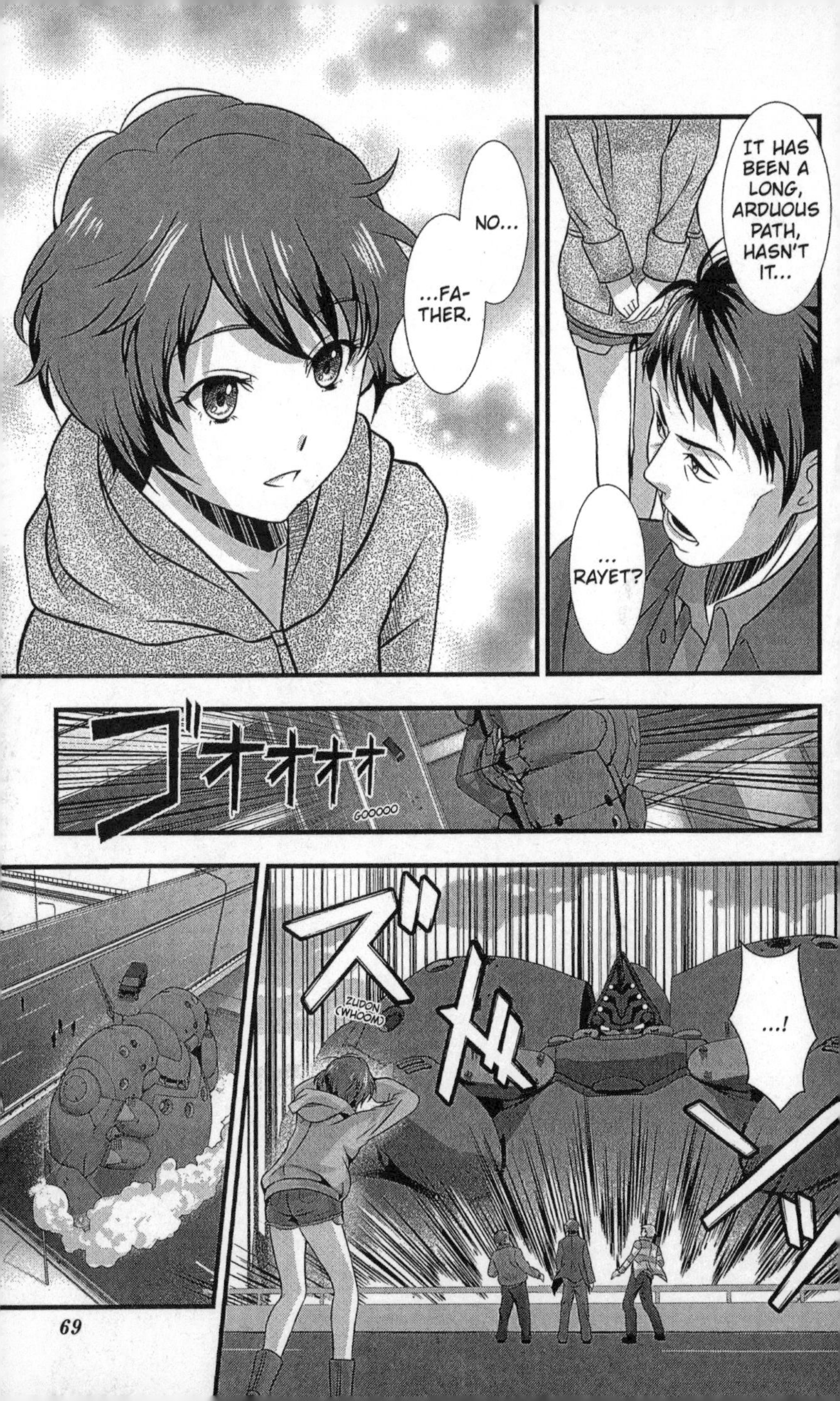
IT HAS BEEN A LONG, ARDUOUS PATH, HASN'T IT...
...RAYET?
NO...
...FA-THER.
ゴオオオオ
GOOOOO
ズドン
ZUDON (WHOOM)
...!

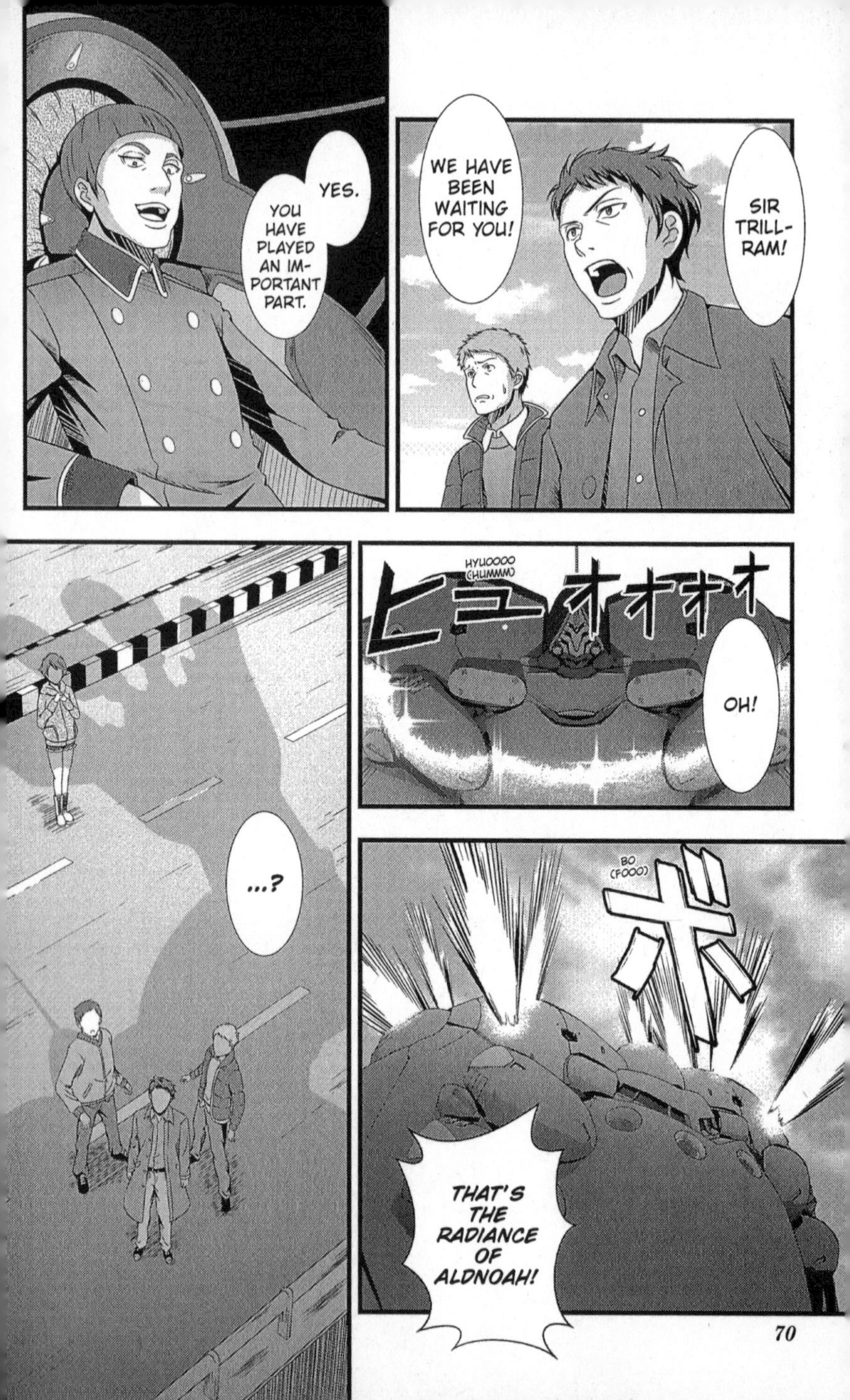
SIR TRILL-RAM!
WE HAVE BEEN WAITING FOR YOU!
YES.
YOU HAVE PLAYED AN IMPORTANT PART.
HYUOOOO (HUMMM)
ヒュオオオオ
OH!
BO (FOOO)
ボ
THAT'S THE RADIANCE OF ALDNOAH!
...?

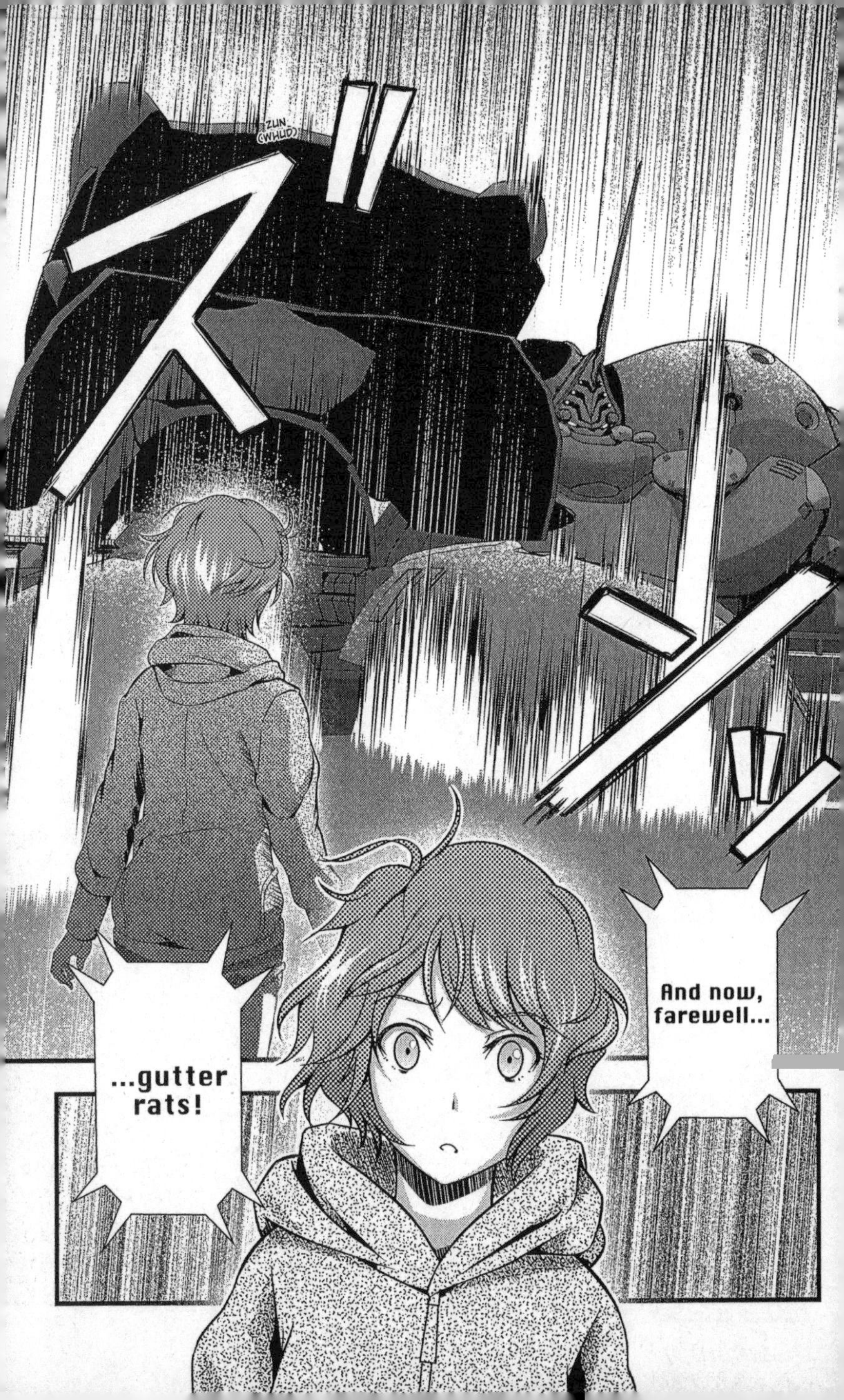
ZUN
(WHUD)
And now, farewell...
...gutter rats!

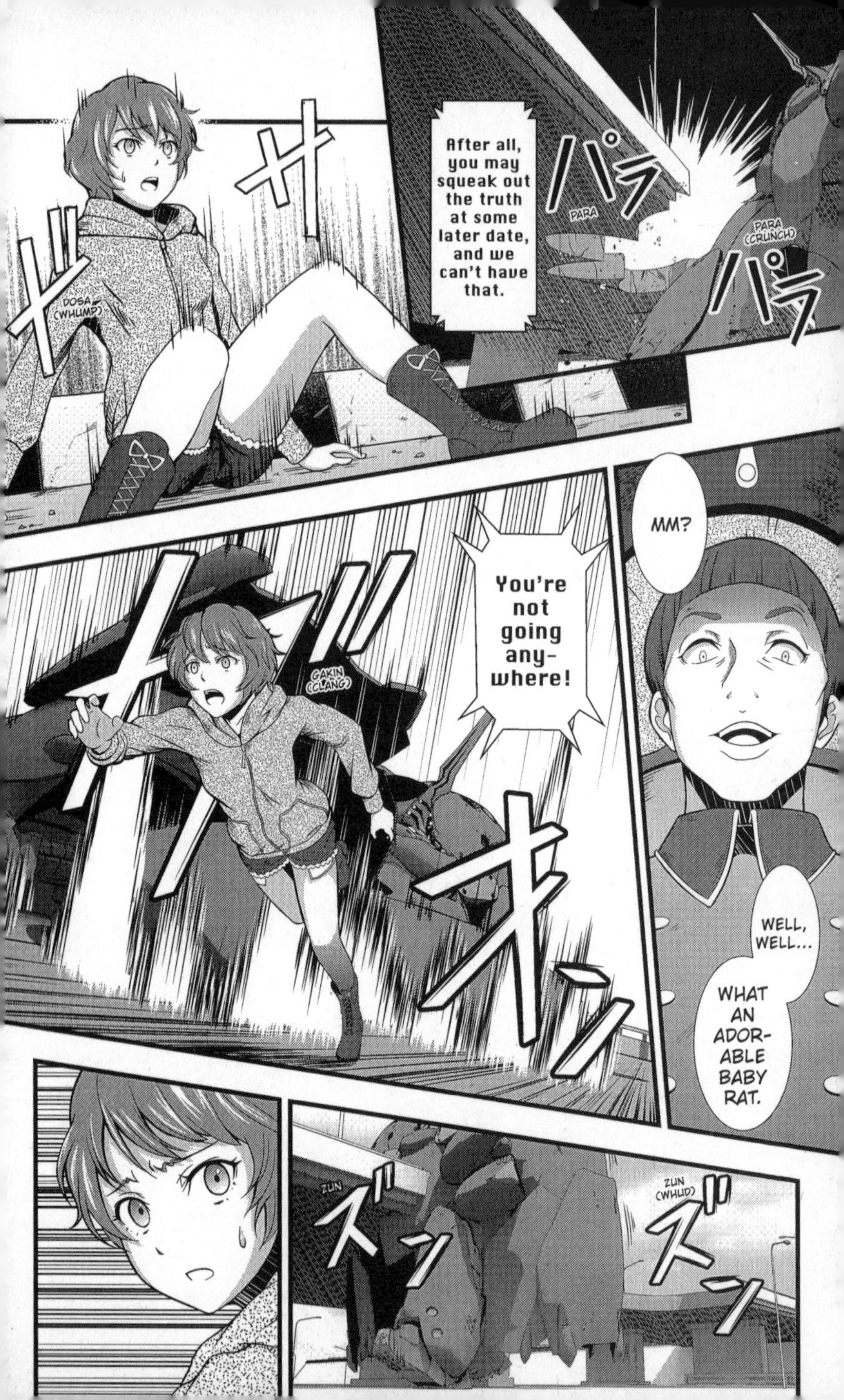
After all, you may squeak out the truth at some later date, and we can't have that.
パラ
PARA
PARA (CRUNCH)
パラ
DOSA (WHUMP)
MM?
WELL, WELL...
WHAT AN ADORABLE BABY RAT.
You're not going any-where!
GAKIN (CLANG)
ZUN (WHUD)
ズン
ZUN
ズン

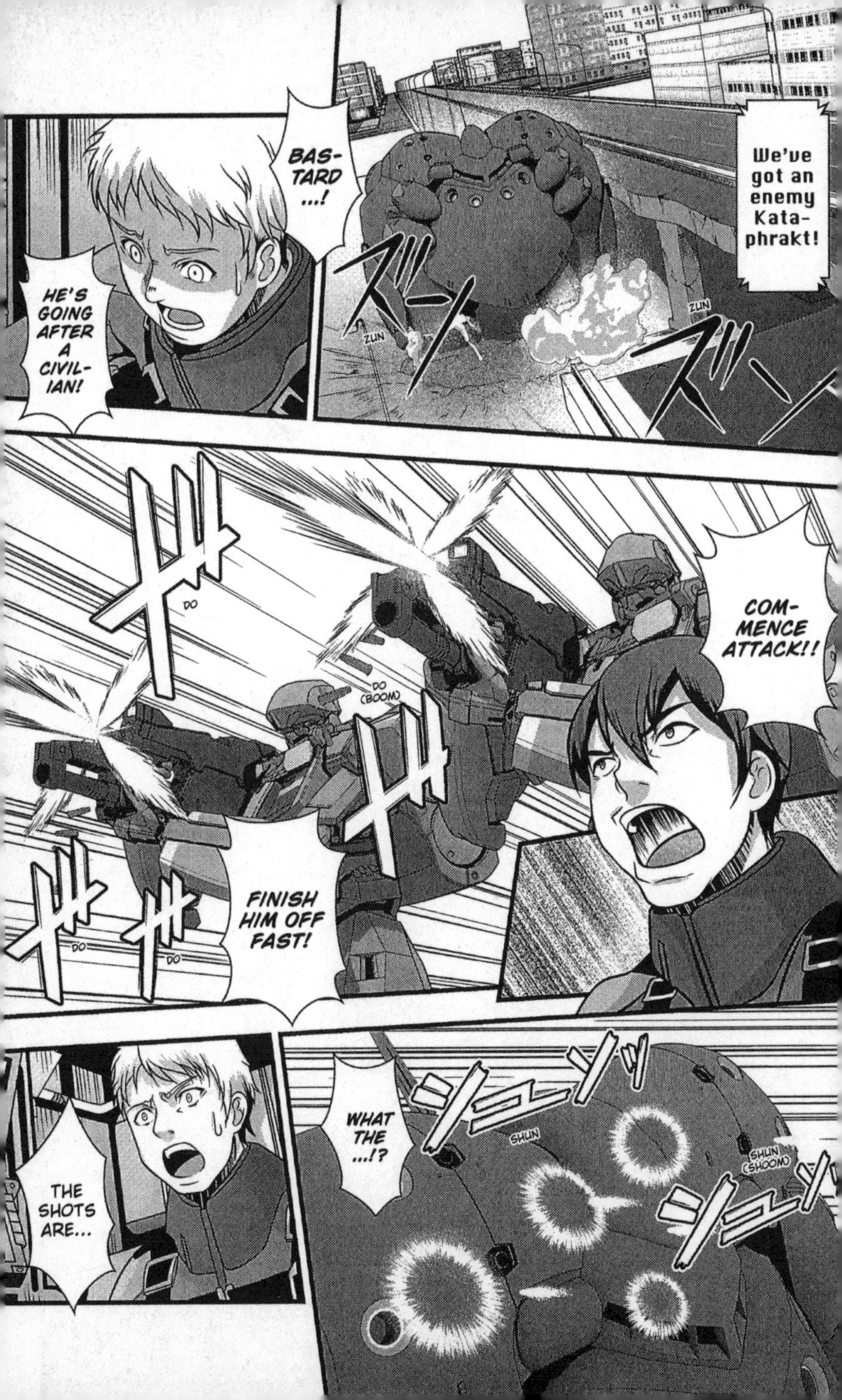
We've got an enemy Kataphrakt!
ZUN
ZUN
BAS-TARD...!
HE'S GOING AFTER A CIVIL-IAN!
COM-MENCE ATTACK!!
DO
DO (BOOM)
FINISH HIM OFF FAST!
DO
DO
WHAT THE...!?
SHUN
SHUN (SHOOM)
THE SHOTS ARE...

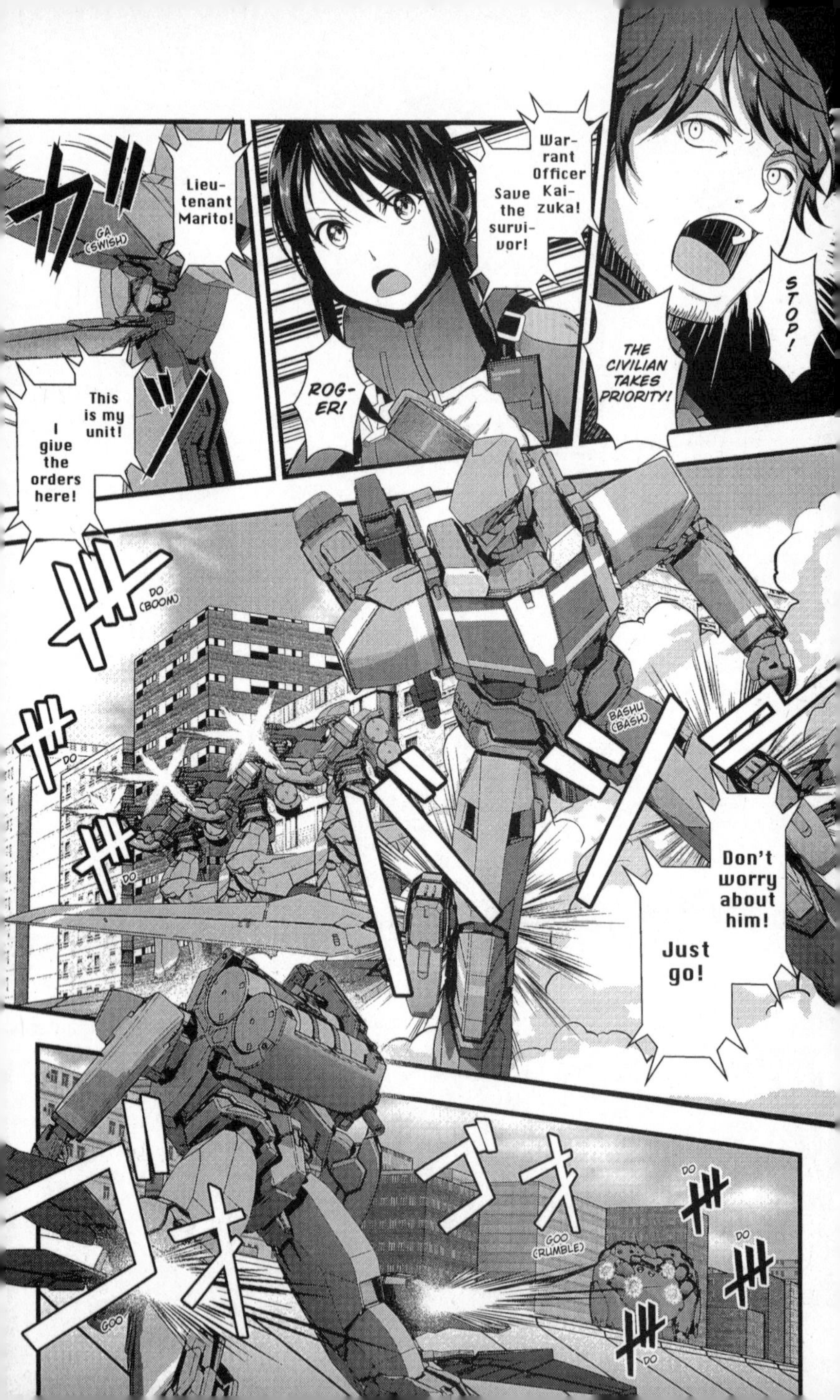
STOP!
THE CIVILIAN TAKES PRIORITY!
Warrant Officer Kaizuka!
Save the survivor!
ROGER!
GA (SWISH)
Lieutenant Marito!
This is my unit!
I give the orders here!
BASHU (BASH)
Don't worry about him!
Just go!
DO (BOOM)
DO
DO
DO
DO
GOO (RUMBLE)
DO
GOO

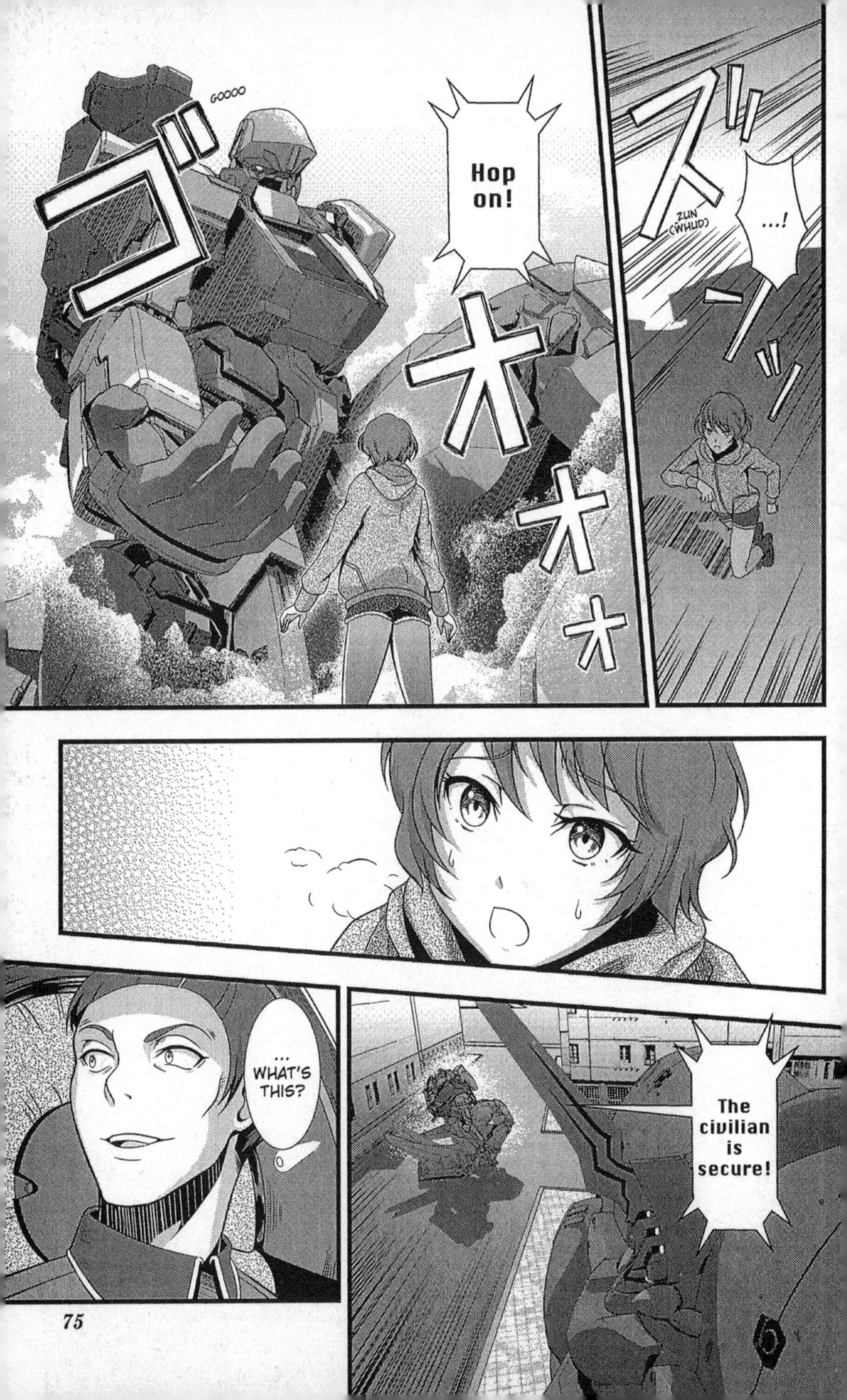
ZUN (WHUD)
...!
GOOOO
Hop on!
The civilian is secure!
... WHAT'S THIS?

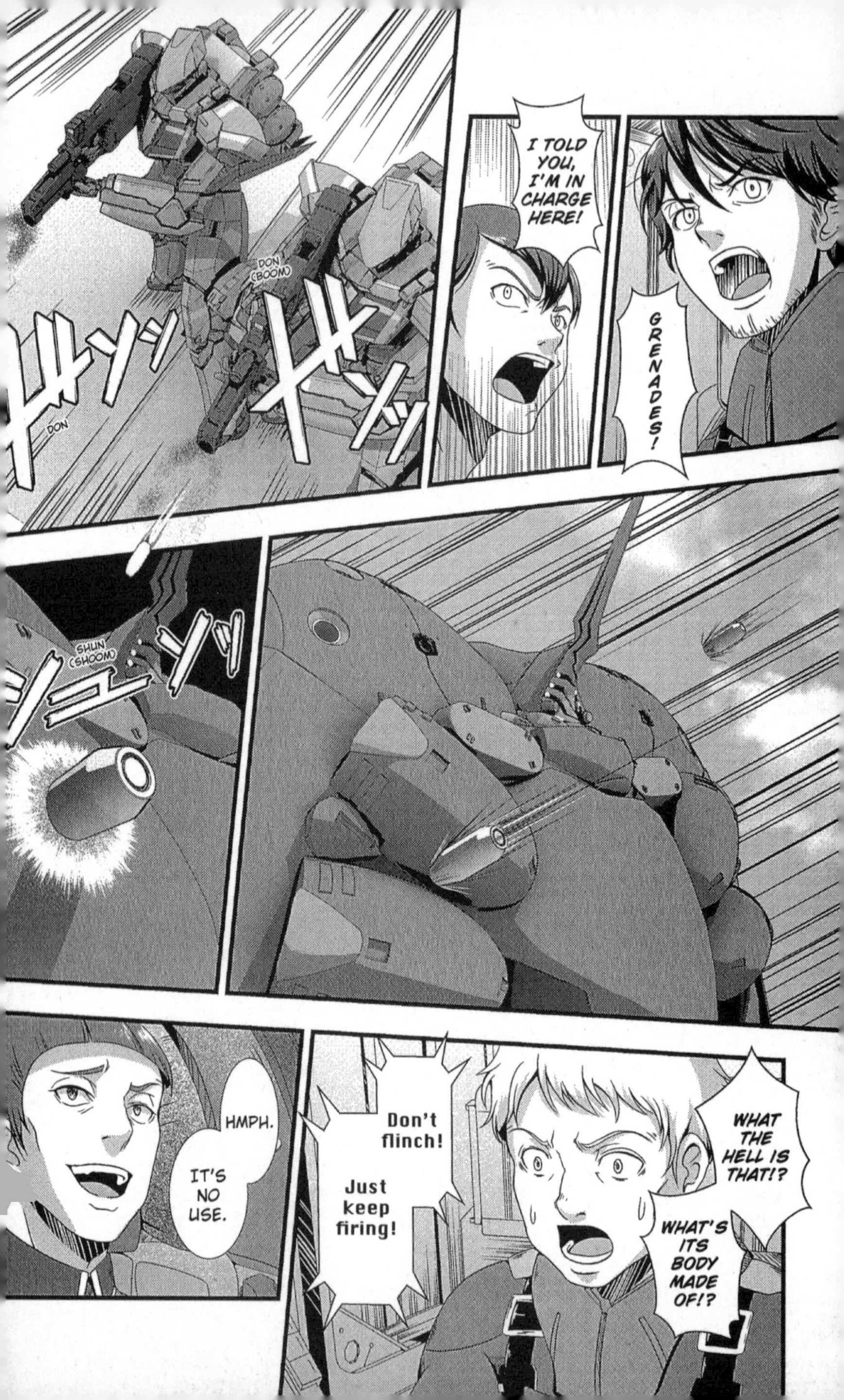
GRENADES!
I TOLD YOU, I'M IN CHARGE HERE!
DON (BOOM)
DON
SHUN (SHOOM)
WHAT THE HELL IS THAT!?
WHAT'S ITS BODY MADE OF!?
Don't flinch!
Just keep firing!
HMPH.
IT'S NO USE.

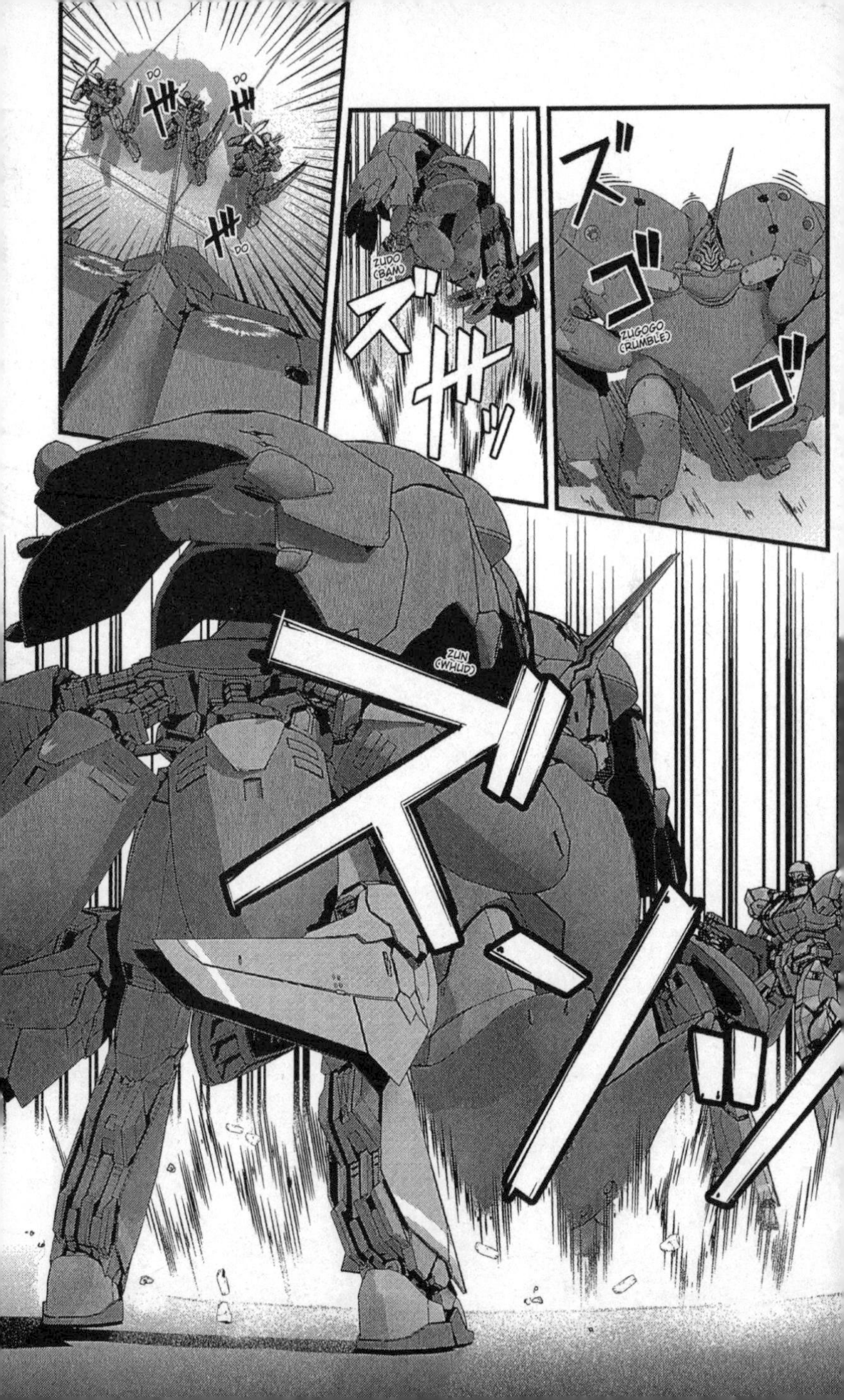
ZUGOGO
(RUMBLE)
ZUDO
(BAM)
DO
DO
DO
ZUN
(WHUD)

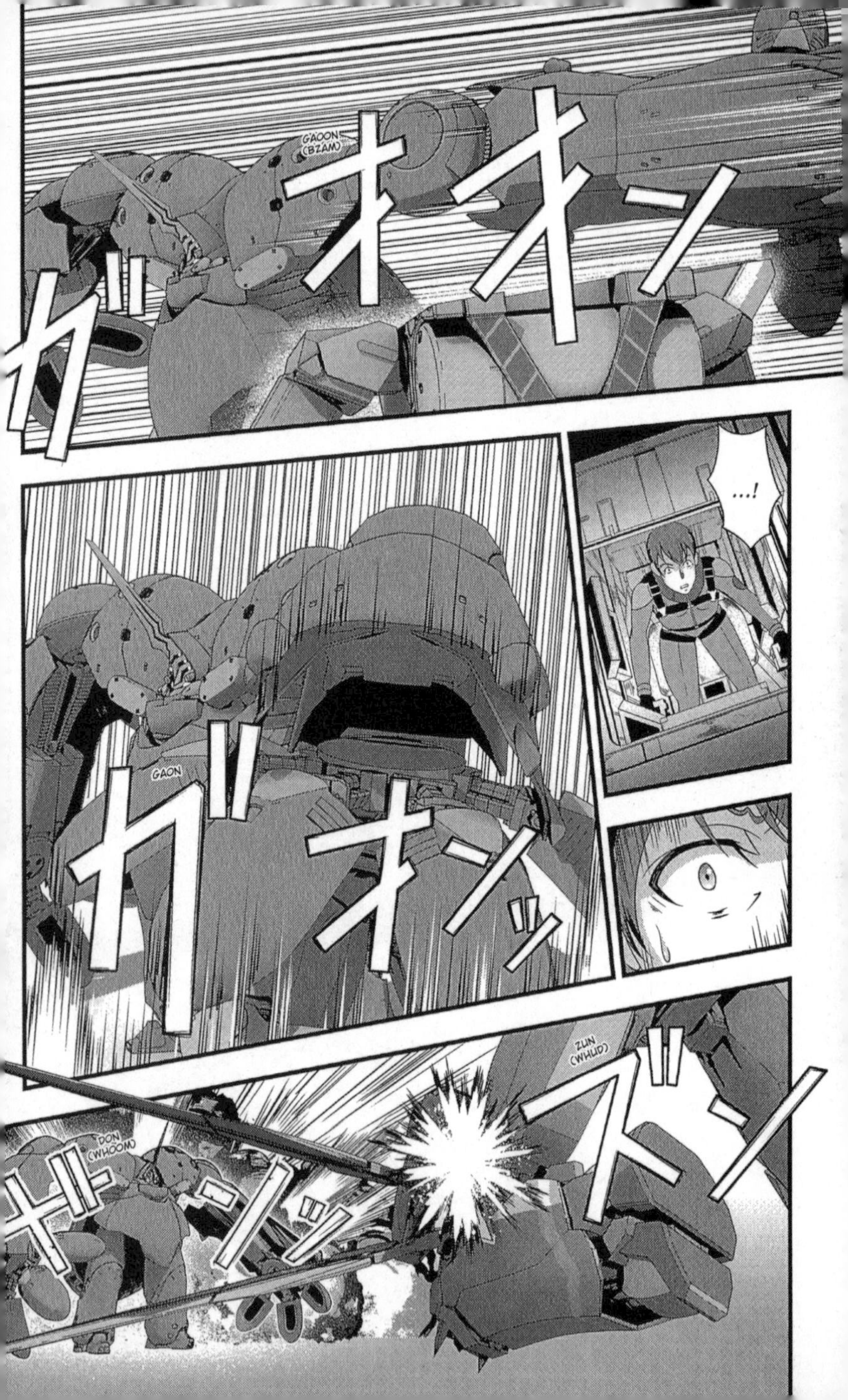
GAOON (BZAM)
...!
GAON
ZUN (WHUD)
DON (WHOOM)

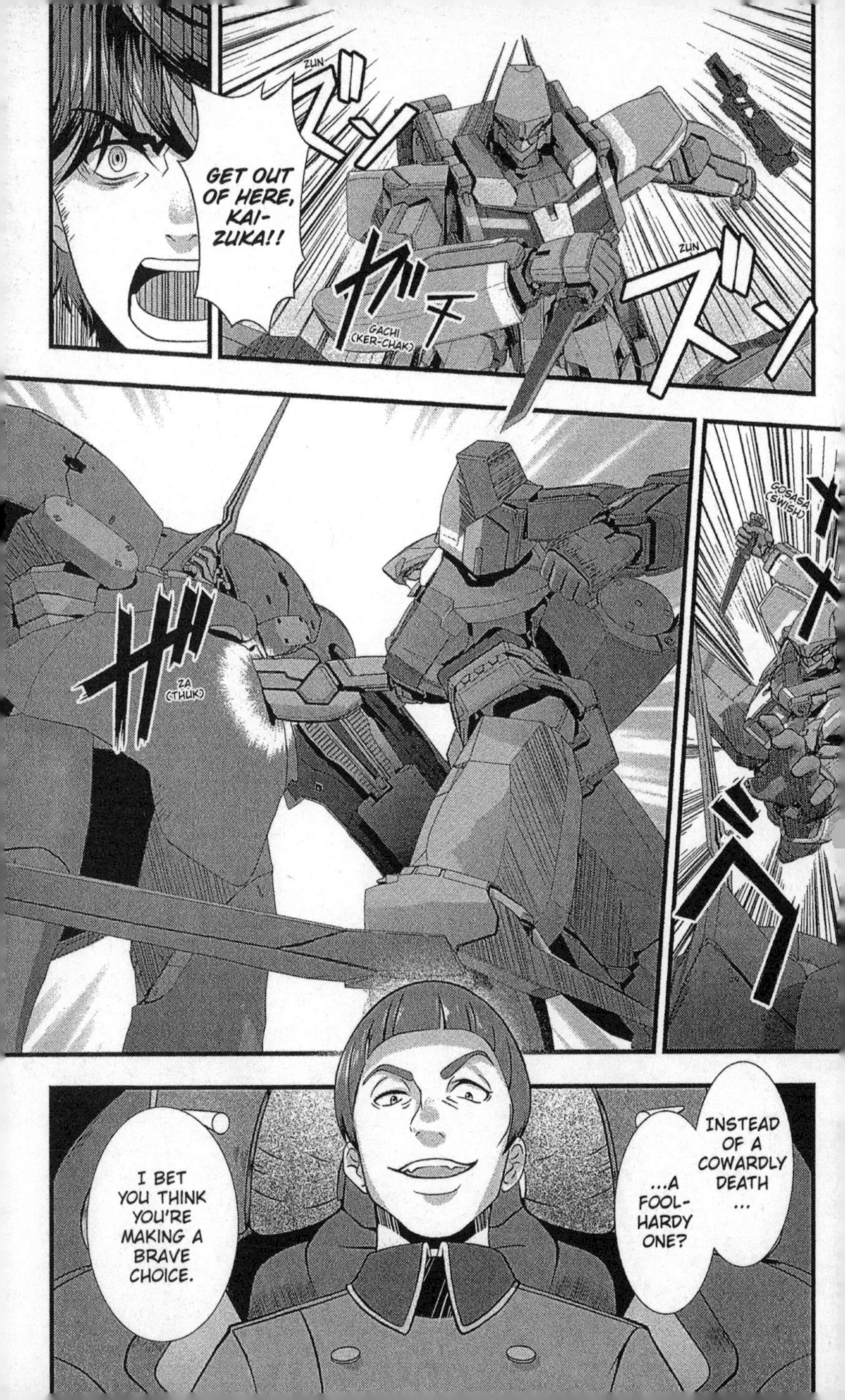
ZUN
ZUN
GACHI (KER-CHAK)
GET OUT OF HERE, KAI-ZUKA!!
GOSASA (SWISH)
ZA (THUK)
INSTEAD OF A COWARDLY DEATH ...
...A FOOL-HARDY ONE?
I BET YOU THINK YOU'RE MAKING A BRAVE CHOICE.

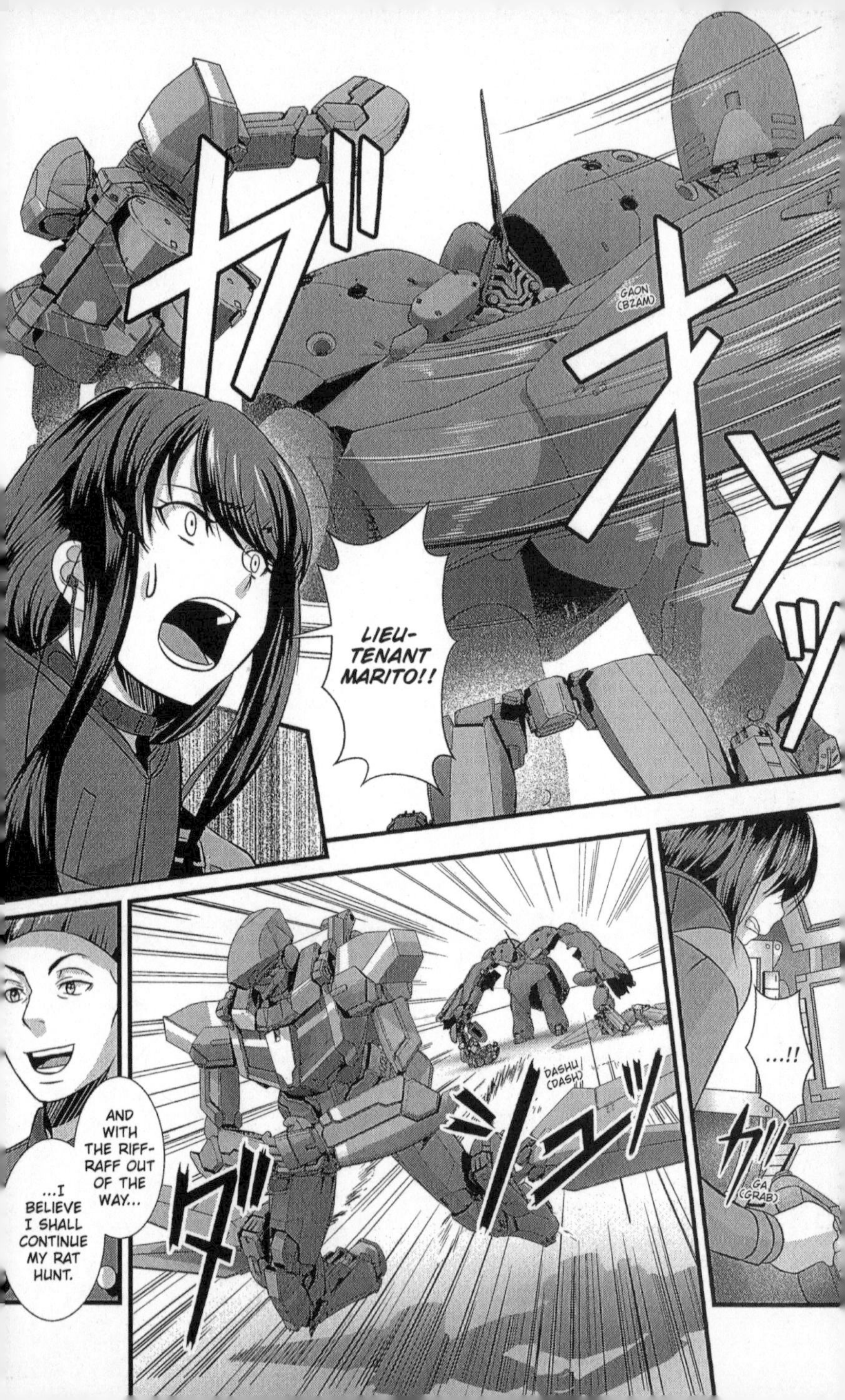
GAON (BZAM)
LIEU-TENANT MARITO!!
...!!
GA (GRAB)
DASHU (DASH)
AND WITH THE RIFF-RAFF OUT OF THE WAY...
...I BELIEVE I SHALL CONTINUE MY RAT HUNT.

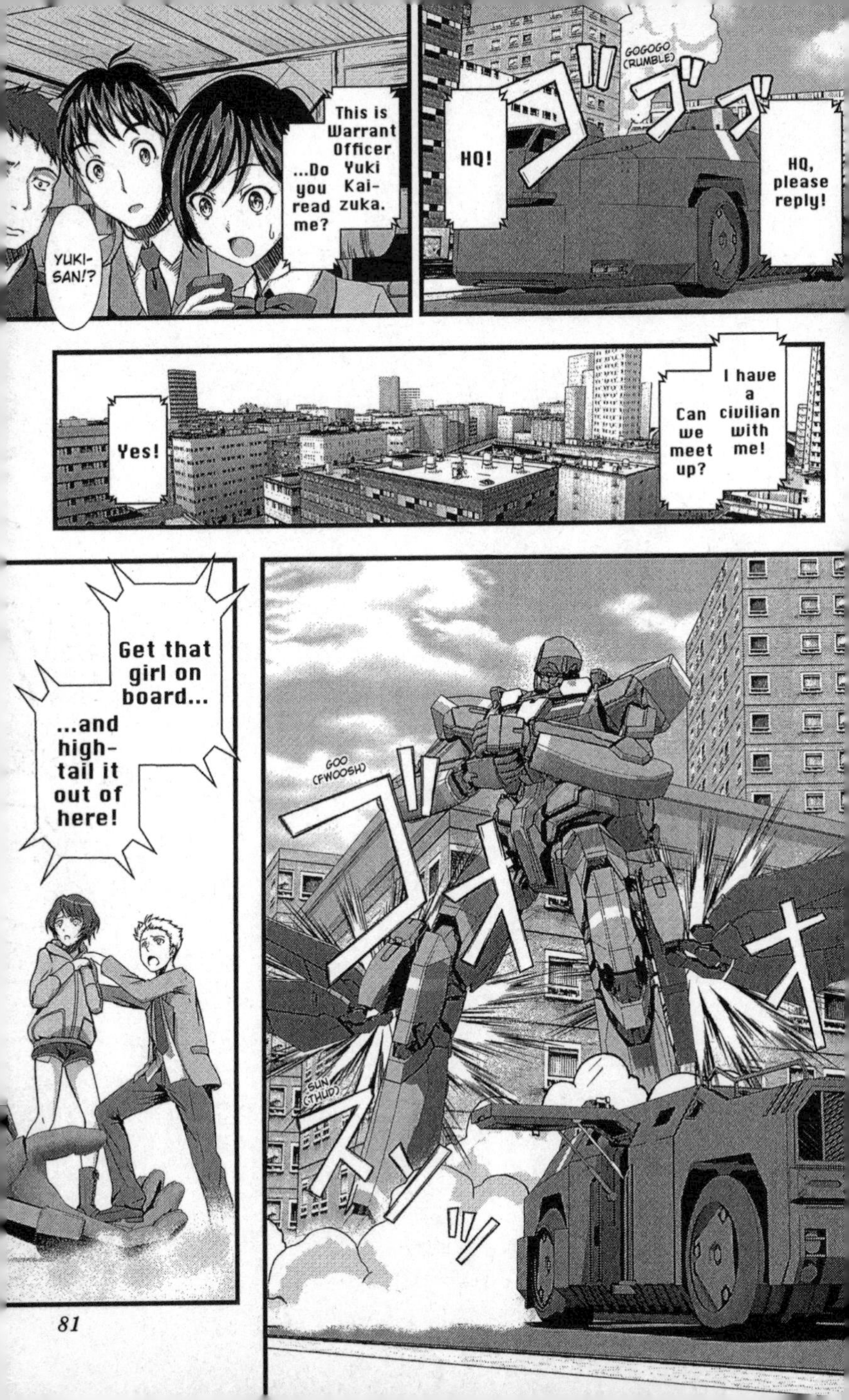
GOGOGO (RUMBLE)
HQ, please reply!
HQ!
This is Warrant Officer Yuki Kai-zuka.
...Do you read me?
YUKI-SAN!?
I have a civilian with me!
Can we meet up?
Yes!
GOO (FWOOSH)
SUN (THUD)
Get that girl on board...
...and high-tail it out of here!

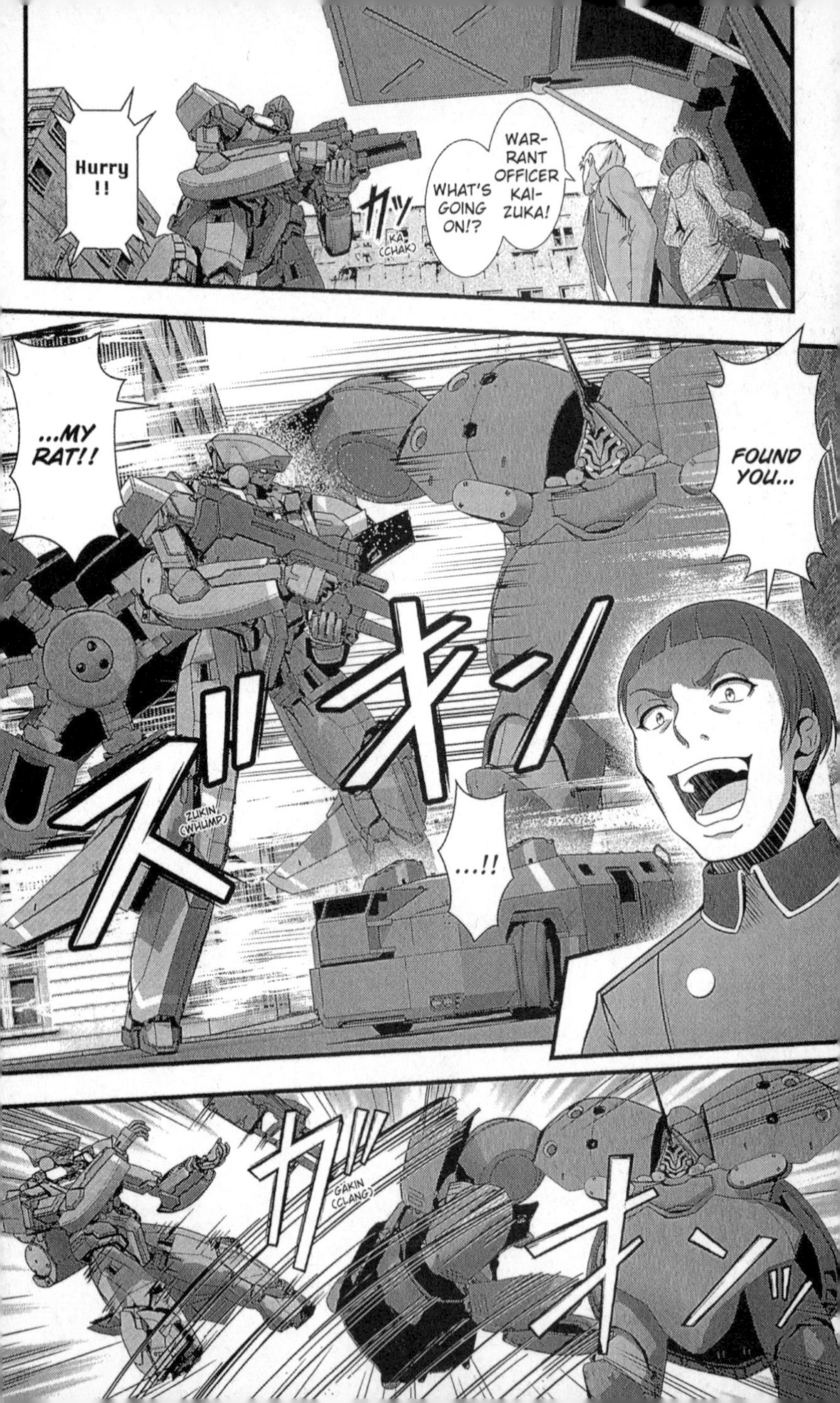
WAR-RANT OFFICER KAI-ZUKA!
WHAT'S GOING ON!?
KA (CHAK)
Hurry !!
FOUND YOU...
...MY RAT!!
...!!
ZUKIN (WHUMP)
GAKIN (CLANG)

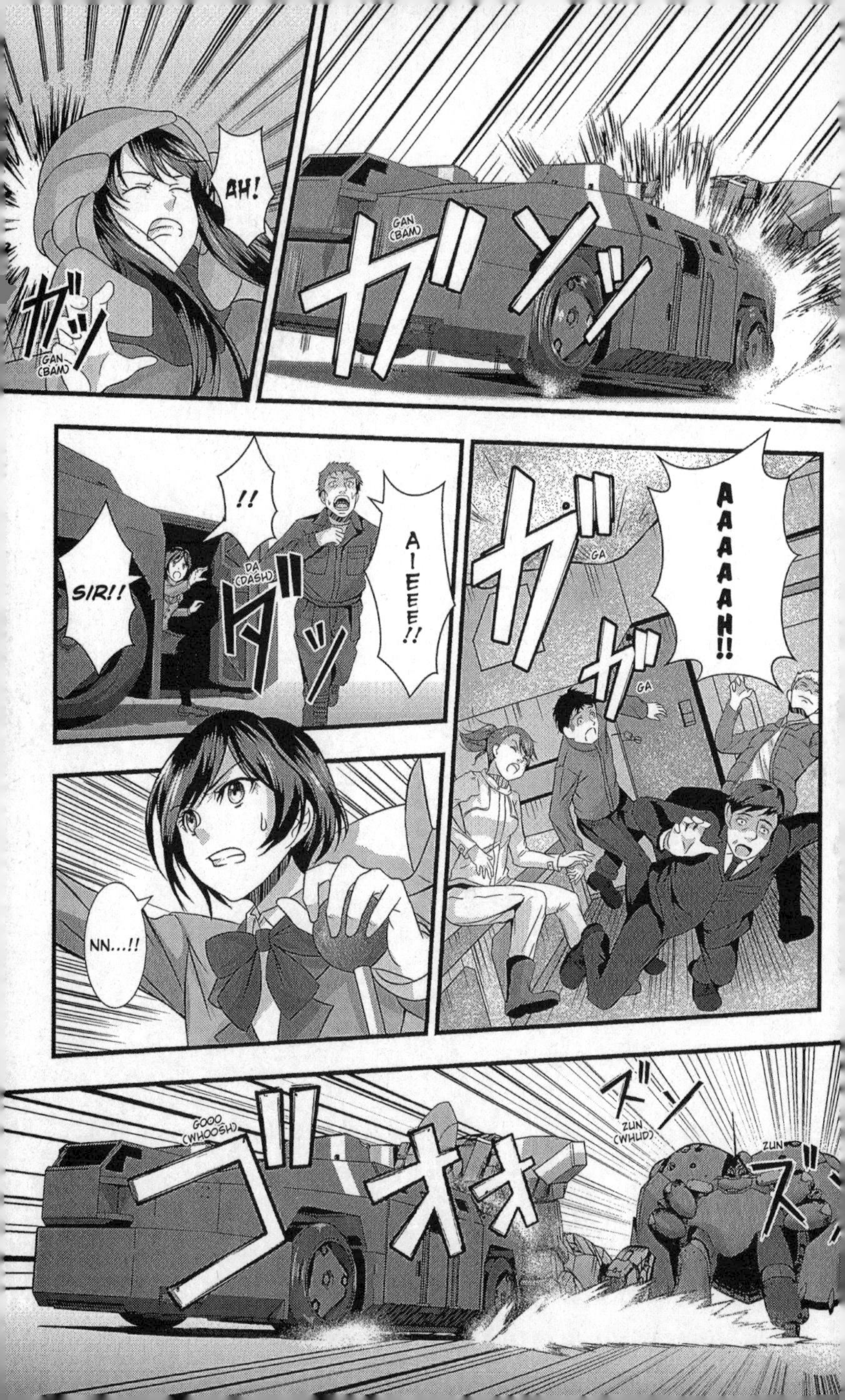
GAN (BAM)
AH!
GAN (BAM)
AAAAAAH!!
GA
GA
!!
AIEEE!!
DA (DASH)
SIR!!
NN...!!
ZUN
ZUN (WHUD)
GOOO (WHOOSH)

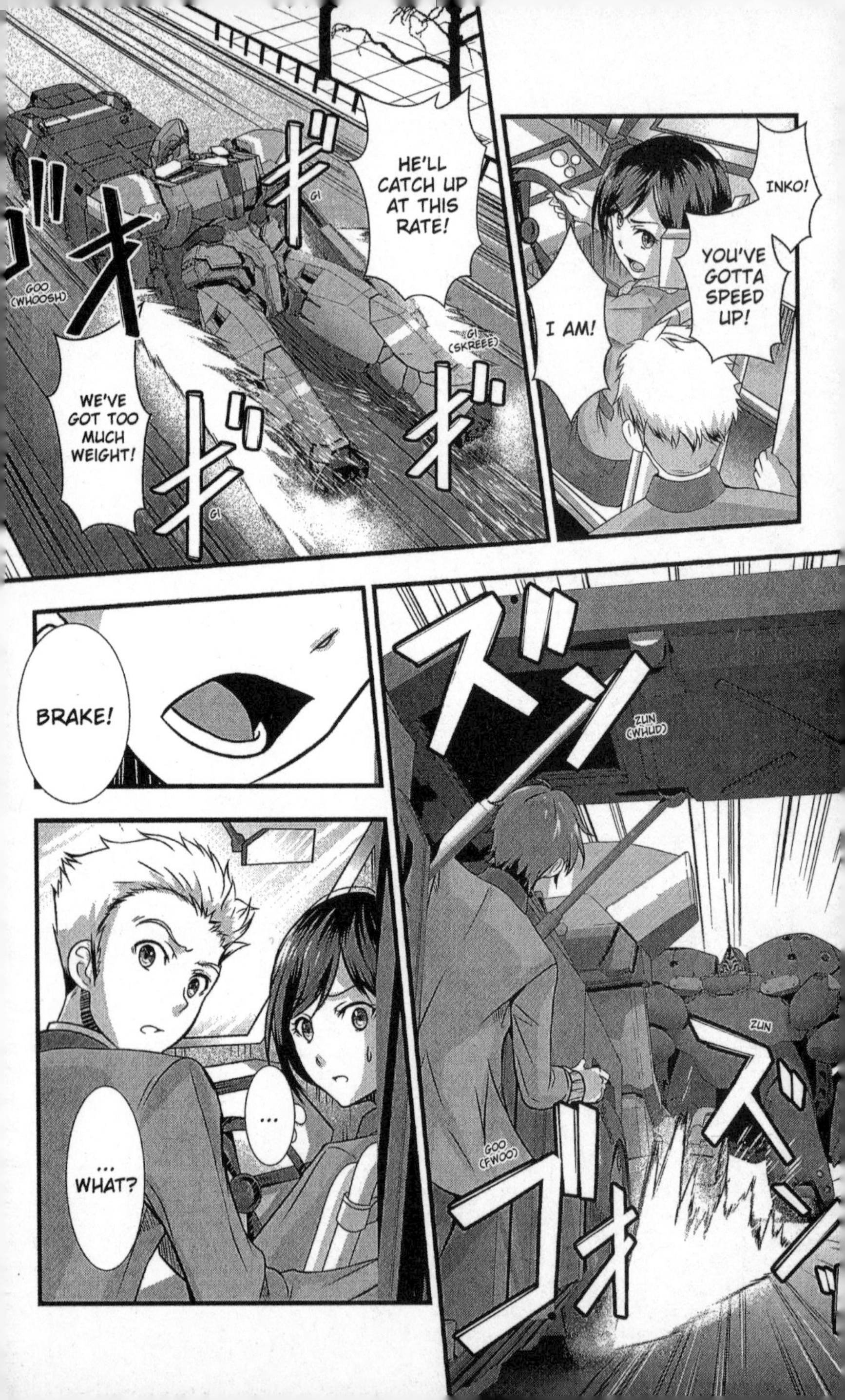
INKO!
YOU'VE GOTTA SPEED UP!
I AM!
HE'LL CATCH UP AT THIS RATE!
GI
GI (SKREEE)
GOO (WHOOSH)
WE'VE GOT TOO MUCH WEIGHT!
GI
ZUN (WHUD)
ZUN
GOO (FWOO)
BRAKE!
...
... WHAT?

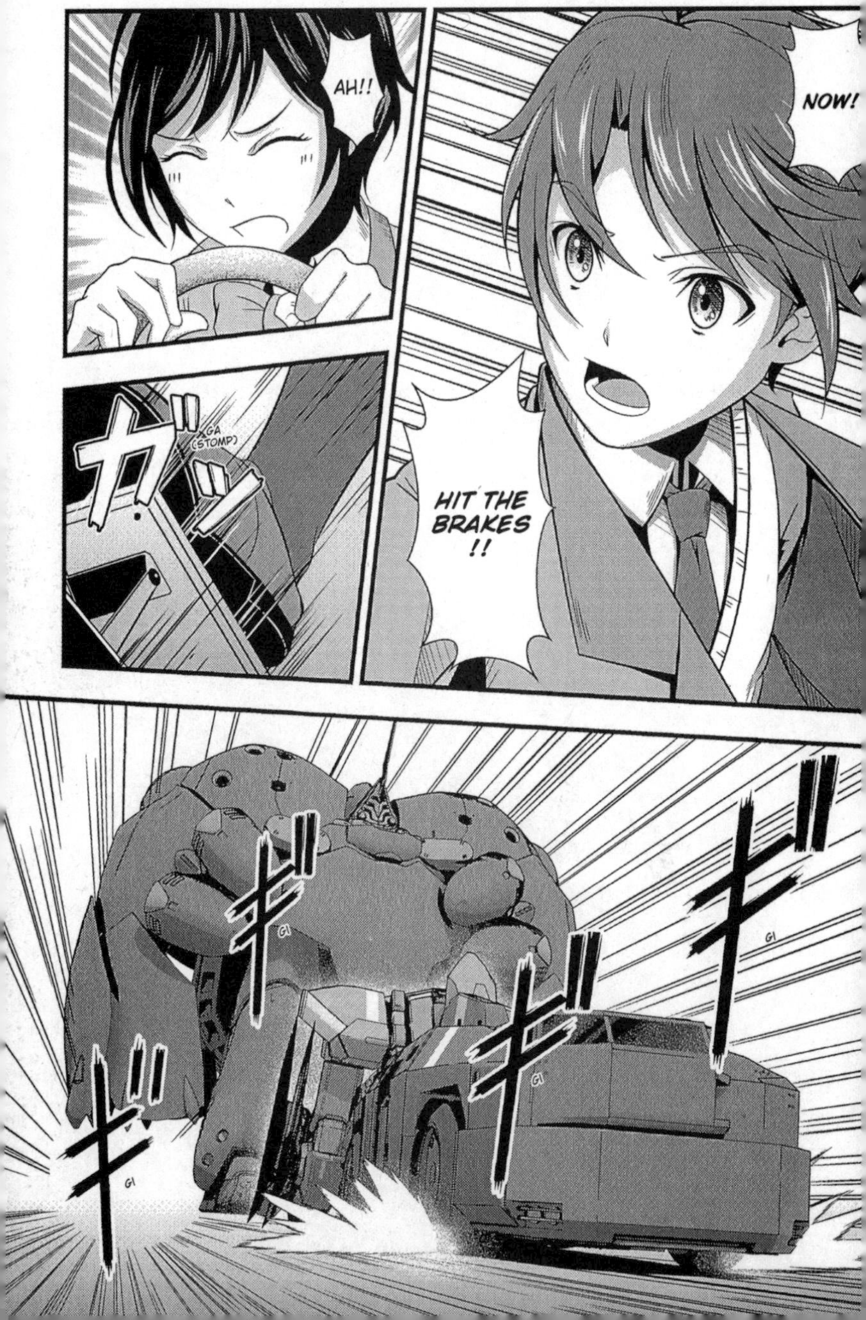
NOW!
HIT THE BRAKES !!
AH!!
GA (STOMP)
GI
GI
GI
GI

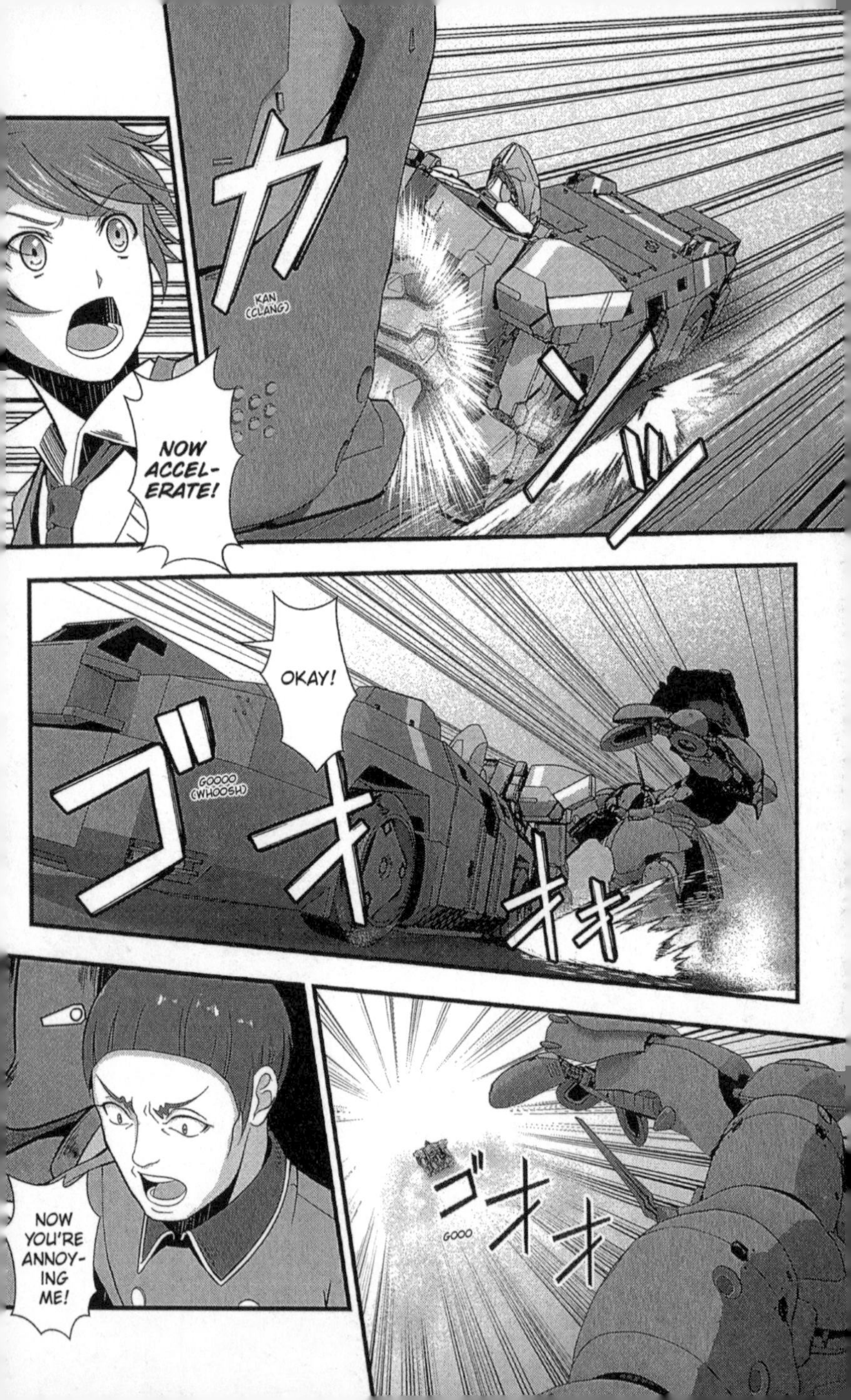
KAN (CLANG)
NOW ACCEL-ERATE!
OKAY!
GOOOO (WHOOSH)
GOOO
NOW YOU'RE ANNOY-ING ME!

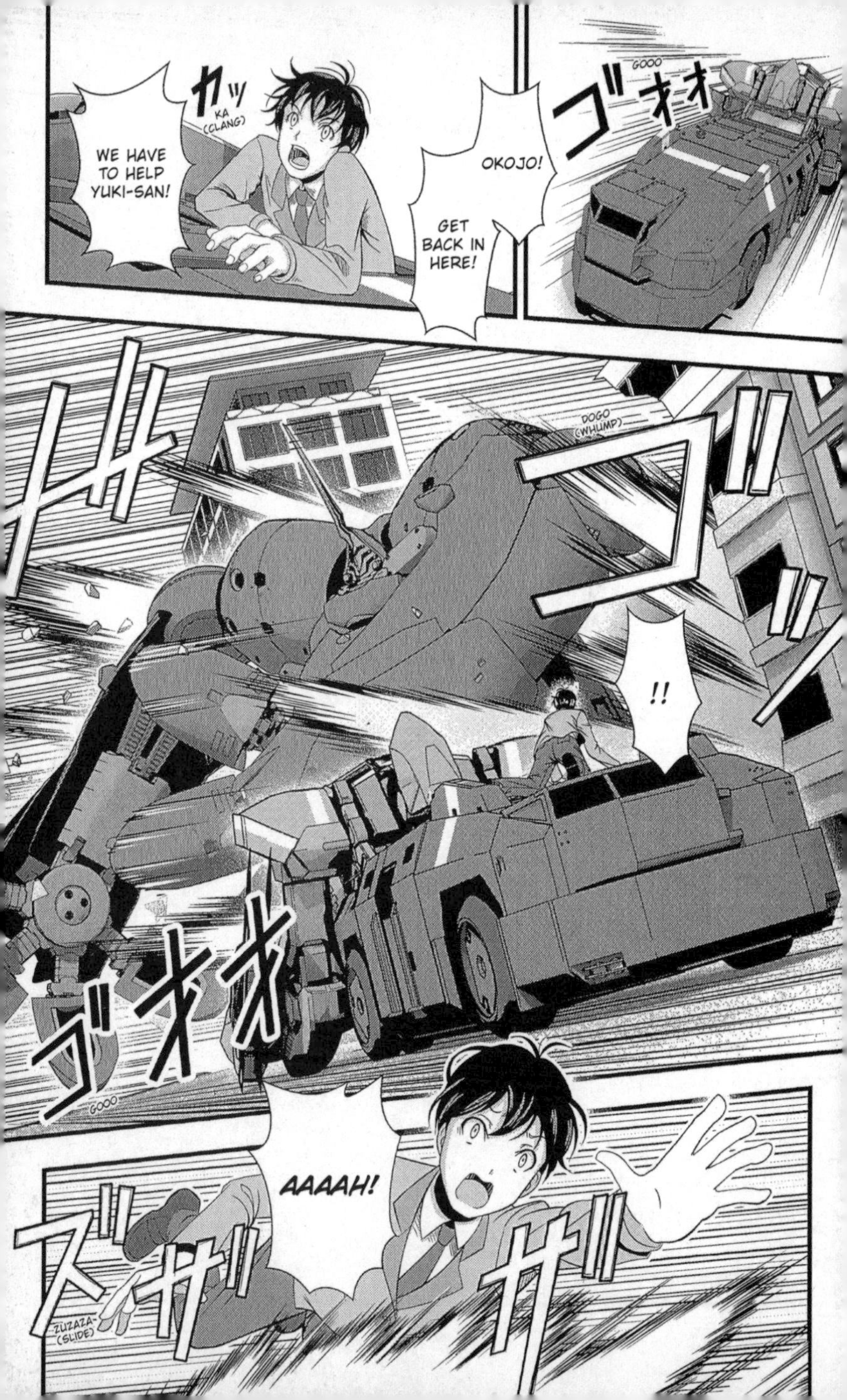
GOOO
OKOJO!
GET BACK IN HERE!
KA (CLANG)
WE HAVE TO HELP YUKI-SAN!
DOGO (WHUMP)
!!
GOOO
AAAAH!
ZUZAZA (SLIDE)

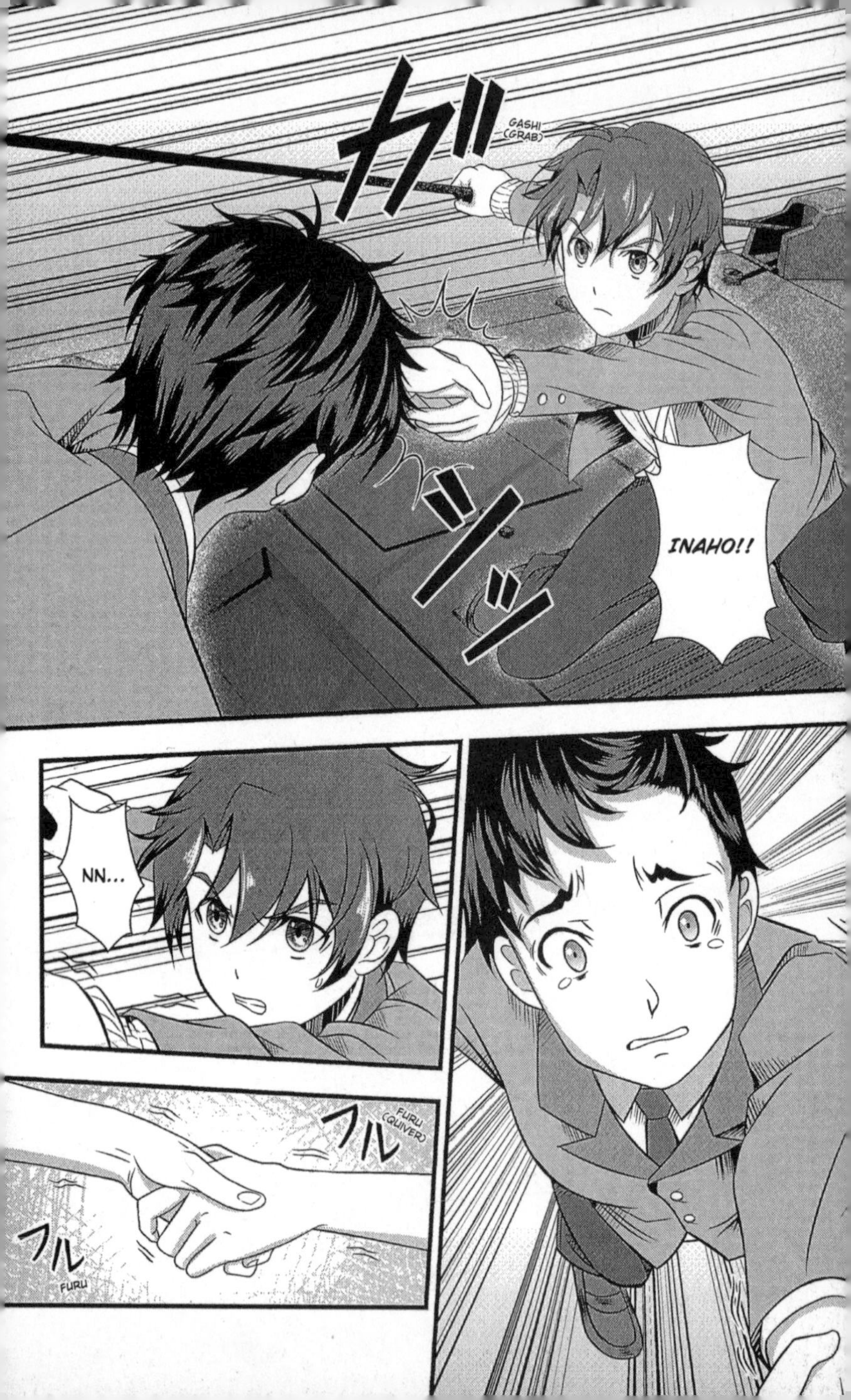
GASHI (GRAB)
INAHO!!
NN...
フル
FURU (QUIVER)
フル
FURU

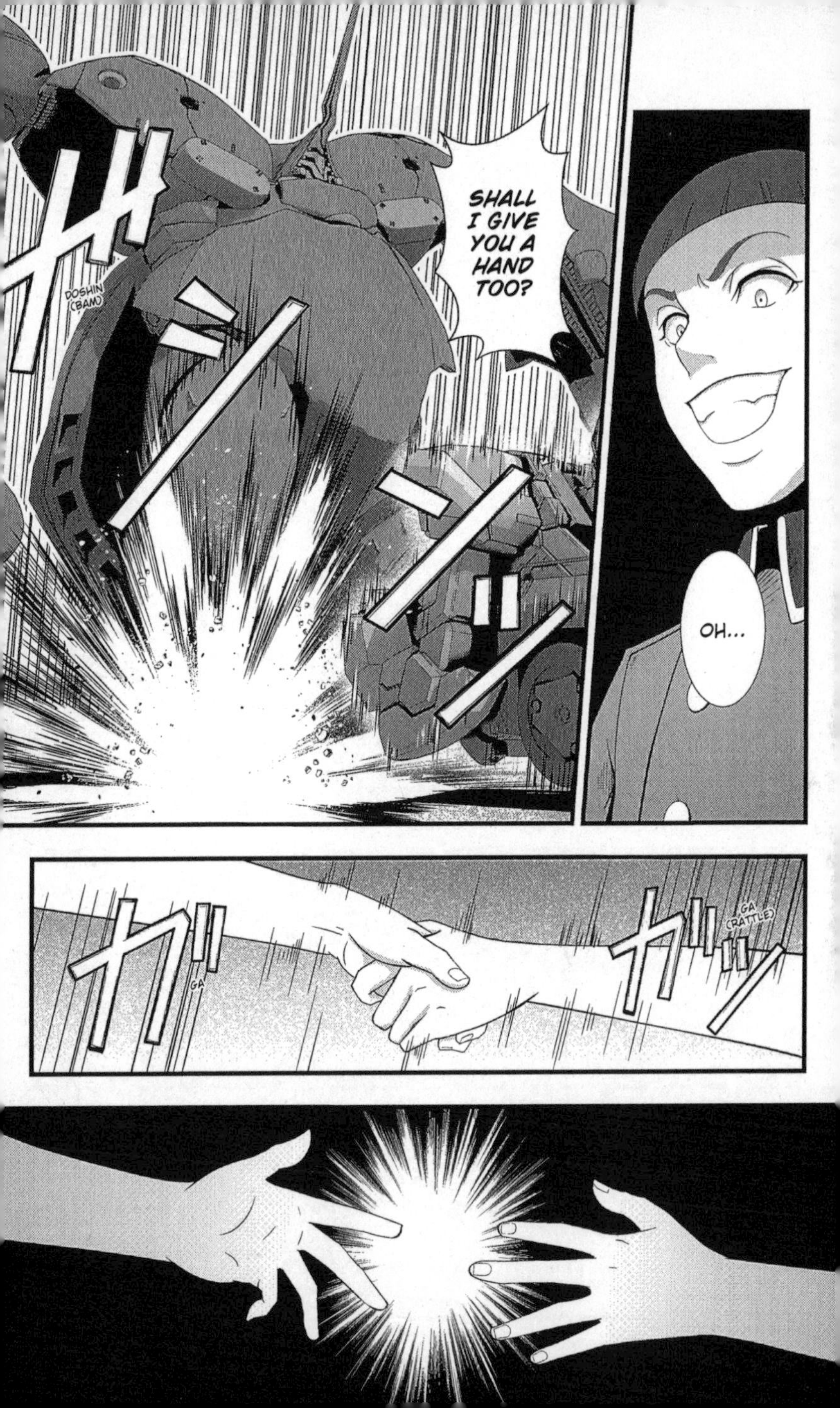
OH...
SHALL I GIVE YOU A HAND TOO?
DOSHIN (BAM)
GA (RATTLE)
GA

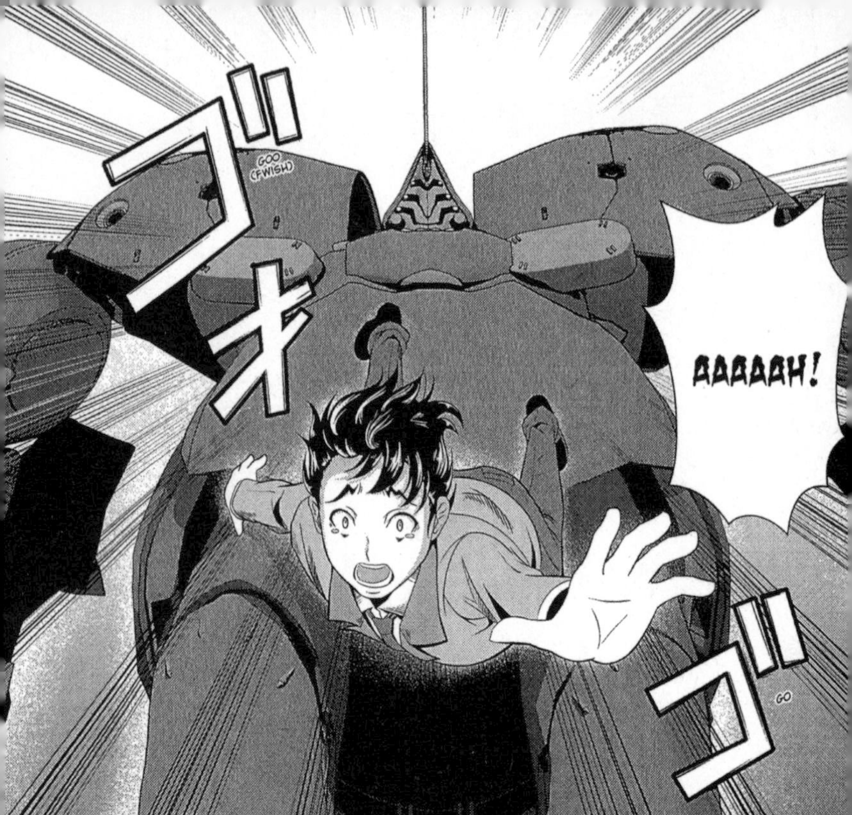
AAAAAH!
ゴオ
GOO (FWISH)
ゴゴ
GO

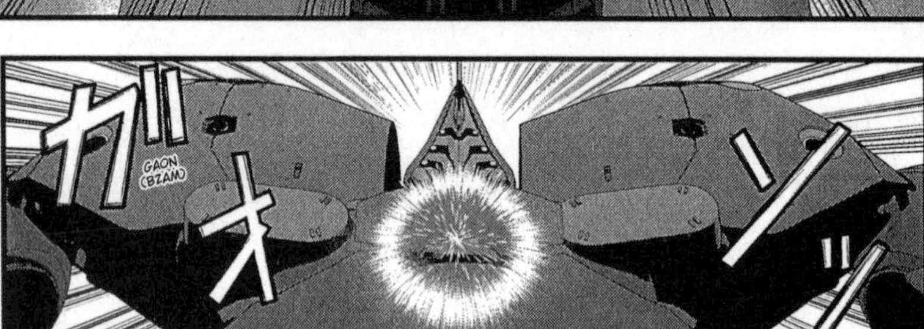
ガオーン
GAON (BZAM)

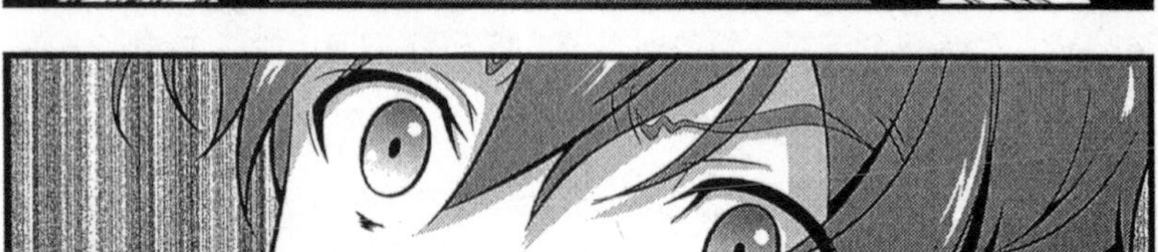

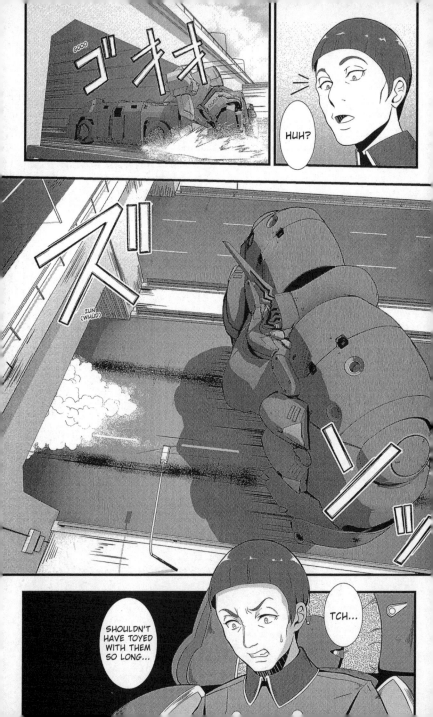

GOOO

HUH?

ZUN
(WHUD)

SHOULDN'T
HAVE TOYED
WITH THEM
SO LONG...

TCH...

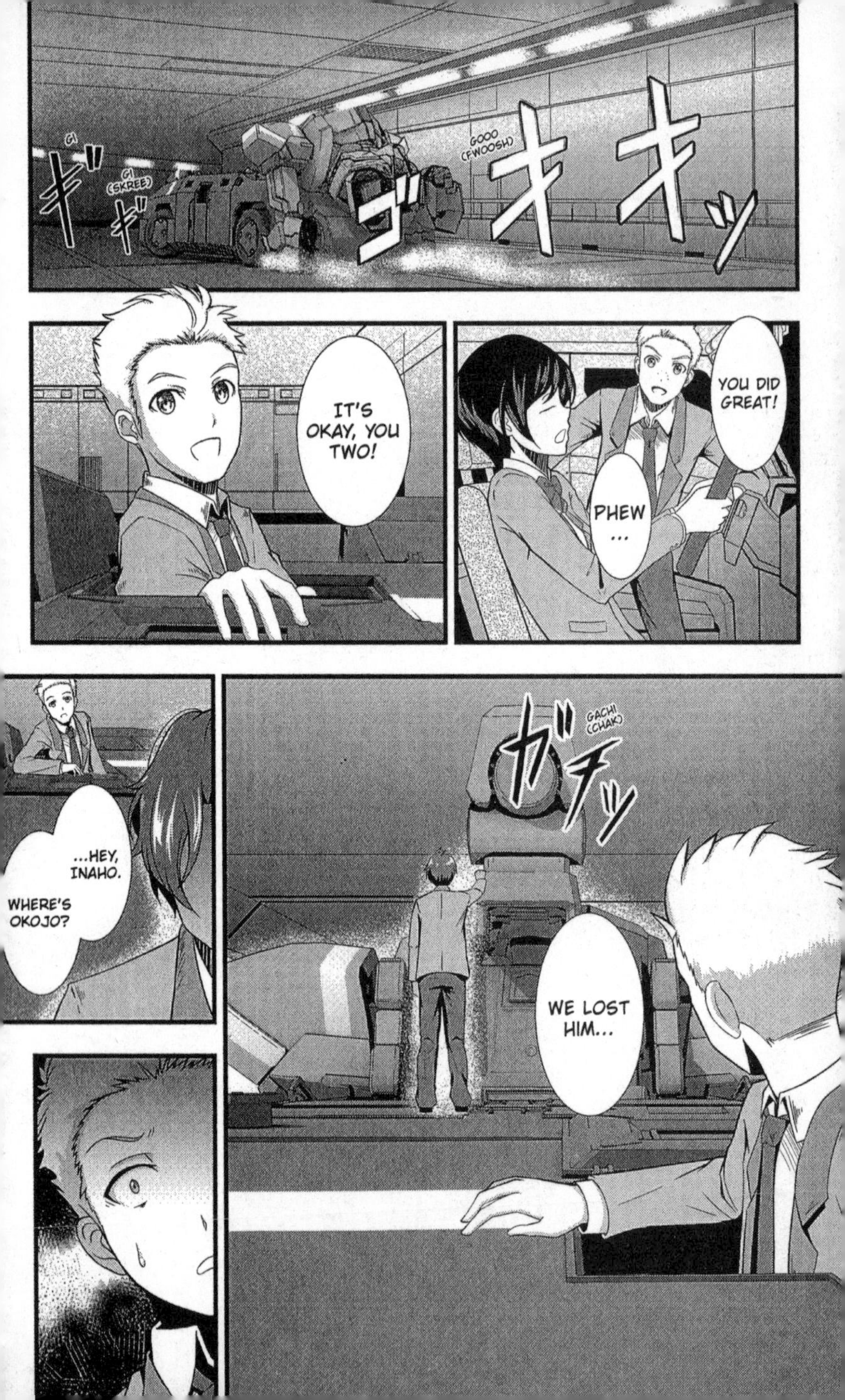
GOOO (FWOOSH)
GI
GI (SKREE)
YOU DID GREAT!
PHEW...
IT'S OKAY, YOU TWO!
GACHI (CHAK)
WE LOST HIM...
...HEY, INAHO.
WHERE'S OKOJO?

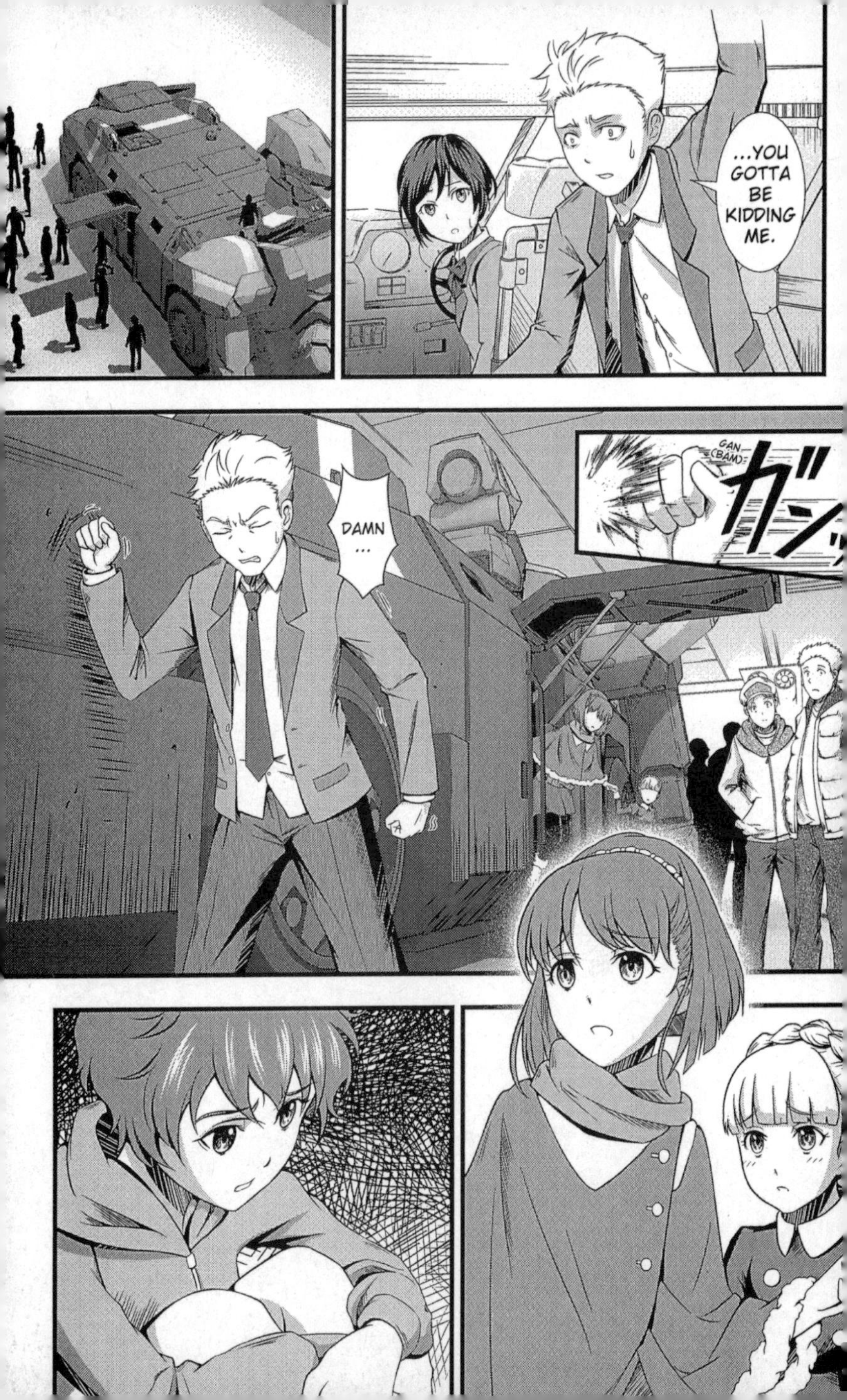
...YOU GOTTA BE KIDDING ME.
GAN (BAM)
ガンッ
DAMN ...

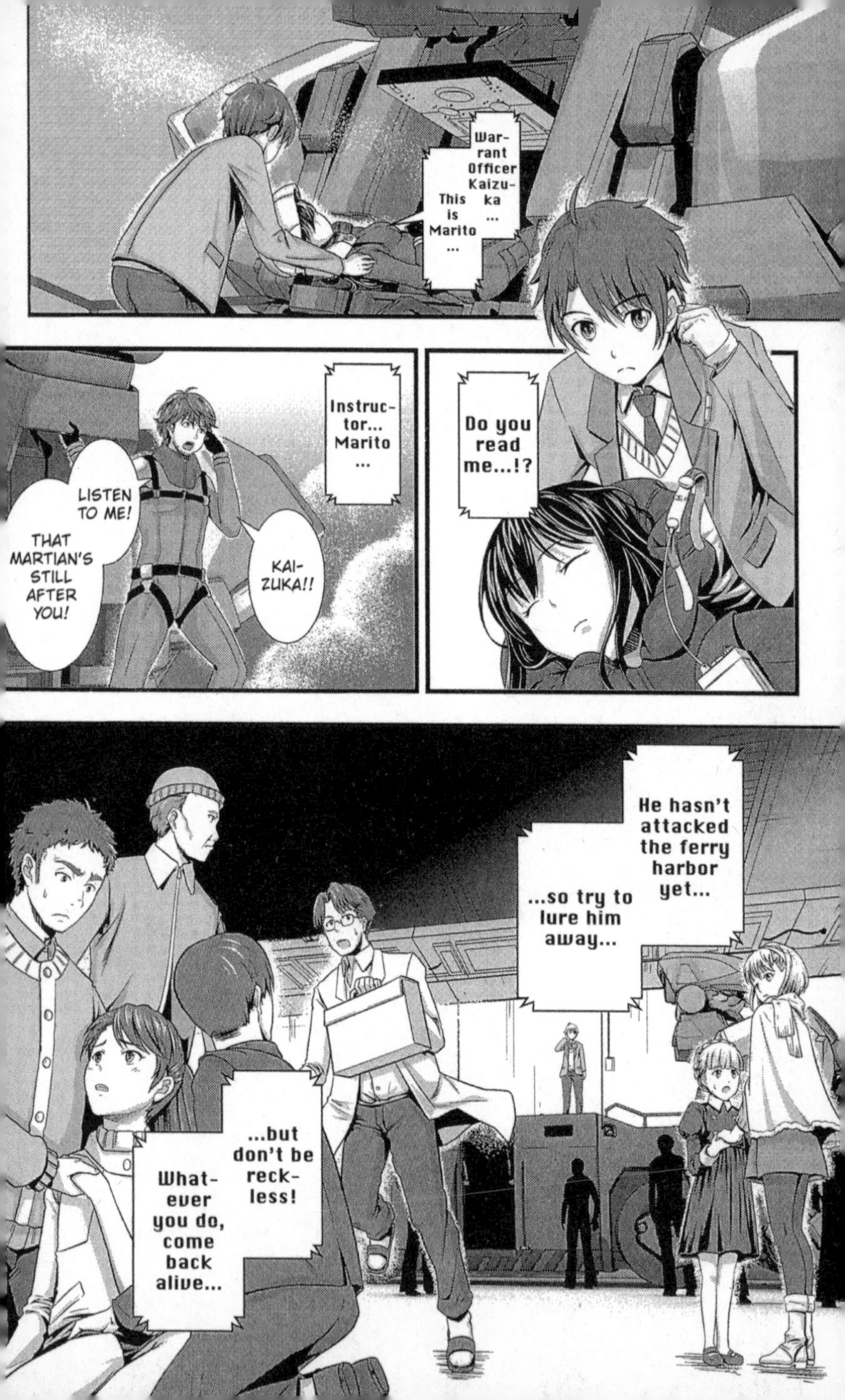

Warrant Officer Kaizuka...
This is Marito...
Do you read me...!?
Instructor... Marito...
KAIZUKA!!
LISTEN TO ME!
THAT MARTIAN'S STILL AFTER YOU!
He hasn't attacked the ferry harbor yet...
...so try to lure him away...
...but don't be reckless!
Whatever you do, come back alive...

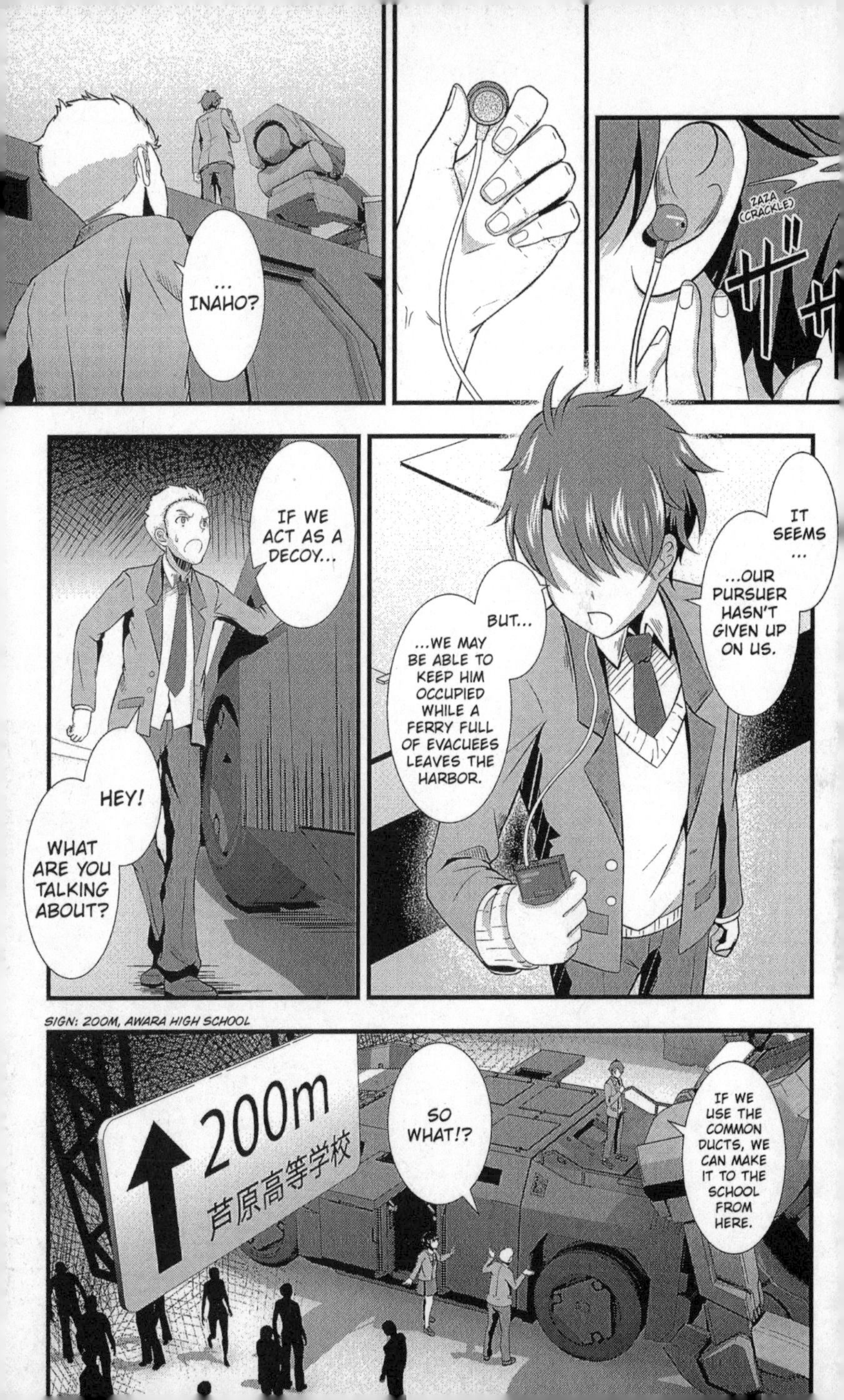
ZAZA (CRACKLE)
ザザ
... INAHO?
IT SEEMS ...
...OUR PURSUER HASN'T GIVEN UP ON US.
BUT...
...WE MAY BE ABLE TO KEEP HIM OCCUPIED WHILE A FERRY FULL OF EVACUEES LEAVES THE HARBOR.
IF WE ACT AS A DECOY...
HEY!
WHAT ARE YOU TALKING ABOUT?
SIGN: 200M, AWARA HIGH SCHOOL
IF WE USE THE COMMON DUCTS, WE CAN MAKE IT TO THE SCHOOL FROM HERE.
SO WHAT!?
200m
芦原高等学校

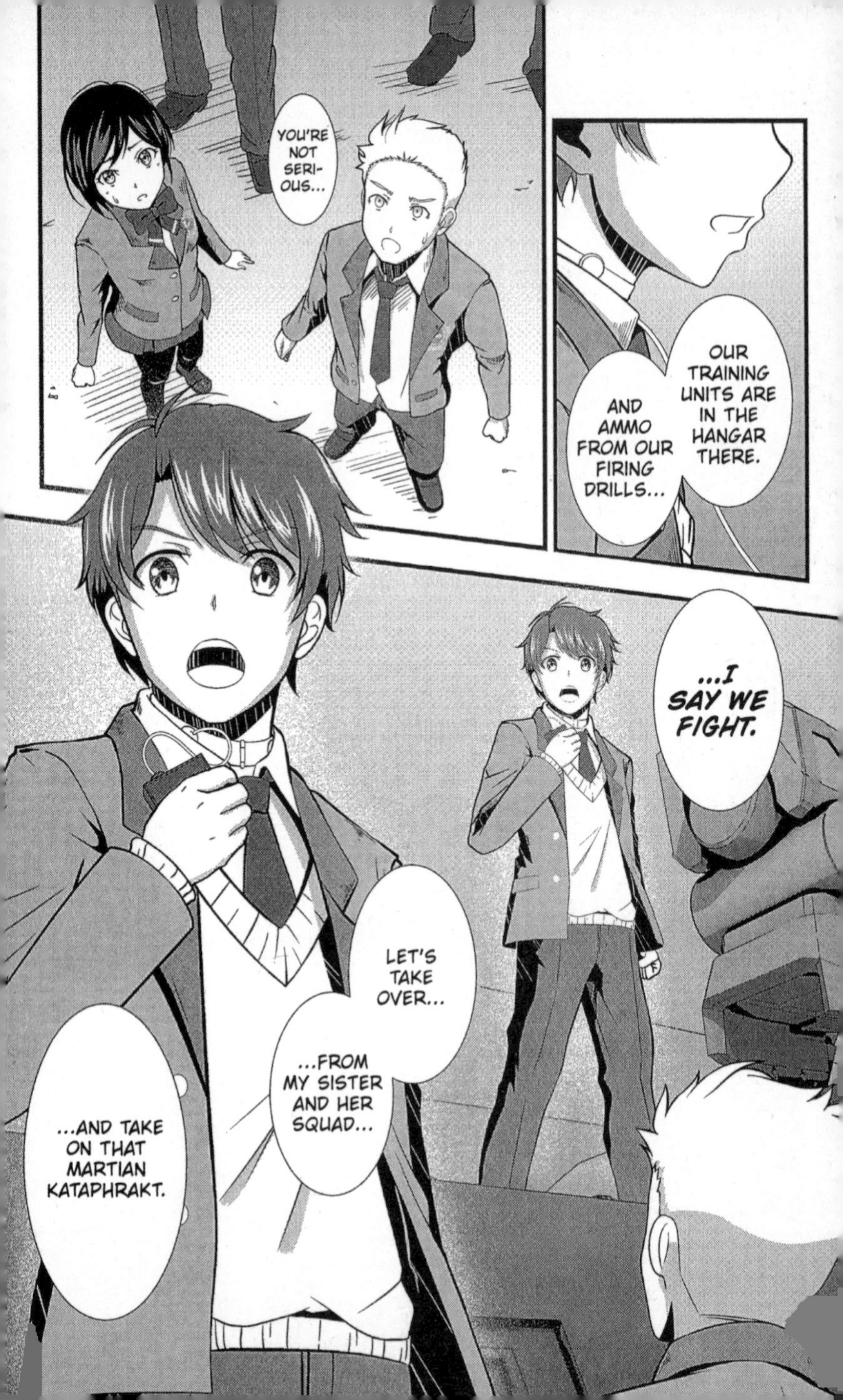
OUR TRAINING UNITS ARE IN THE HANGAR THERE.
AND AMMO FROM OUR FIRING DRILLS...
YOU'RE NOT SERI-OUS...
...I SAY WE FIGHT.
LET'S TAKE OVER...
...FROM MY SISTER AND HER SQUAD...
...AND TAKE ON THAT MARTIAN KATAPHRAKT.

EP03 Children on the Battlefield — The Children's Echelon —

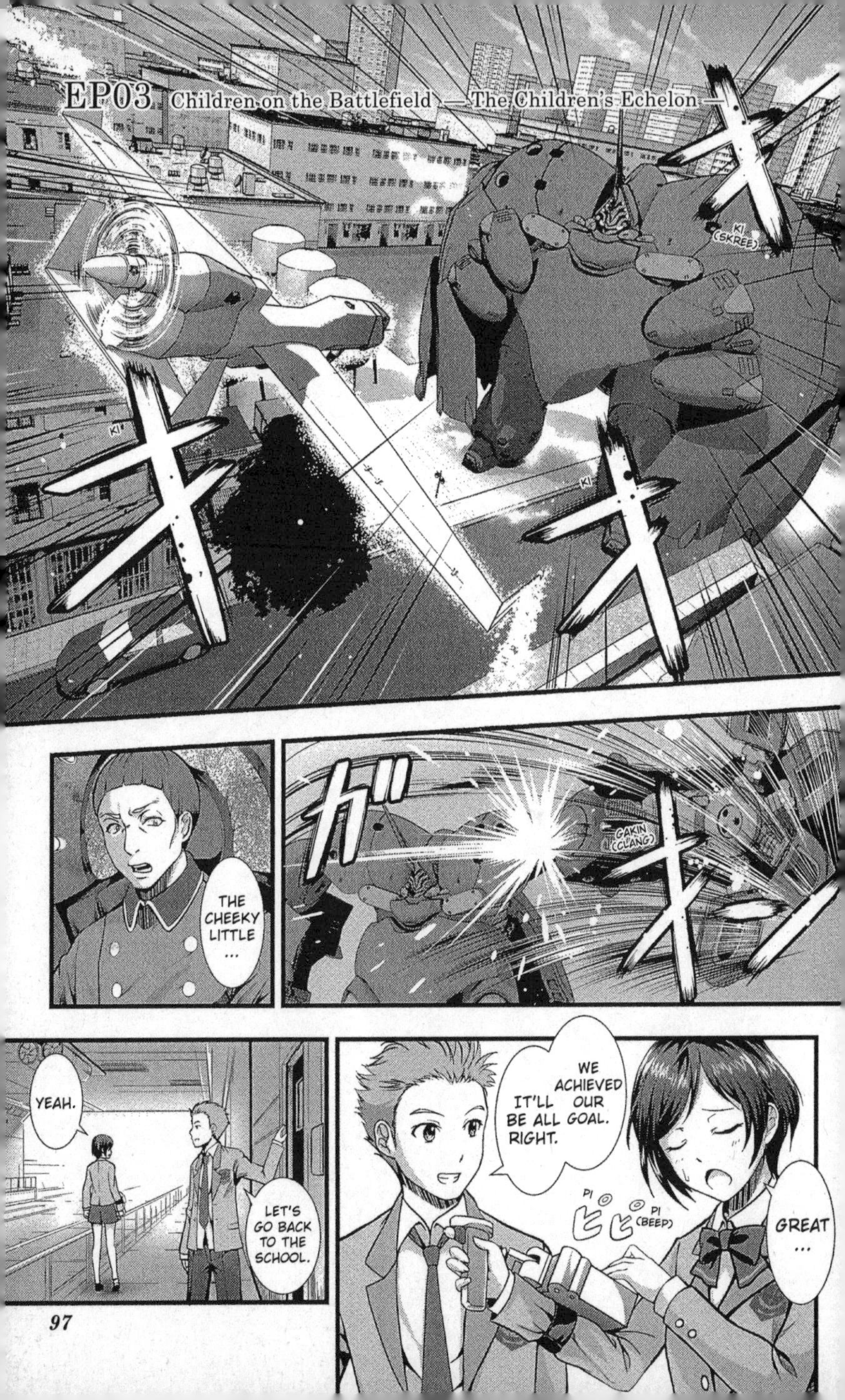
KI (SKREE)
KI
KI
ガ
GAKIN (CLANG)
THE CHEEKY LITTLE ...
WE ACHIEVED OUR GOAL. IT'LL BE ALL RIGHT.
GREAT ...
PI PI (BEEP)
LET'S GO BACK TO THE SCHOOL.
YEAH.

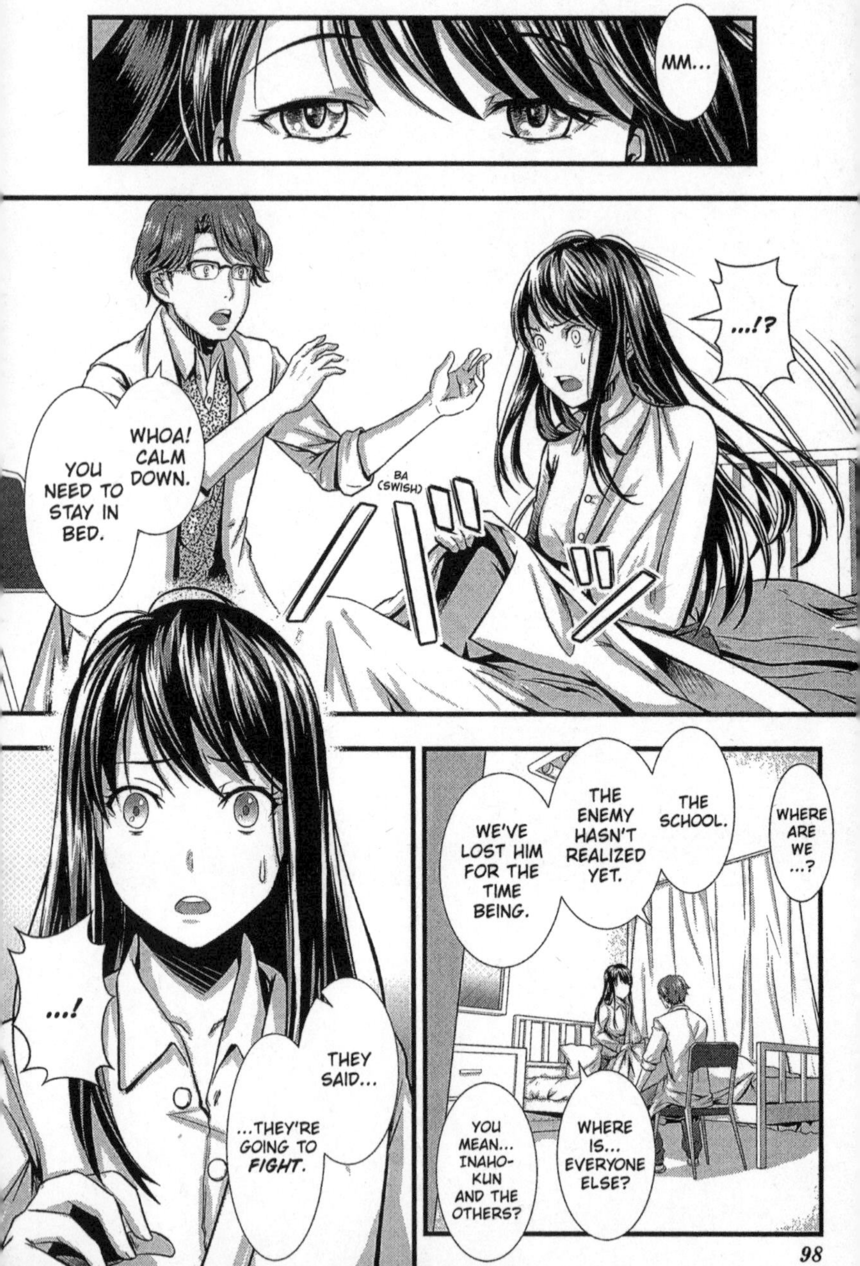
MM...
...!?
BA (SWISH)
WHOA! CALM DOWN.
YOU NEED TO STAY IN BED.
WHERE ARE WE ...?
THE SCHOOL.
THE ENEMY HASN'T REALIZED YET.
WE'VE LOST HIM FOR THE TIME BEING.
WHERE IS... EVERYONE ELSE?
YOU MEAN... INAHO-KUN AND THE OTHERS?
...!
THEY SAID...
...THEY'RE GOING TO *FIGHT*.

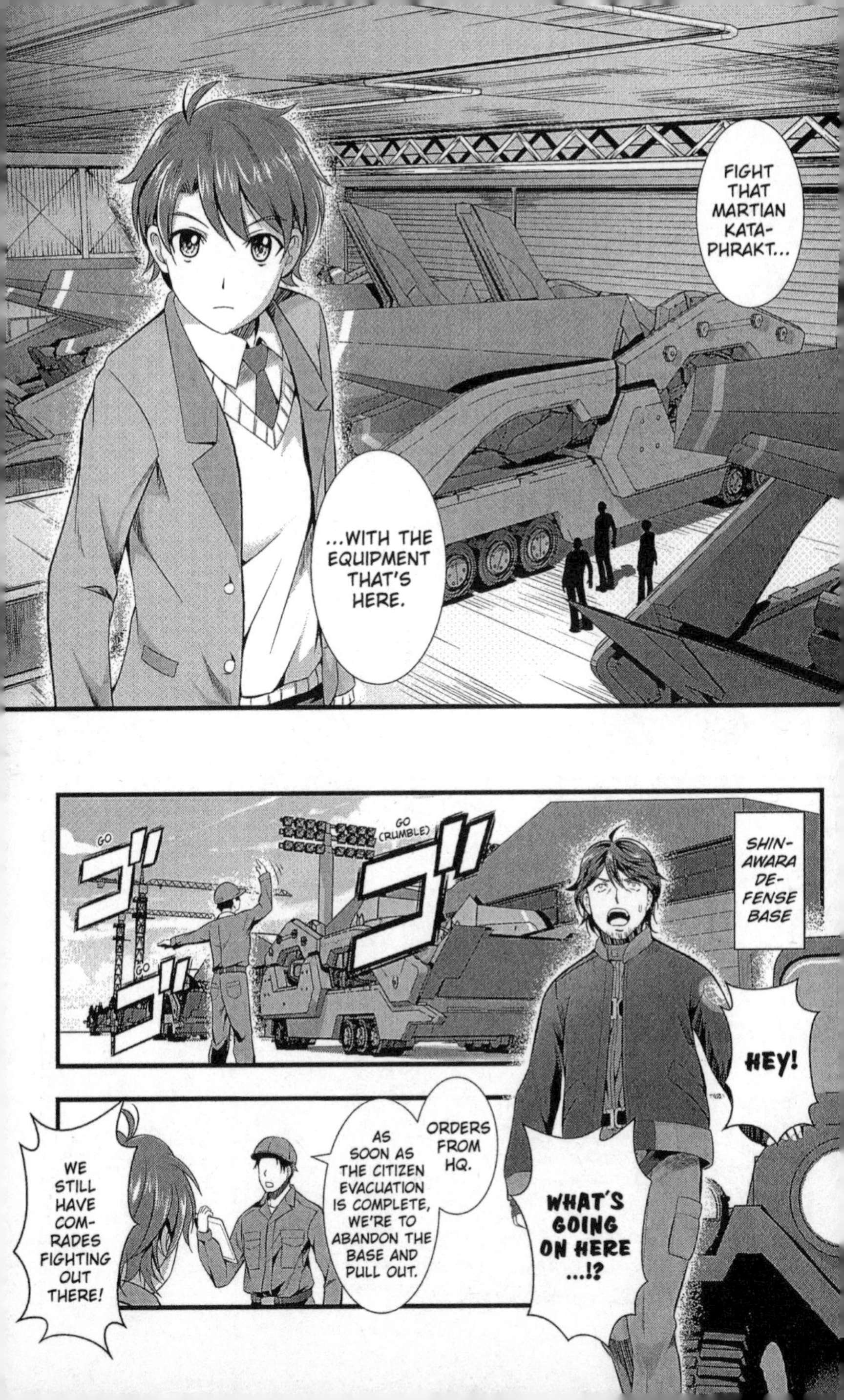

FIGHT THAT MARTIAN KATA-PHRAKT...
...WITH THE EQUIPMENT THAT'S HERE.
SHIN-AWARA DEFENSE BASE
GO (RUMBLE)
GO
GO
HEY!
WHAT'S GOING ON HERE ...!?
ORDERS FROM HQ.
AS SOON AS THE CITIZEN EVACUATION IS COMPLETE, WE'RE TO ABANDON THE BASE AND PULL OUT.
WE STILL HAVE COM-RADES FIGHTING OUT THERE!

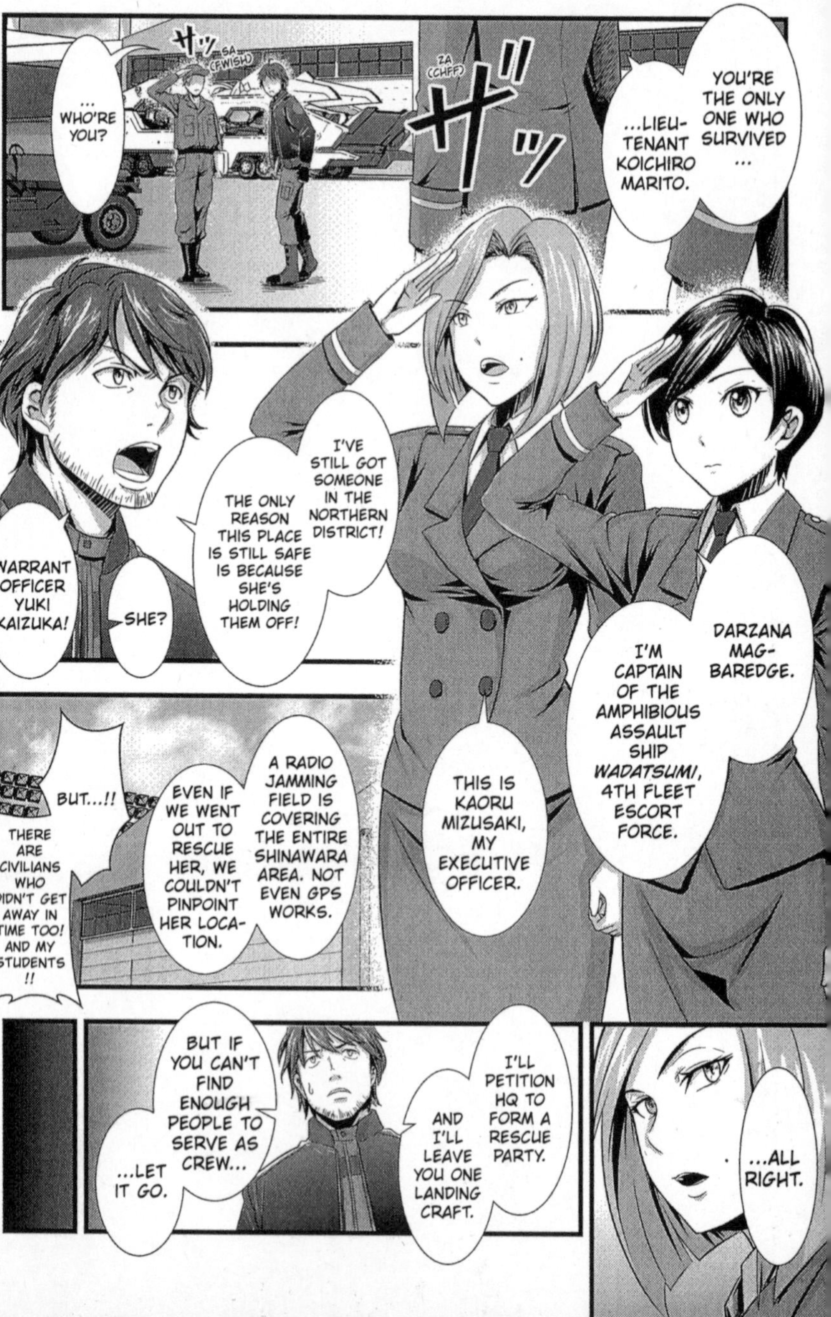
YOU'RE THE ONLY ONE WHO SURVIVED...
...LIEUTENANT KOICHIRO MARITO.
ZA (CHFF)
SA (FWISH)
...WHO'RE YOU?
DARZANA MAG-BAREDGE.
I'M CAPTAIN OF THE AMPHIBIOUS ASSAULT SHIP *WADATSUMI*, 4TH FLEET ESCORT FORCE.
THIS IS KAORU MIZUSAKI, MY EXECUTIVE OFFICER.
I'VE STILL GOT SOMEONE IN THE NORTHERN DISTRICT!
THE ONLY REASON THIS PLACE IS STILL SAFE IS BECAUSE SHE'S HOLDING THEM OFF!
SHE?
WARRANT OFFICER YUKI KAIZUKA!
A RADIO JAMMING FIELD IS COVERING THE ENTIRE SHINAWARA AREA. NOT EVEN GPS WORKS.
EVEN IF WE WENT OUT TO RESCUE HER, WE COULDN'T PINPOINT HER LOCA-TION.
BUT...!!
THERE ARE CIVILIANS WHO DIDN'T GET AWAY IN TIME TOO! AND MY STUDENTS!!
...ALL RIGHT.
I'LL PETITION HQ TO FORM A RESCUE PARTY.
AND I'LL LEAVE YOU ONE LANDING CRAFT.
BUT IF YOU CAN'T FIND ENOUGH PEOPLE TO SERVE AS CREW...
...LET IT GO.

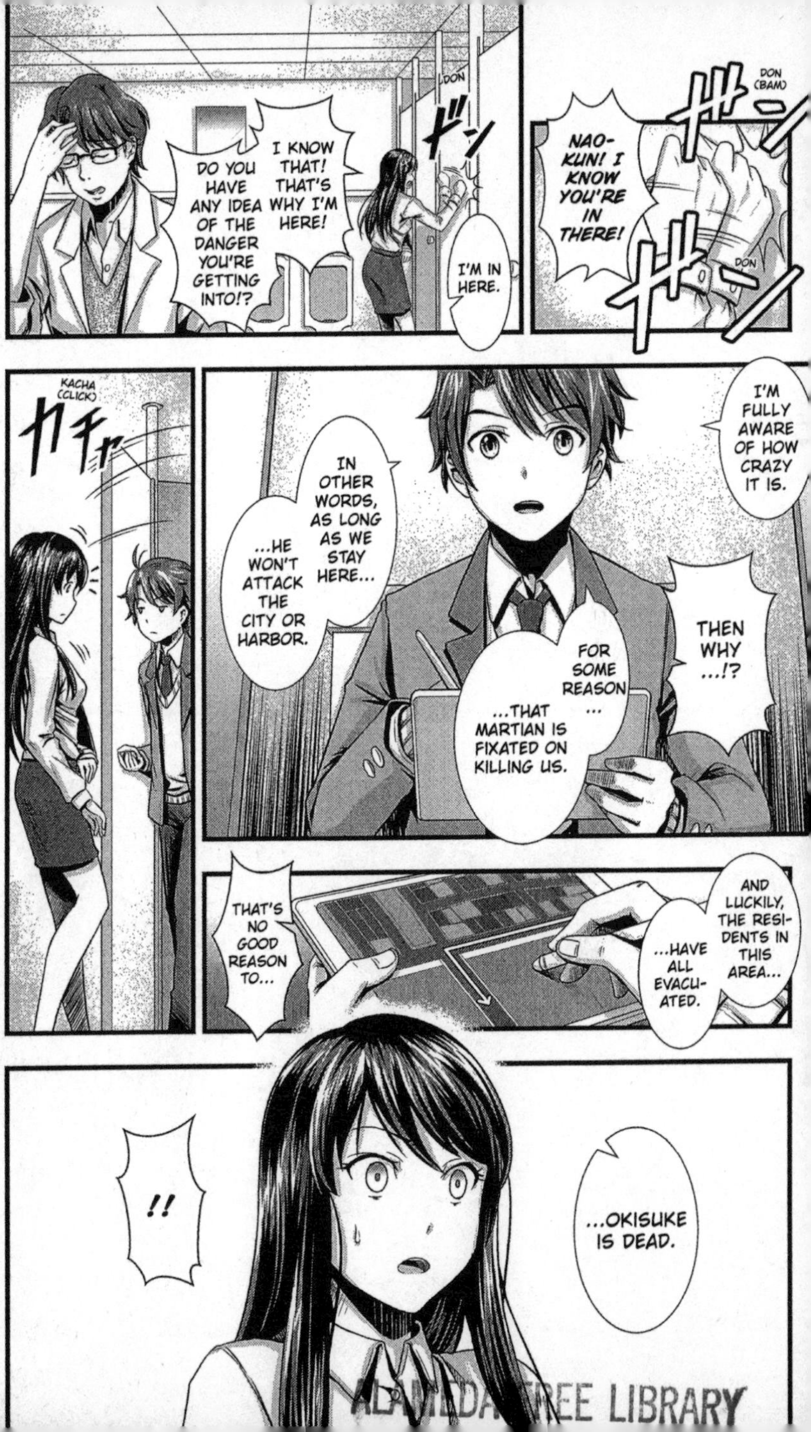
DON (BAM)
NAO-KUN! I KNOW YOU'RE IN THERE!
DON
I'M IN HERE.
DON
I KNOW THAT! THAT'S WHY I'M HERE!
DO YOU HAVE ANY IDEA OF THE DANGER YOU'RE GETTING INTO!?
I'M FULLY AWARE OF HOW CRAZY IT IS.
THEN WHY ...!?
FOR SOME REASON ...
...THAT MARTIAN IS FIXATED ON KILLING US.
IN OTHER WORDS, AS LONG AS WE STAY HERE...
...HE WON'T ATTACK THE CITY OR HARBOR.
AND LUCKILY, THE RESIDENTS IN THIS AREA...
...HAVE ALL EVACUATED.
THAT'S NO GOOD REASON TO...
KACHA (CLICK)
...OKISUKE IS DEAD.
!!

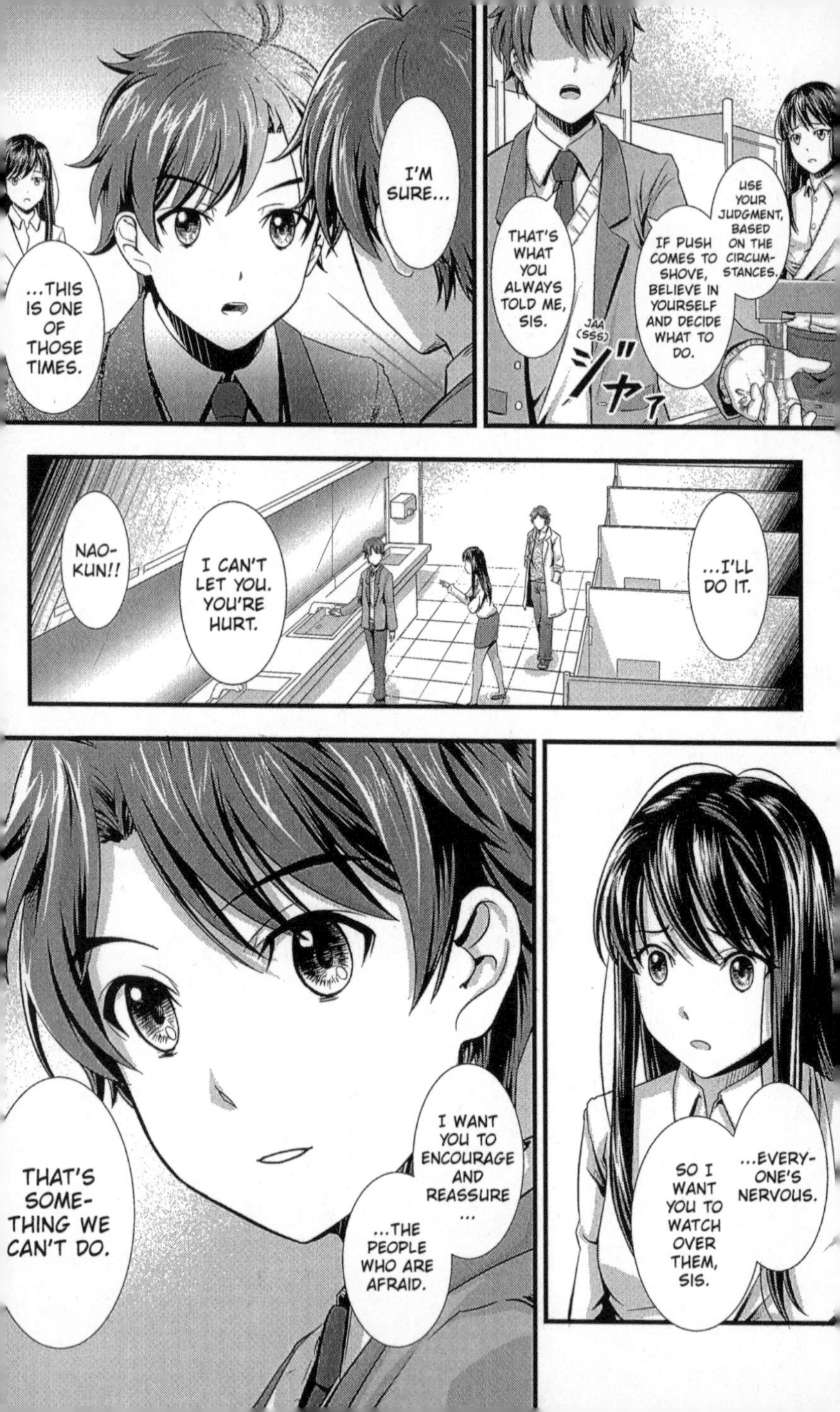

USE YOUR JUDGMENT, BASED ON THE CIRCUMSTANCES.
IF PUSH COMES TO SHOVE, BELIEVE IN YOURSELF AND DECIDE WHAT TO DO.
JAA (SSS)
THAT'S WHAT YOU ALWAYS TOLD ME, SIS.
I'M SURE...
...THIS IS ONE OF THOSE TIMES.
...I'LL DO IT.
I CAN'T LET YOU. YOU'RE HURT.
NAO-KUN!!
...EVERYONE'S NERVOUS.
SO I WANT YOU TO WATCH OVER THEM, SIS.
I WANT YOU TO ENCOURAGE AND REASSURE...
...THE PEOPLE WHO ARE AFRAID.
THAT'S SOMETHING WE CAN'T DO.

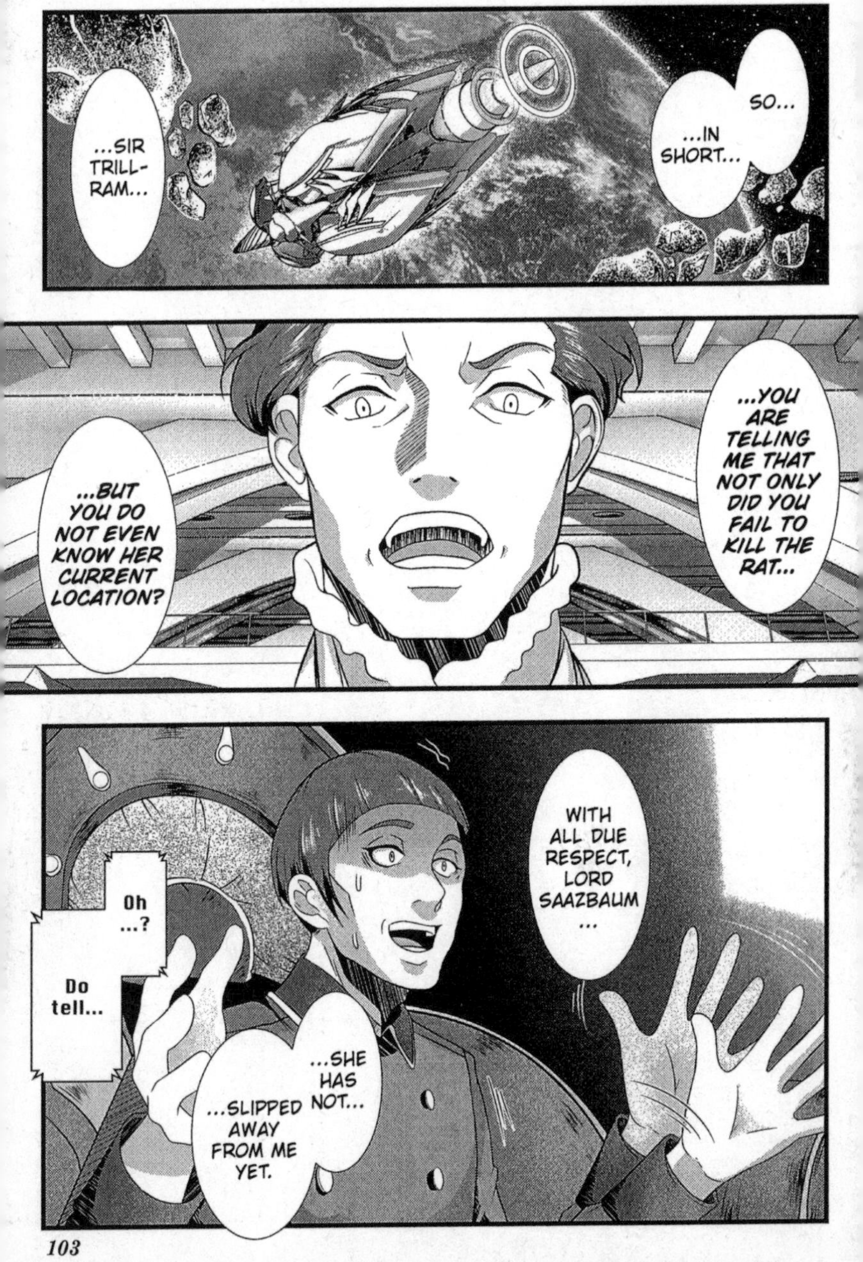
SO...
...IN SHORT...
...SIR TRILL-RAM...
...YOU ARE TELLING ME THAT NOT ONLY DID YOU FAIL TO KILL THE RAT...
...BUT YOU DO NOT EVEN KNOW HER CURRENT LOCATION?
WITH ALL DUE RESPECT, LORD SAAZBAUM...
...SHE HAS NOT...
...SLIPPED AWAY FROM ME YET.
Oh ...?
Do tell...

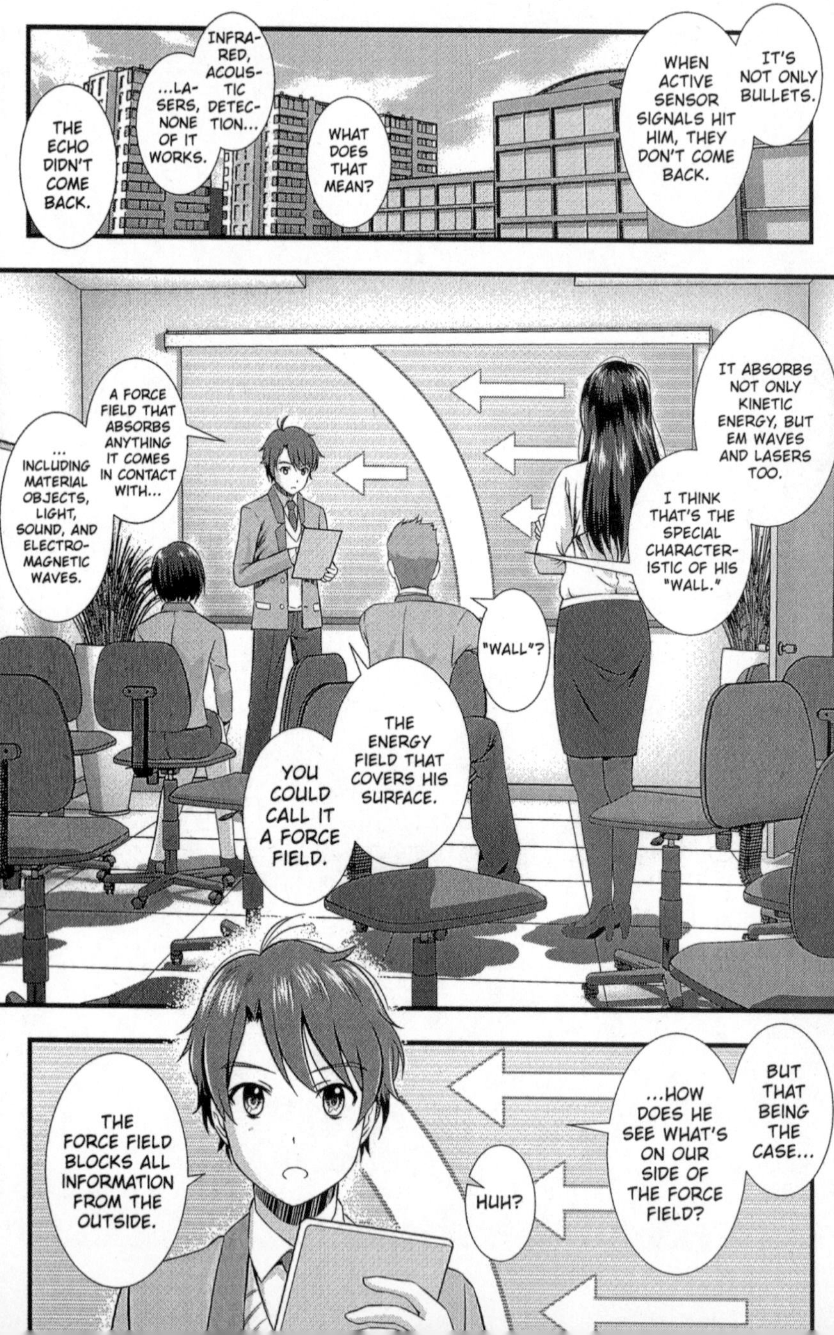
IT'S NOT ONLY BULLETS.
WHEN ACTIVE SENSOR SIGNALS HIT HIM, THEY DON'T COME BACK.
WHAT DOES THAT MEAN?
INFRA-RED, ACOUS-TIC DETEC-TION...
...LA-SERS, NONE OF IT WORKS.
THE ECHO DIDN'T COME BACK.
IT ABSORBS NOT ONLY KINETIC ENERGY, BUT EM WAVES AND LASERS TOO.
I THINK THAT'S THE SPECIAL CHARACTER-ISTIC OF HIS "WALL."
"WALL"?
THE ENERGY FIELD THAT COVERS HIS SURFACE.
YOU COULD CALL IT A FORCE FIELD.
A FORCE FIELD THAT ABSORBS ANYTHING IT COMES IN CONTACT WITH...
...INCLUDING MATERIAL OBJECTS, LIGHT, SOUND, AND ELECTRO-MAGNETIC WAVES.
BUT THAT BEING THE CASE...
...HOW DOES HE SEE WHAT'S ON OUR SIDE OF THE FORCE FIELD?
HUH?
THE FORCE FIELD BLOCKS ALL INFORMATION FROM THE OUTSIDE.

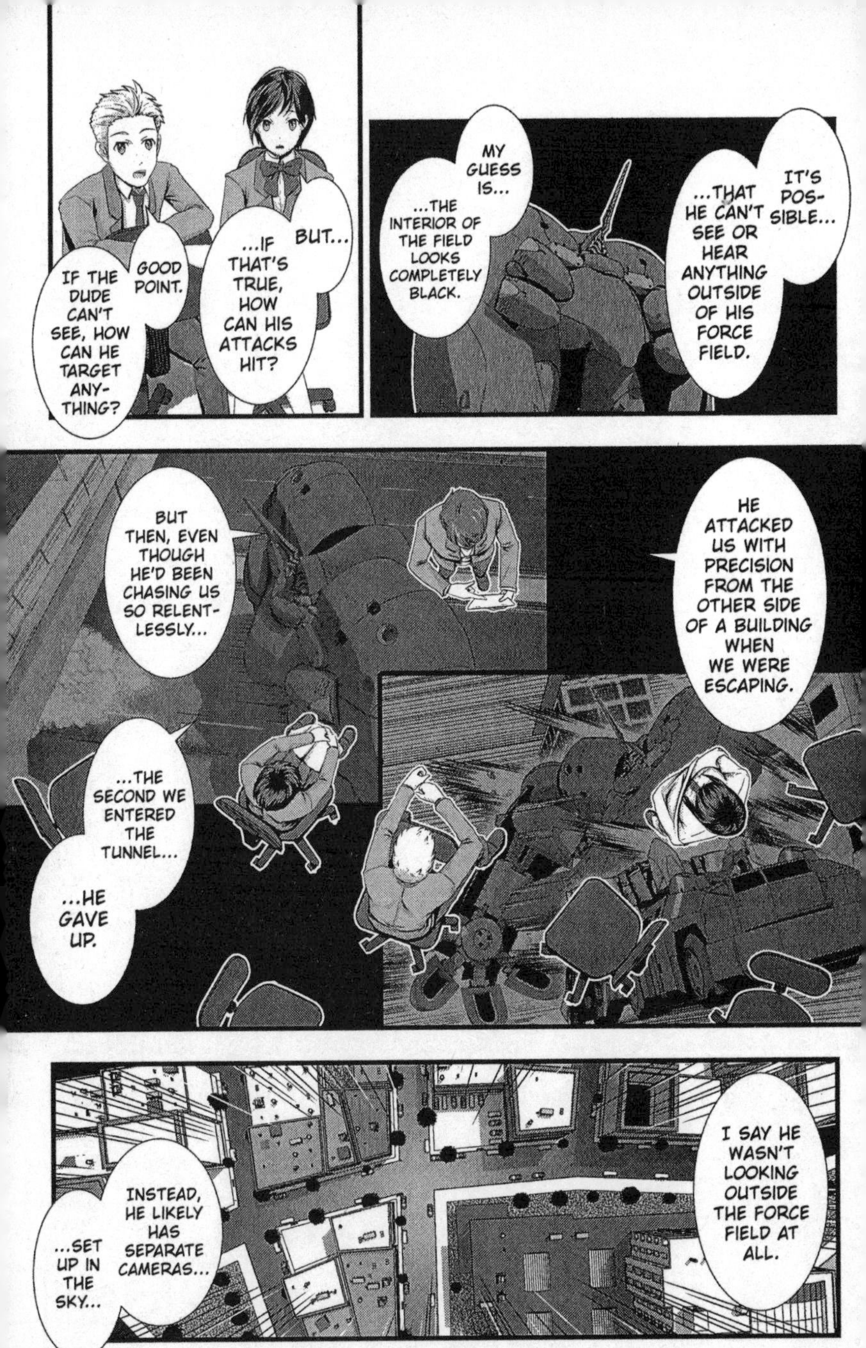
IT'S POSSIBLE...
...THAT HE CAN'T SEE OR HEAR ANYTHING OUTSIDE OF HIS FORCE FIELD.
MY GUESS IS...
...THE INTERIOR OF THE FIELD LOOKS COMPLETELY BLACK.
BUT...
...IF THAT'S TRUE, HOW CAN HIS ATTACKS HIT?
GOOD POINT.
IF THE DUDE CAN'T SEE, HOW CAN HE TARGET ANYTHING?
HE ATTACKED US WITH PRECISION FROM THE OTHER SIDE OF A BUILDING WHEN WE WERE ESCAPING.
BUT THEN, EVEN THOUGH HE'D BEEN CHASING US SO RELENTLESSLY...
...THE SECOND WE ENTERED THE TUNNEL...
...HE GAVE UP.
I SAY HE WASN'T LOOKING OUTSIDE THE FORCE FIELD AT ALL.
INSTEAD, HE LIKELY HAS SEPARATE CAMERAS...
...SET UP IN THE SKY...

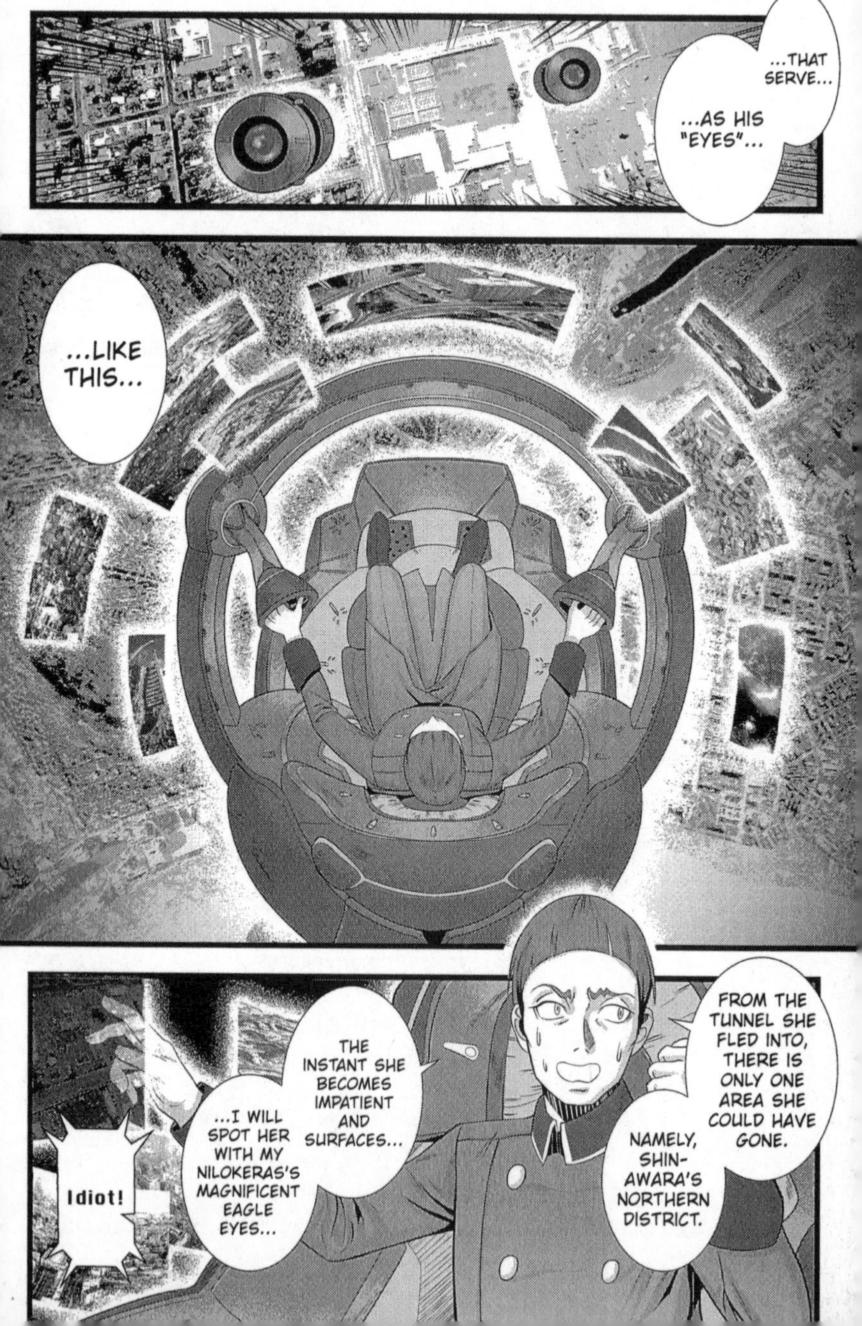
...THAT SERVE... ...AS HIS "EYES"...
...LIKE THIS...
FROM THE TUNNEL SHE FLED INTO, THERE IS ONLY ONE AREA SHE COULD HAVE GONE.
NAMELY, SHIN-AWARA'S NORTHERN DISTRICT.
THE INSTANT SHE BECOMES IMPATIENT AND SURFACES...
...I WILL SPOT HER WITH MY NILOKERAS'S MAGNIFICENT EAGLE EYES...
Idiot!

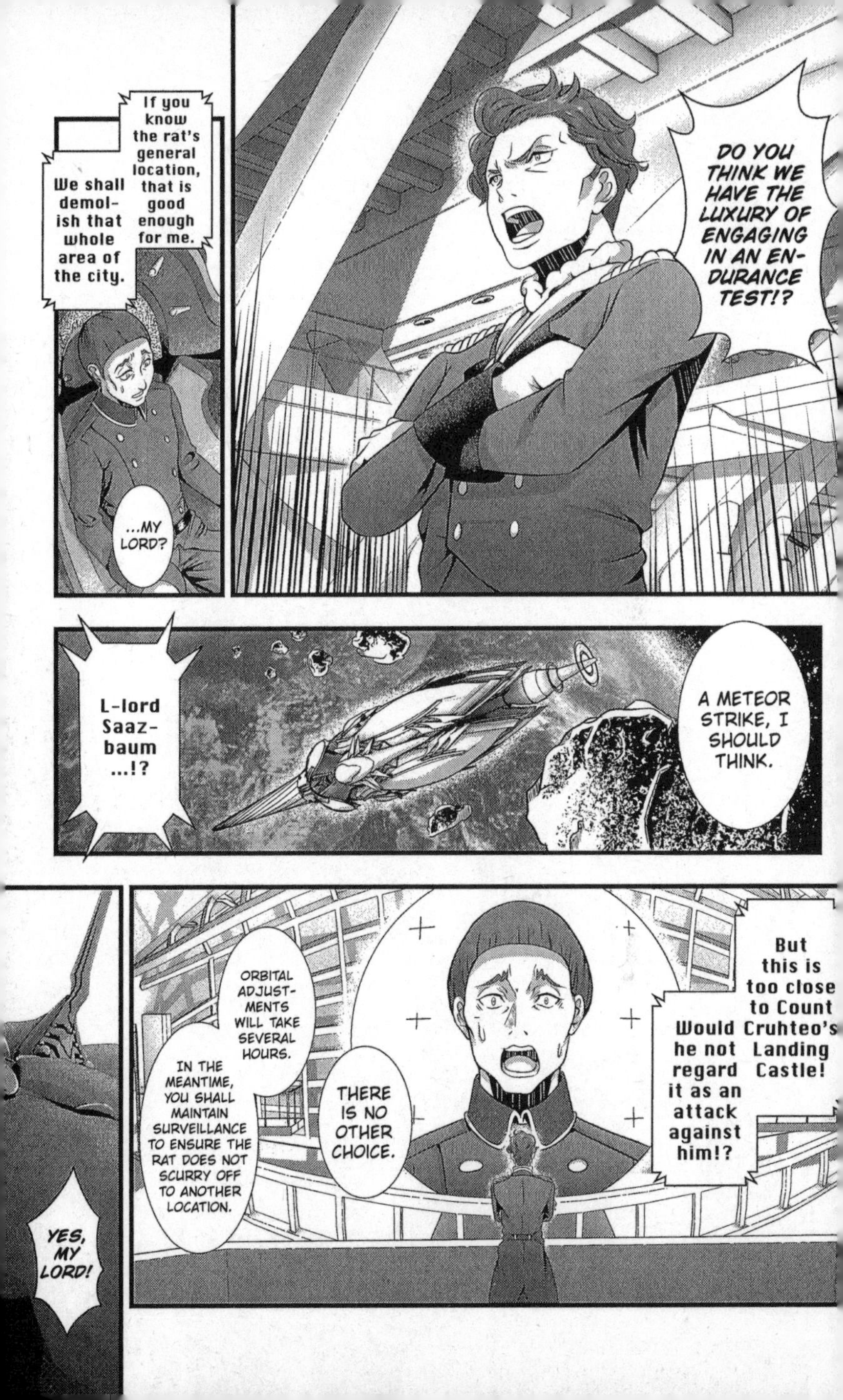
DO YOU THINK WE HAVE THE LUXURY OF ENGAGING IN AN ENDURANCE TEST!?
If you know the rat's general location, that is good enough for me.
We shall demolish that whole area of the city.
...MY LORD?
A METEOR STRIKE, I SHOULD THINK.
L-lord Saazbaum ...!?
But this is too close to Count Cruhteo's Landing Castle!
Would he not regard it as an attack against him!?
THERE IS NO OTHER CHOICE.
ORBITAL ADJUSTMENTS WILL TAKE SEVERAL HOURS.
IN THE MEANTIME, YOU SHALL MAINTAIN SURVEILLANCE TO ENSURE THE RAT DOES NOT SCURRY OFF TO ANOTHER LOCATION.
YES, MY LORD!

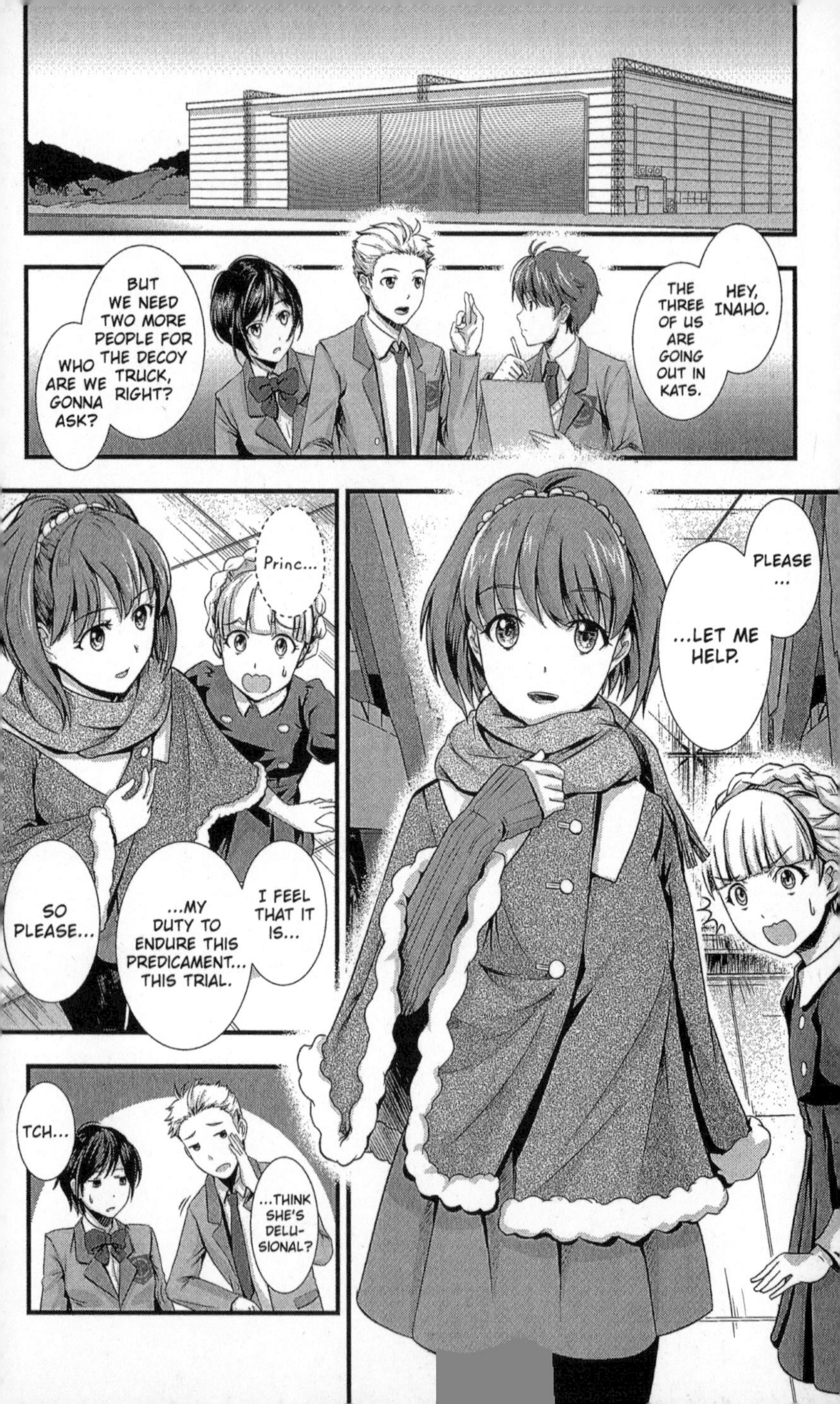
HEY, INAHO.
THE THREE OF US ARE GOING OUT IN KATS.
BUT WE NEED TWO MORE PEOPLE FOR THE DECOY TRUCK, RIGHT?
WHO ARE WE GONNA ASK?
PLEASE ...
...LET ME HELP.
Princ...
I FEEL THAT IT IS...
...MY DUTY TO ENDURE THIS PREDICAMENT... THIS TRIAL.
SO PLEASE...
TCH...
...THINK SHE'S DELUSIONAL?

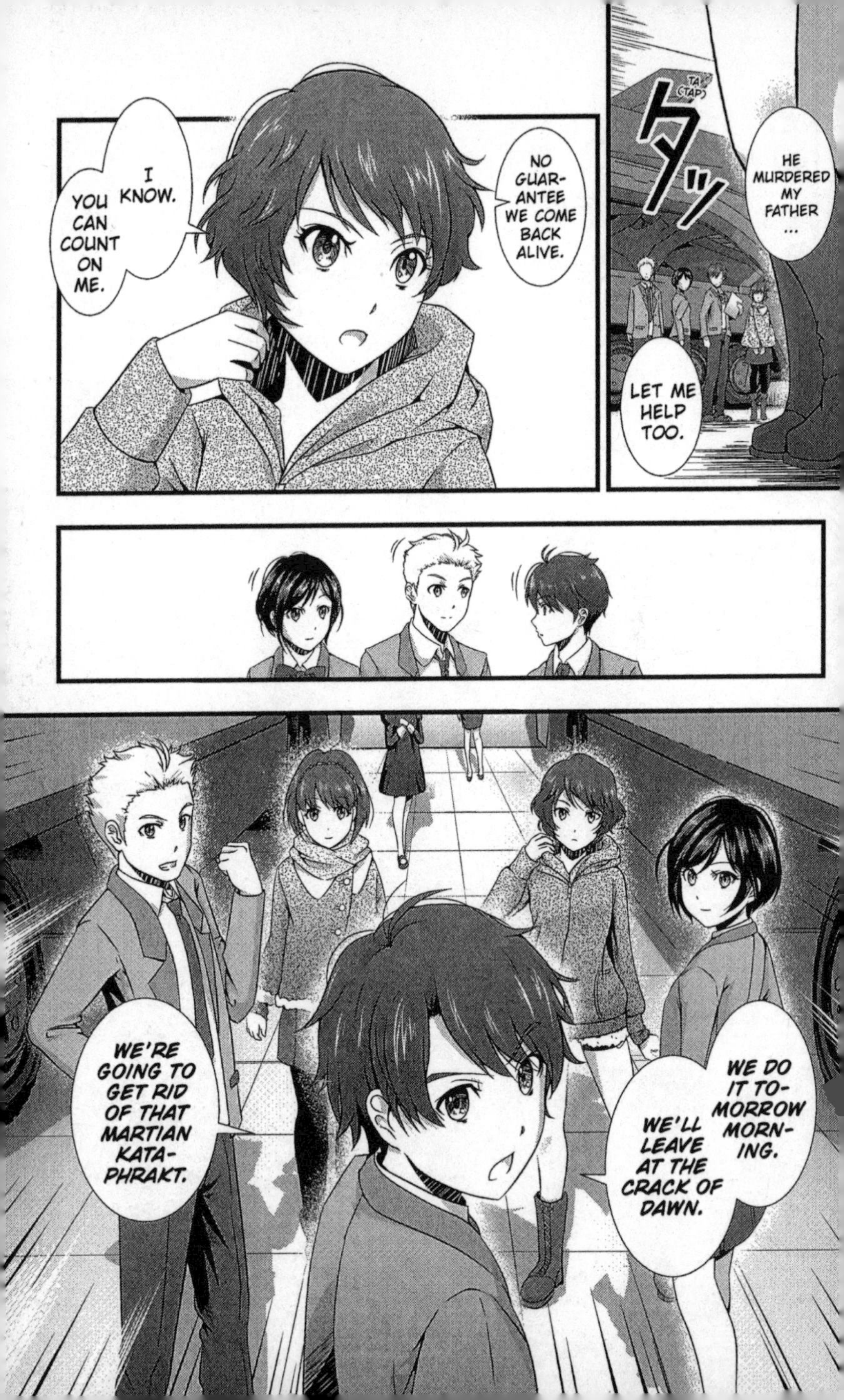
タッ
TA (TAP)
HE MURDERED MY FATHER ...
LET ME HELP TOO.
NO GUARANTEE WE COME BACK ALIVE.
I KNOW.
YOU CAN COUNT ON ME.
WE DO IT TOMORROW MORNING.
WE'LL LEAVE AT THE CRACK OF DAWN.
WE'RE GOING TO GET RID OF THAT MARTIAN KATAPHRAKT.

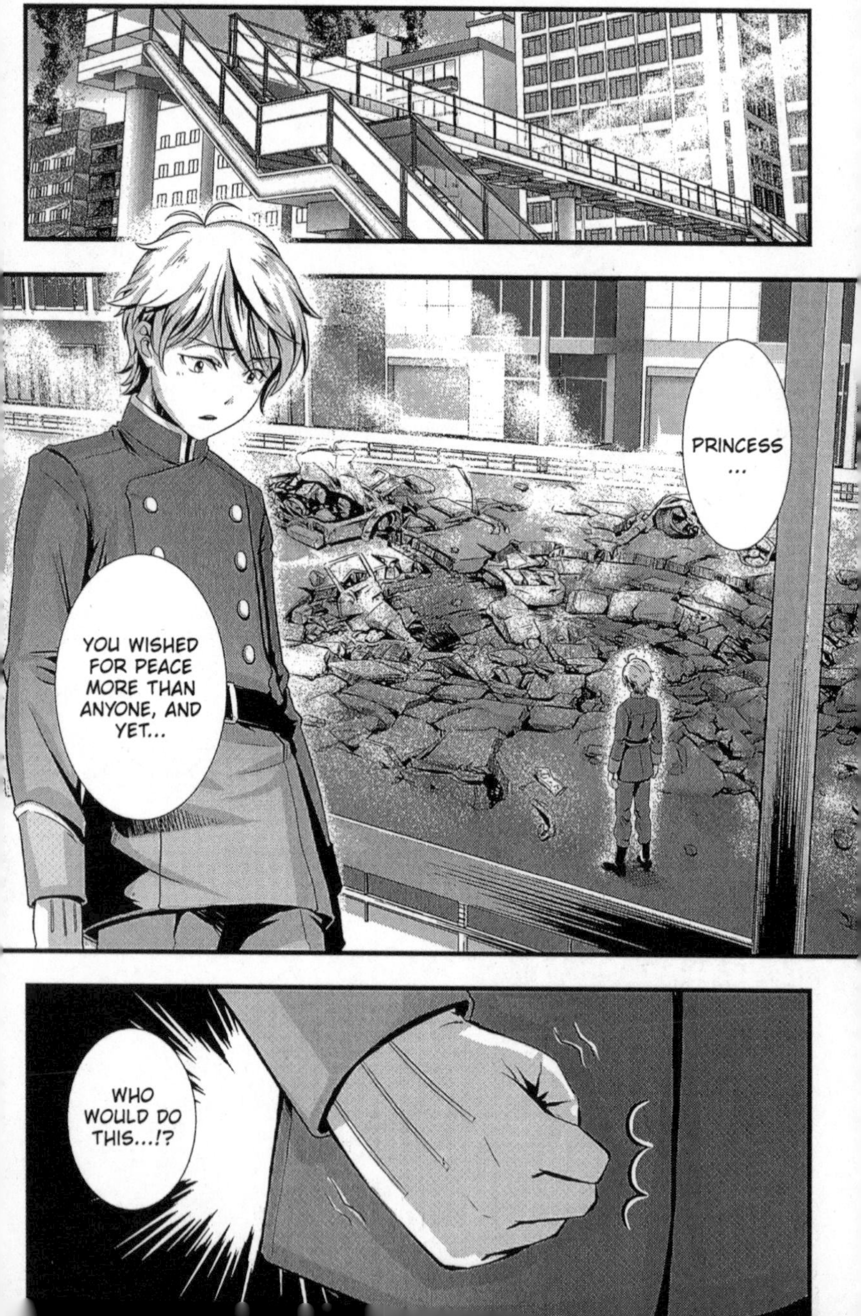
PRINCESS...
YOU WISHED FOR PEACE MORE THAN ANYONE, AND YET...
WHO WOULD DO THIS...!?

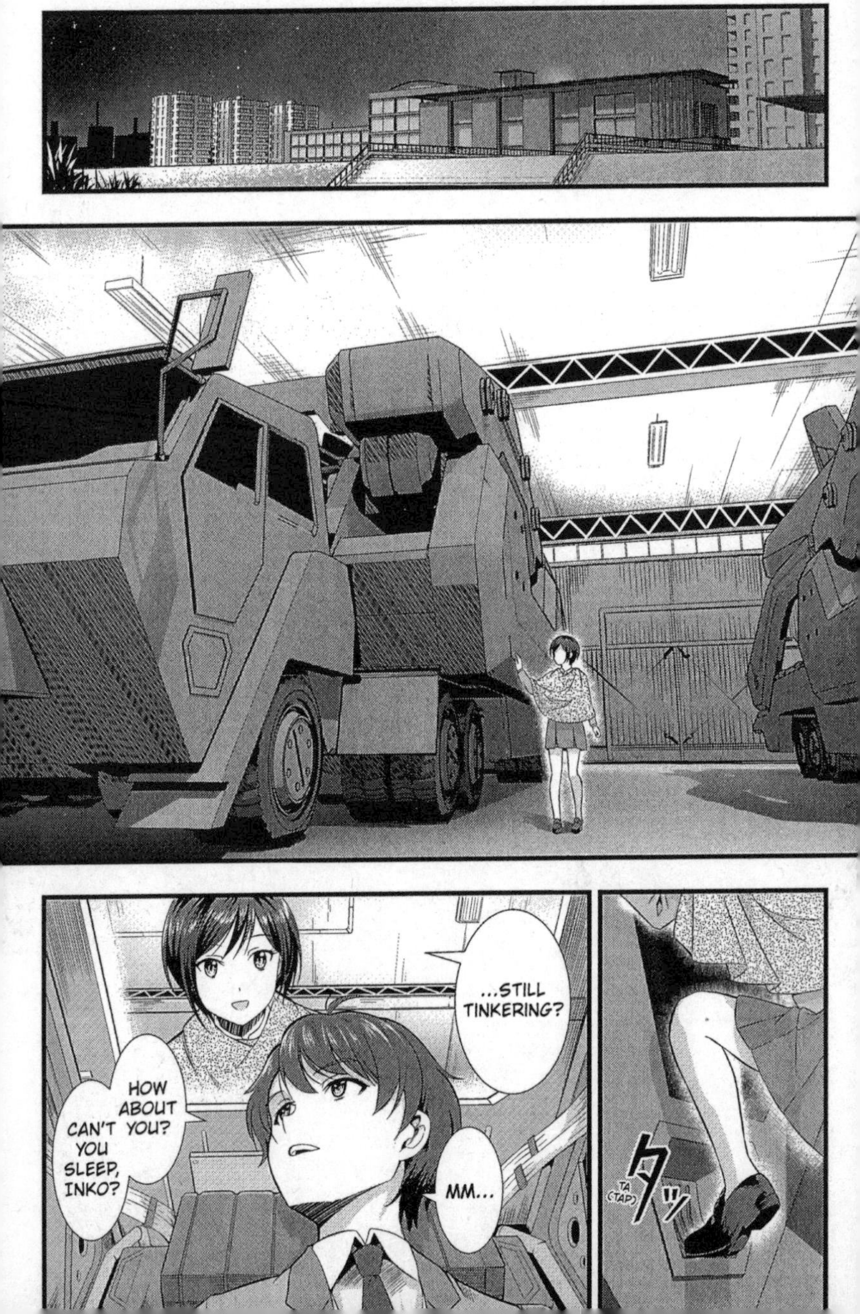
タッ
TA (TAP)
...STILL TINKERING?
MM...
HOW ABOUT YOU? CAN'T YOU SLEEP, INKO?

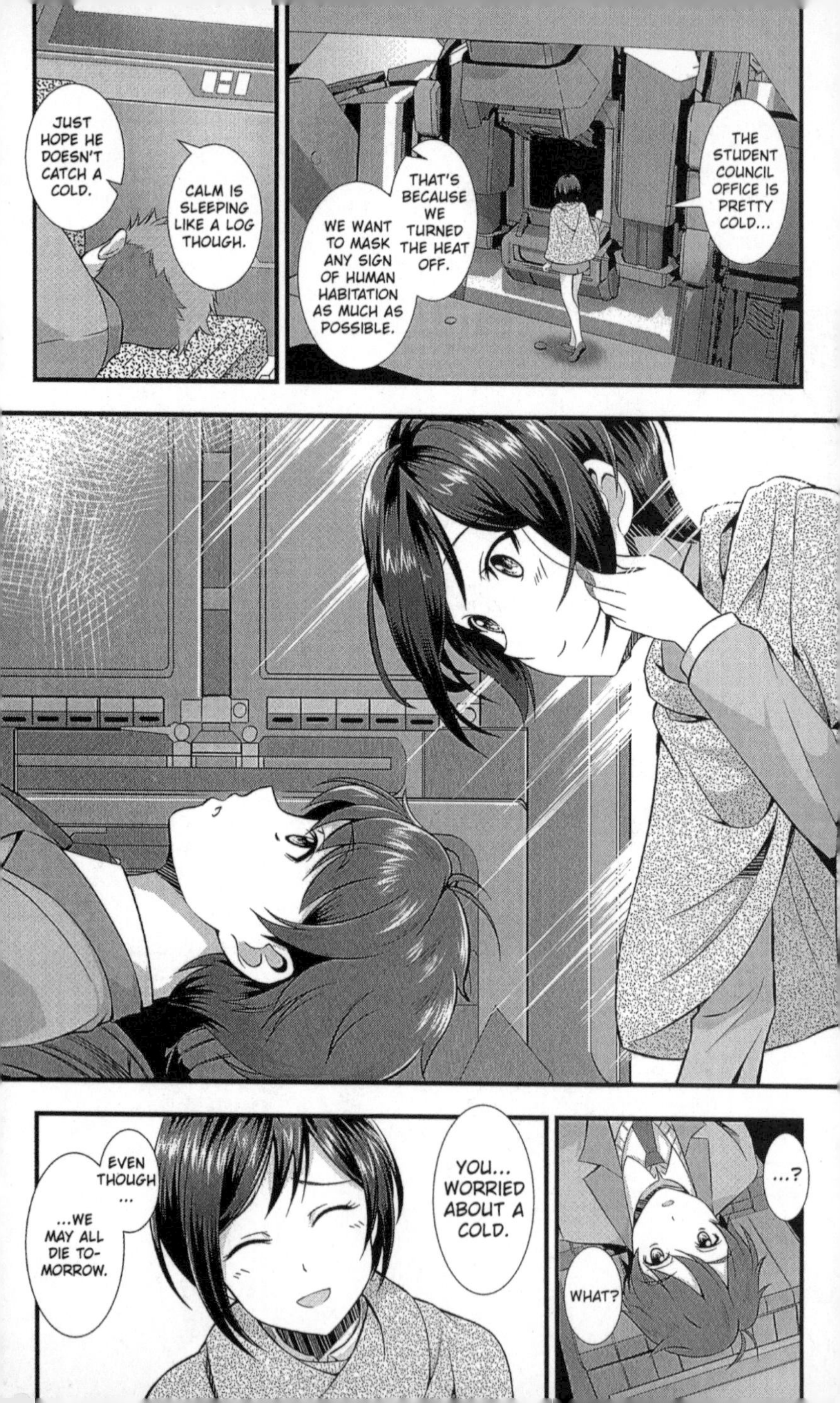
THE STUDENT COUNCIL OFFICE IS PRETTY COLD...
THAT'S BECAUSE WE TURNED THE HEAT OFF.
WE WANT TO MASK ANY SIGN OF HUMAN HABITATION AS MUCH AS POSSIBLE.
CALM IS SLEEPING LIKE A LOG THOUGH.
JUST HOPE HE DOESN'T CATCH A COLD.
...?
WHAT?
YOU... WORRIED ABOUT A COLD.
EVEN THOUGH...
...WE MAY ALL DIE TO-MORROW.

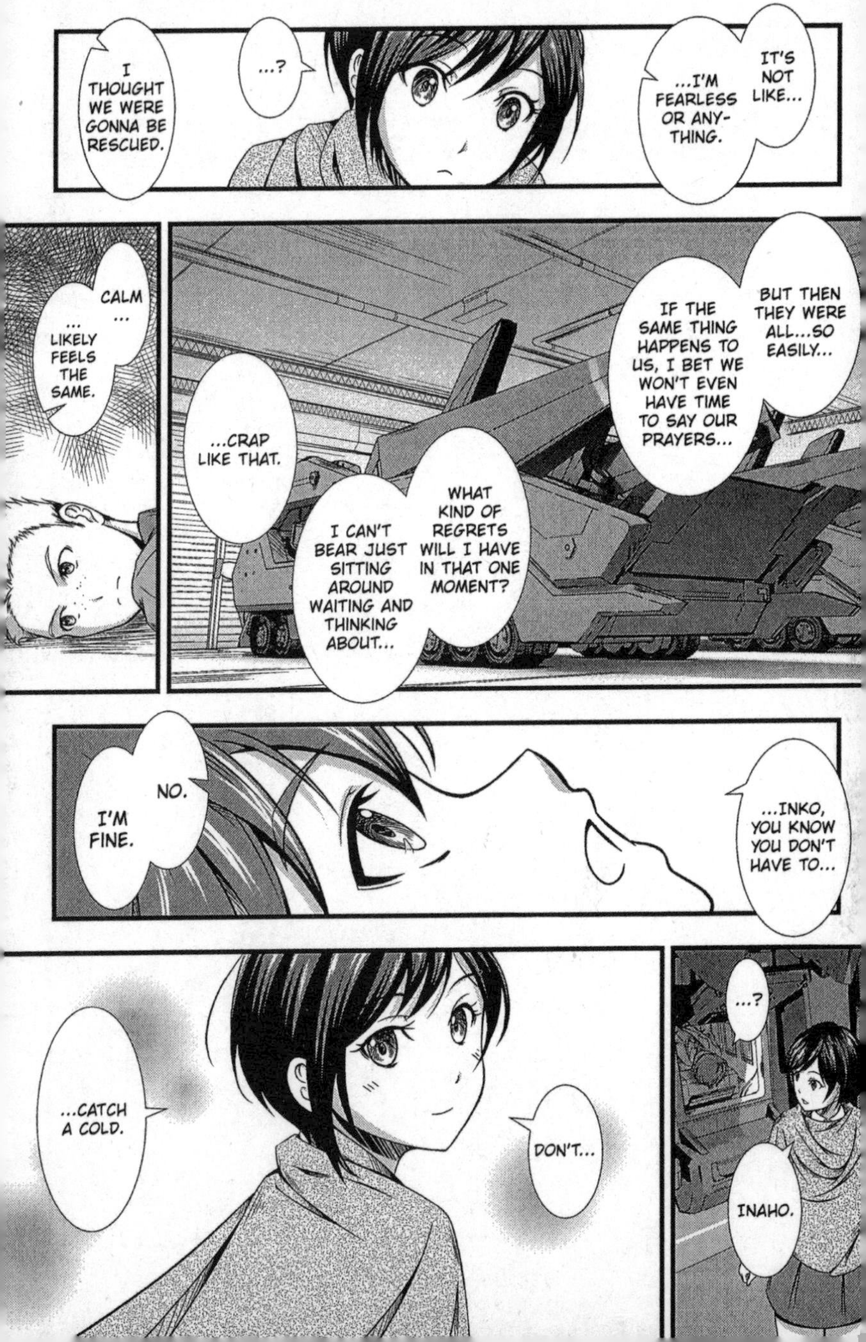
IT'S NOT LIKE...
...I'M FEARLESS OR ANYTHING.
...?
I THOUGHT WE WERE GONNA BE RESCUED.
BUT THEN THEY WERE ALL...SO EASILY...
IF THE SAME THING HAPPENS TO US, I BET WE WON'T EVEN HAVE TIME TO SAY OUR PRAYERS...
WHAT KIND OF REGRETS WILL I HAVE IN THAT ONE MOMENT?
I CAN'T BEAR JUST SITTING AROUND WAITING AND THINKING ABOUT...
...CRAP LIKE THAT.
CALM ... LIKELY FEELS THE SAME.
...INKO, YOU KNOW YOU DON'T HAVE TO...
NO.
I'M FINE.
...?
INAHO.
DON'T...
...CATCH A COLD.

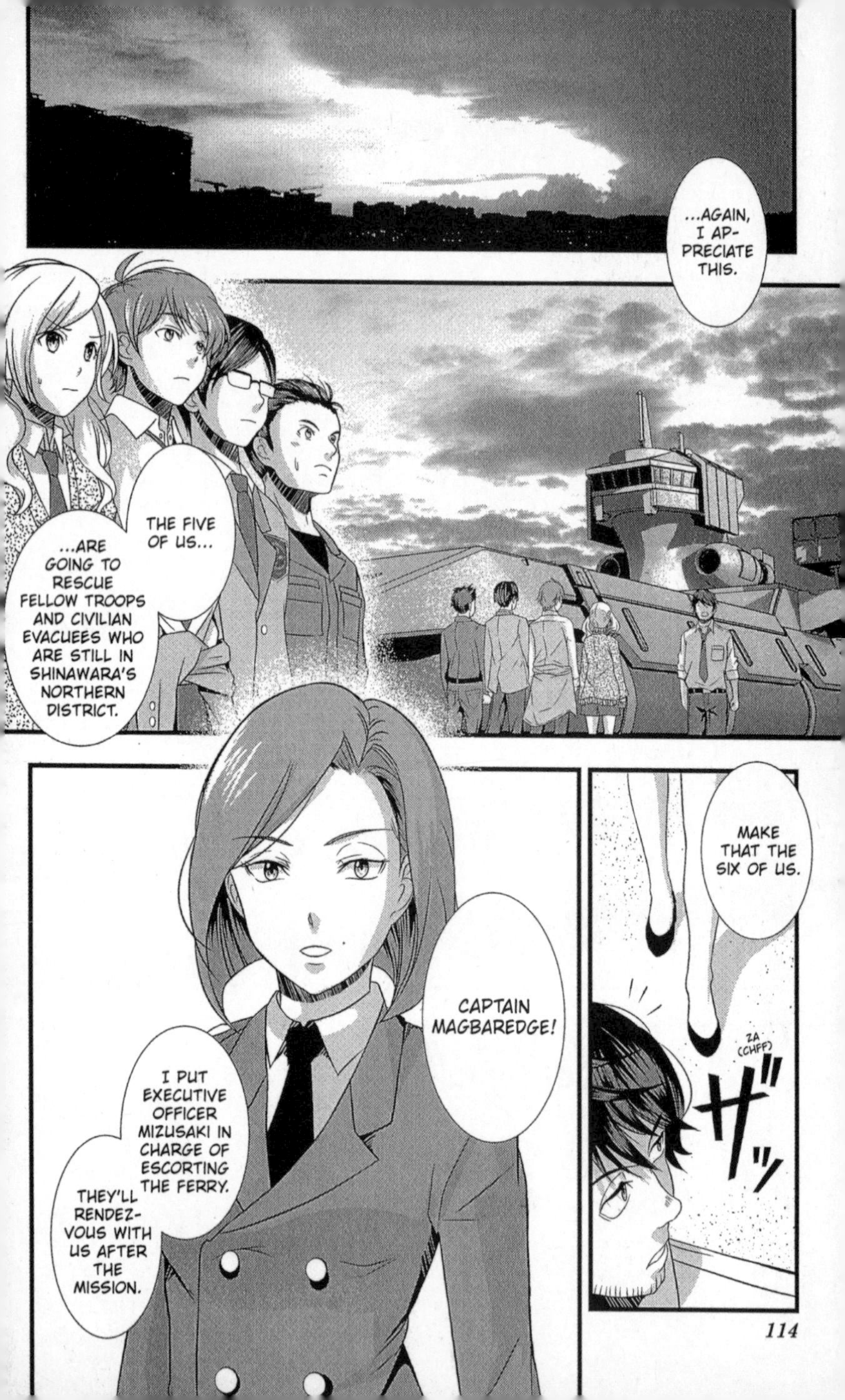
...AGAIN, I AP- PRECIATE THIS.
THE FIVE OF US...
...ARE GOING TO RESCUE FELLOW TROOPS AND CIVILIAN EVACUEES WHO ARE STILL IN SHINAWARA'S NORTHERN DISTRICT.
MAKE THAT THE SIX OF US.
ザッ
ZA (CHFF)
CAPTAIN MAGBAREDGE!
I PUT EXECUTIVE OFFICER MIZUSAKI IN CHARGE OF ESCORTING THE FERRY.
THEY'LL RENDEZ- VOUS WITH US AFTER THE MISSION.

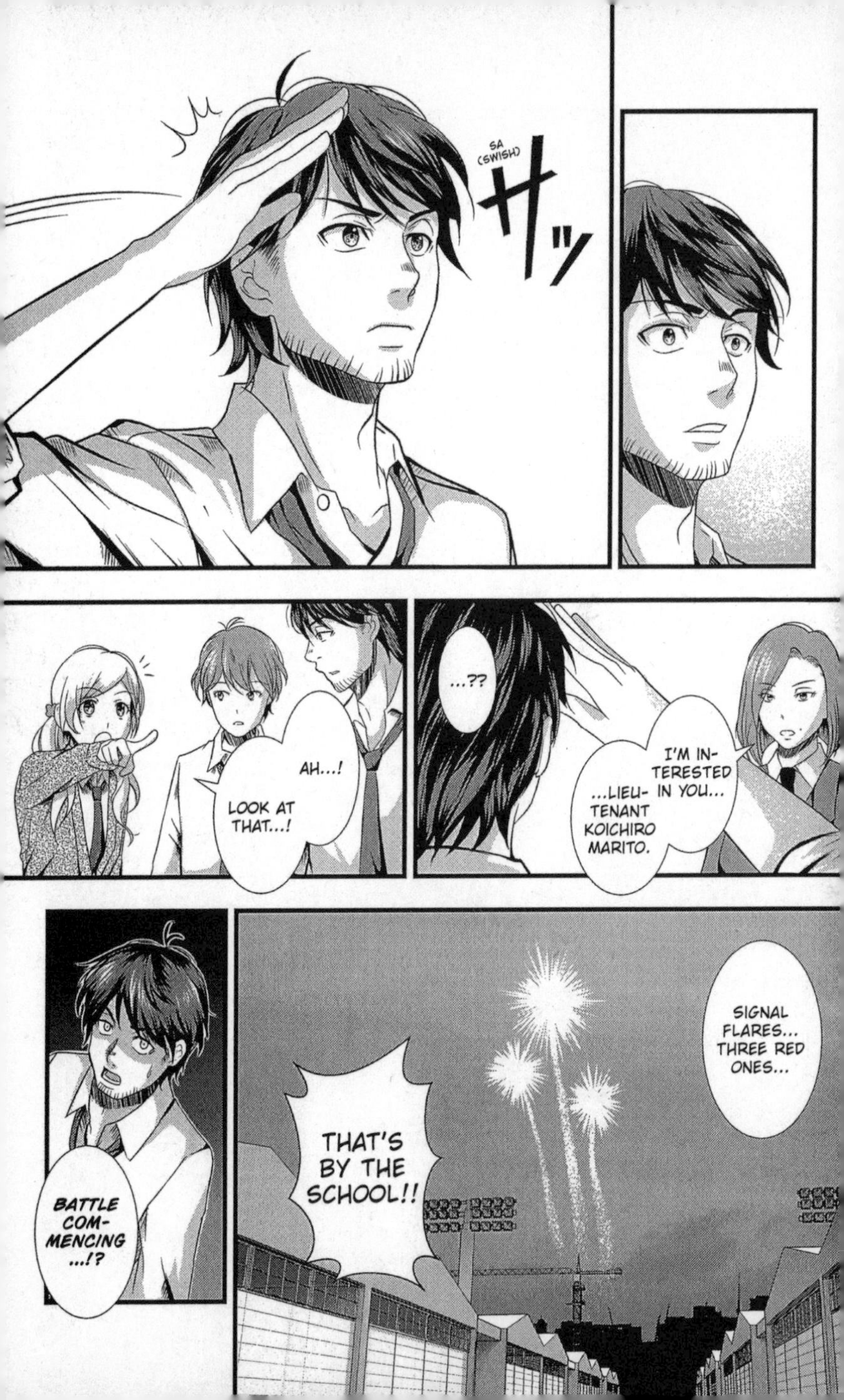
SA (SWISH)
サッ
...??
I'M INTERESTED IN YOU...
...LIEUTENANT KOICHIRO MARITO.
AH...!
LOOK AT THAT...!
SIGNAL FLARES... THREE RED ONES...
THAT'S BY THE SCHOOL!!
BATTLE COMMENCING...!?

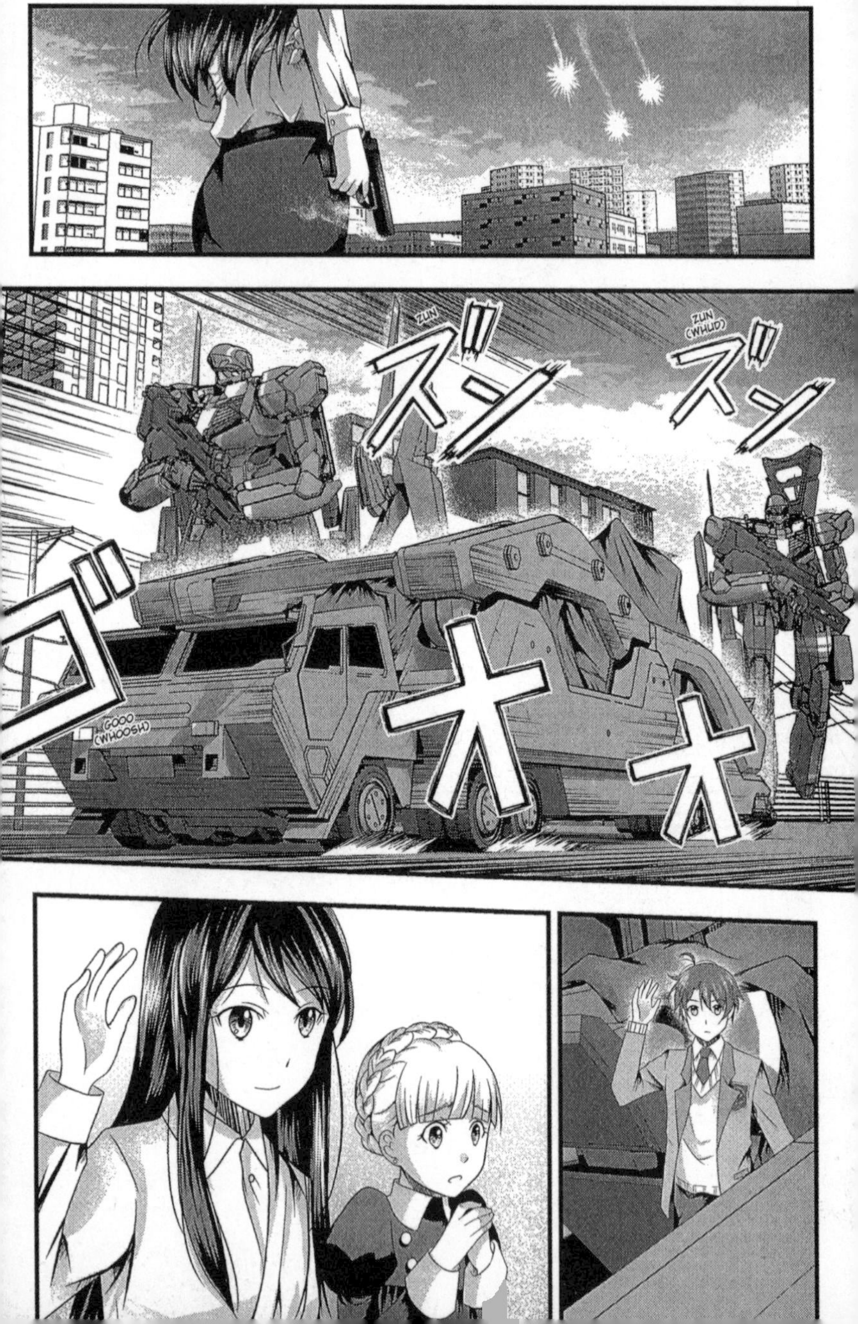
ズン
ZUN
(WHUD)
ズン
ZUN
ゴオオ
GOOO
(WHOOSH)

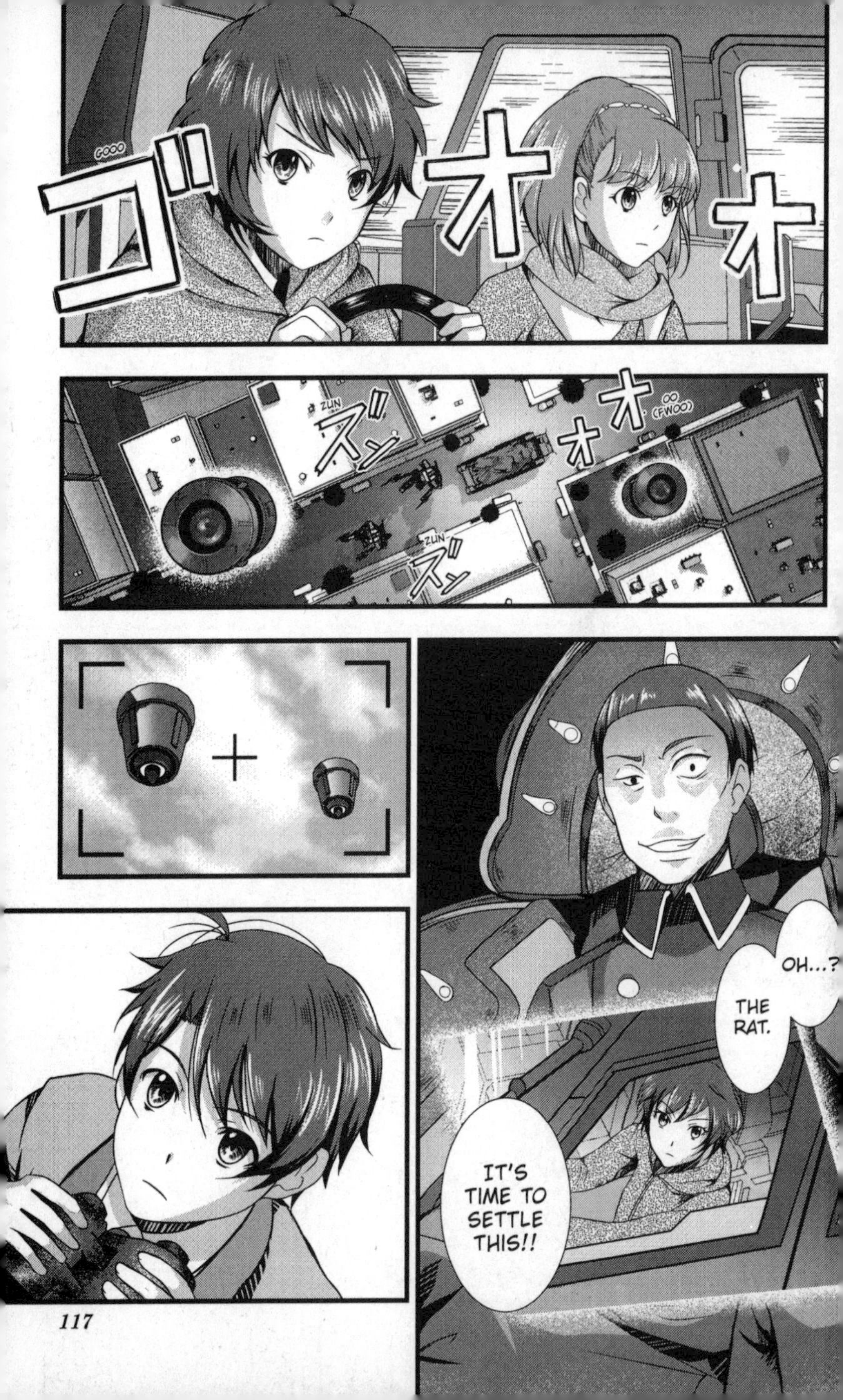
GOOO
ZUN
OO (FWOO)
ZUN
OH...?
THE RAT.
IT'S TIME TO SETTLE THIS!!

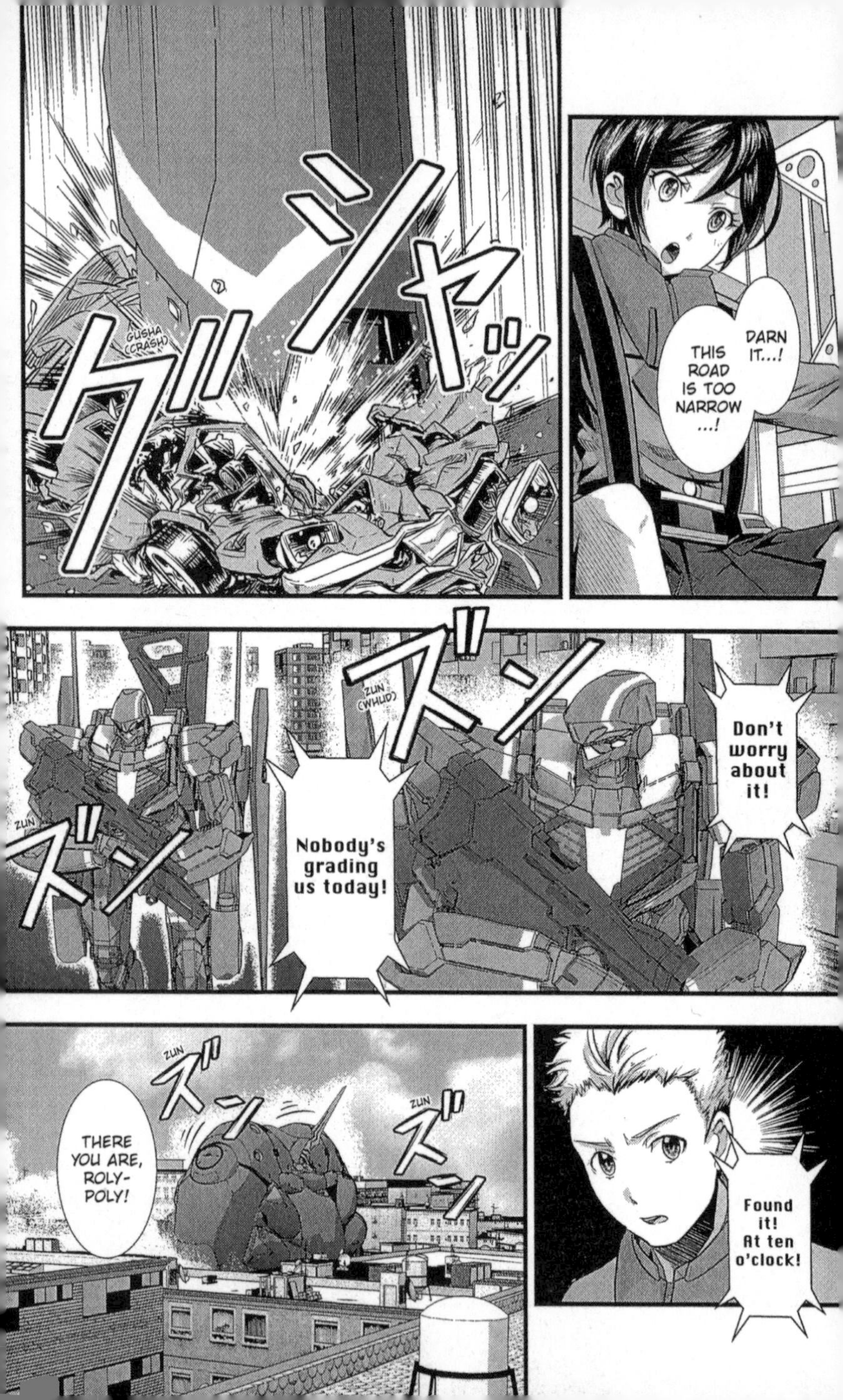
DARN IT...! THIS ROAD IS TOO NARROW ...!
GUSHA (CRASH)
Don't worry about it!
ZUN (WHUD)
Nobody's grading us today!
ZUN
Found it! At ten o'clock!
ZUN
ZUN
THERE YOU ARE, ROLY-POLY!

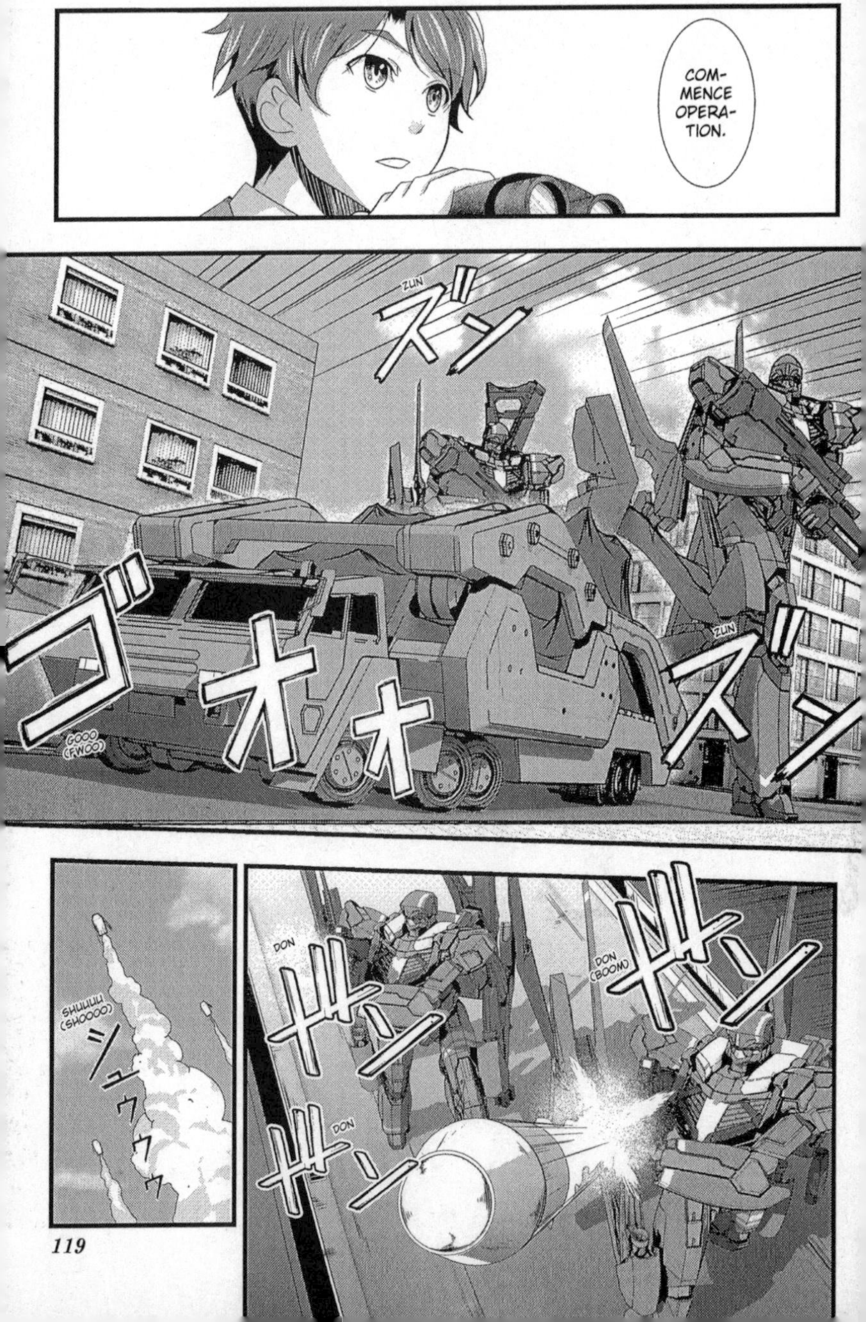
COM-MENCE OPERA-TION.
ZUN
ZUN
GOOO (FWOO)
DON (BOOM)
DON
DON
SHUUUU (SHOOOO)

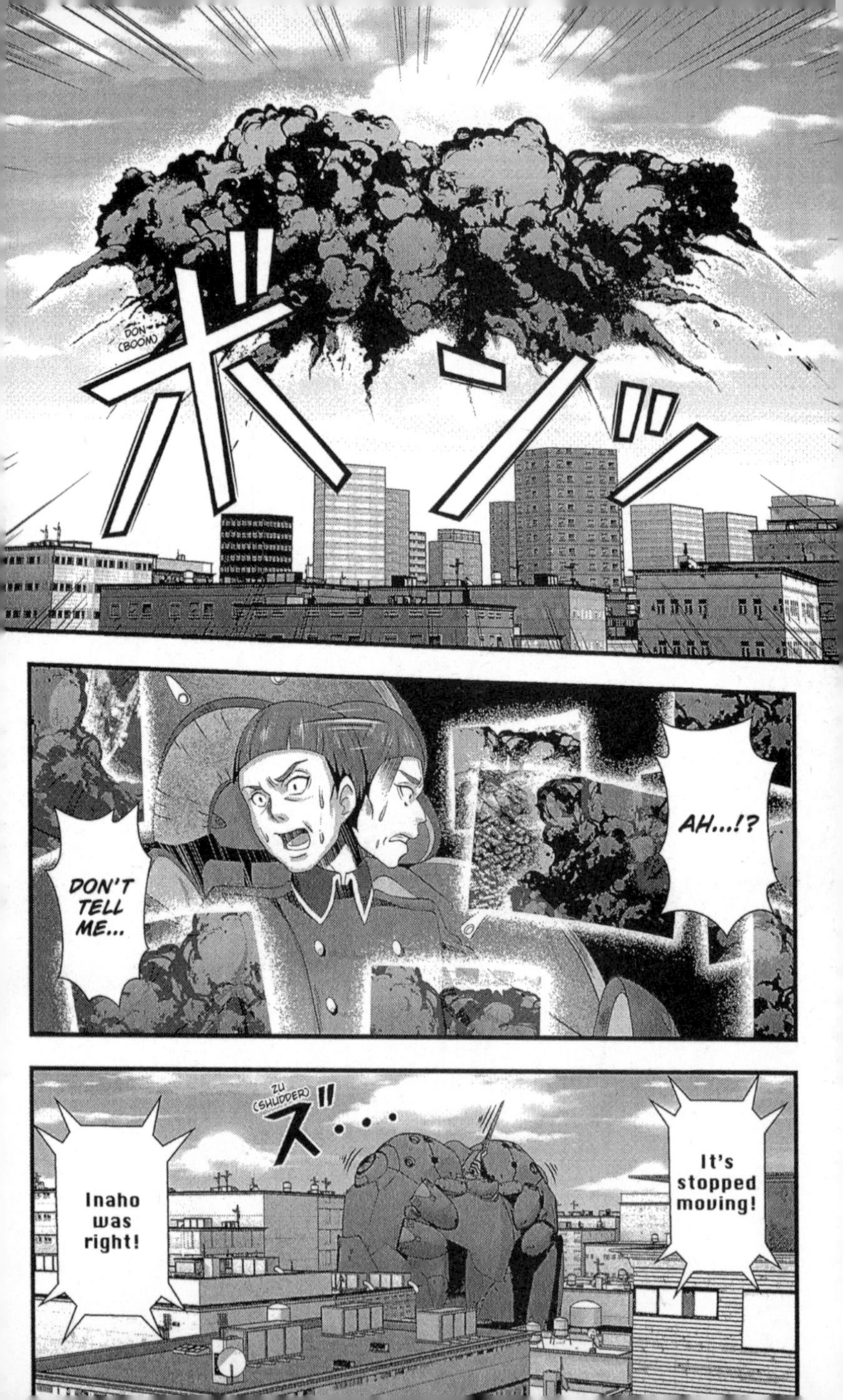
DON (BOOM)
AH...!?
DON'T TELL ME...
It's stopped moving!
ZU (SHUDDER)
Inaho was right!

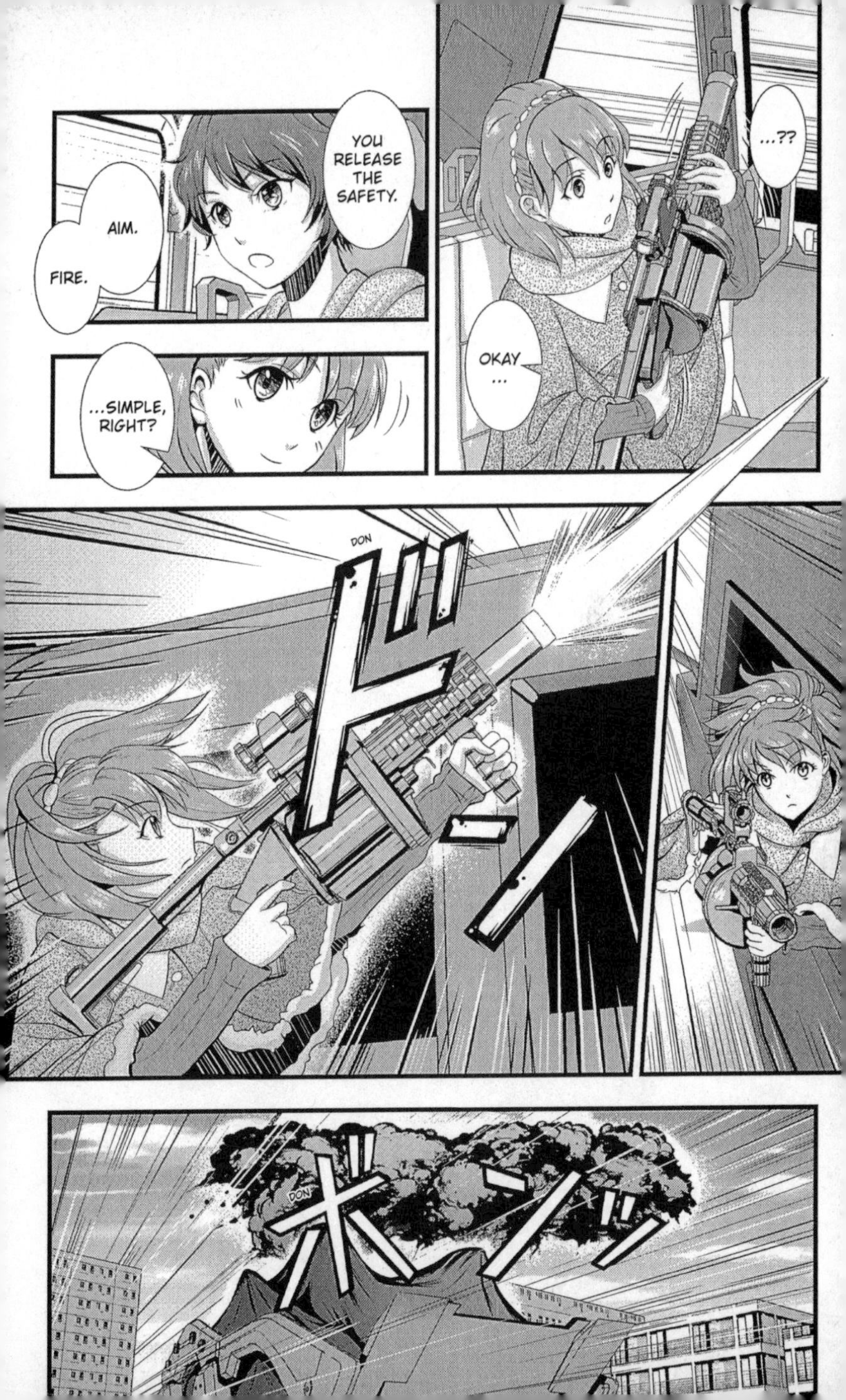
...??
OKAY ...
YOU RELEASE THE SAFETY.
AIM.
FIRE.
...SIMPLE, RIGHT?
DON
DON

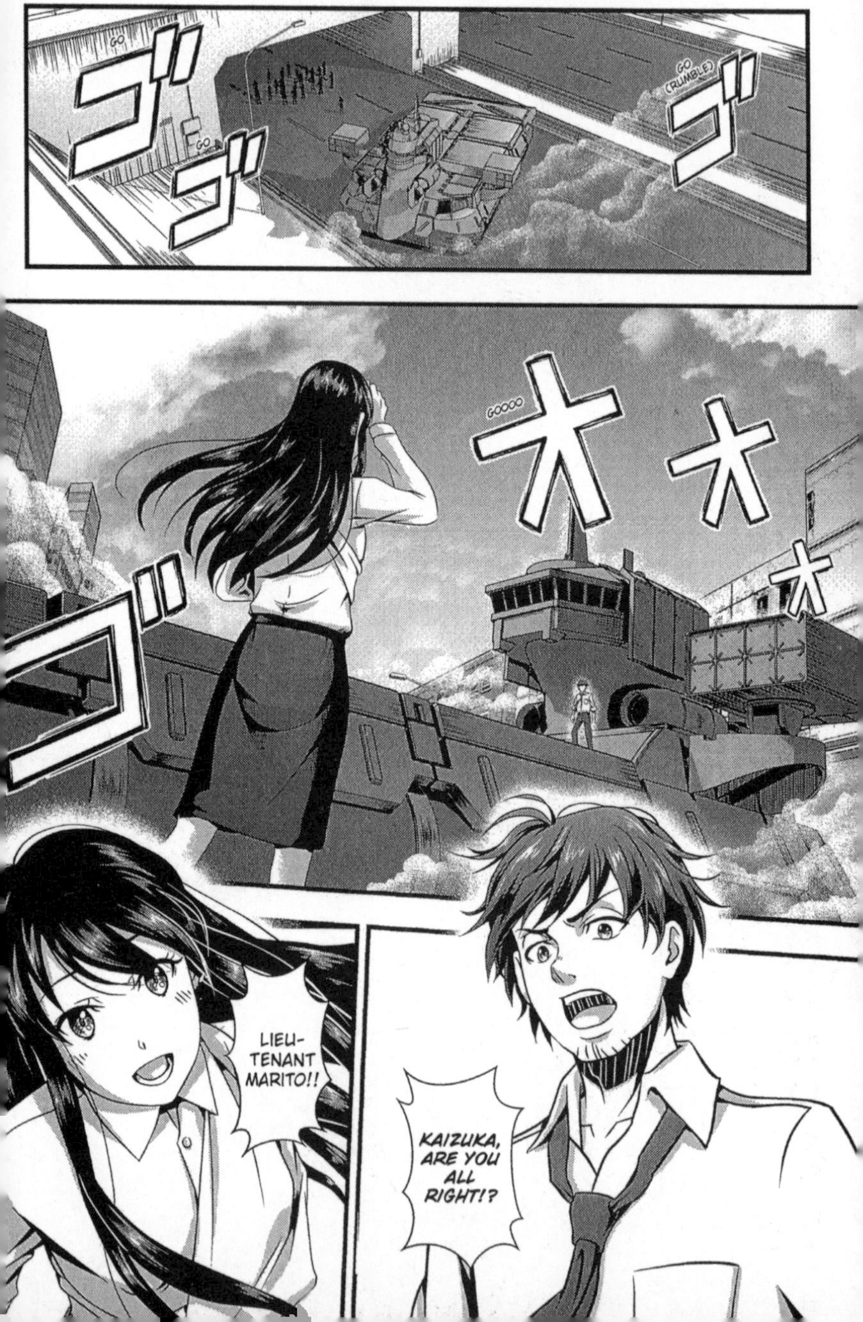
GO (RUMBLE)
GO
GO
GOOOO
KAIZUKA, ARE YOU ALL RIGHT!?
LIEU-TENANT MARITO!!

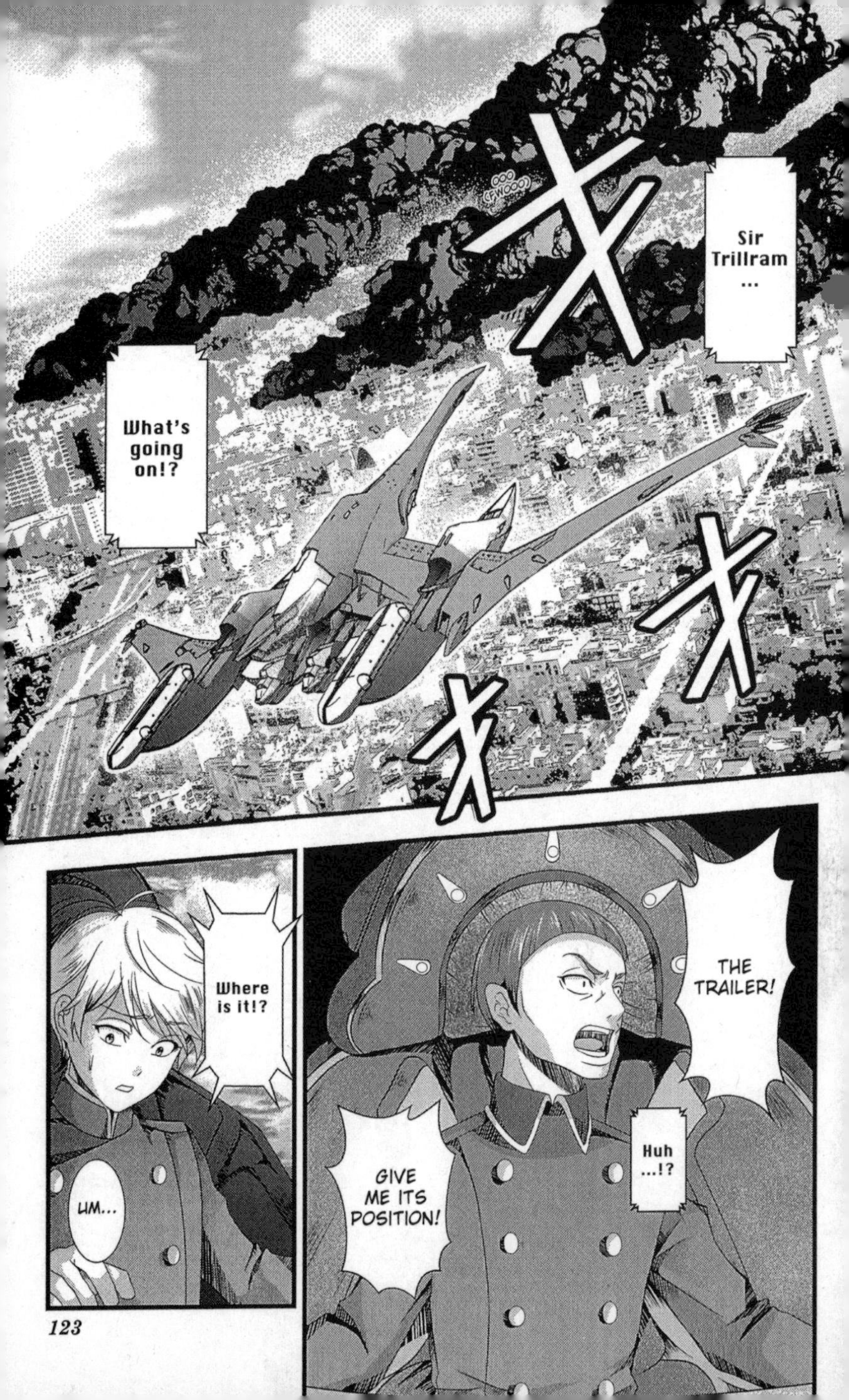
Sir Trillram ...
GOO (FWOOO)
What's going on!?
THE TRAILER!
Huh ...!?
GIVE ME ITS POSITION!
Where is it!?
UM...

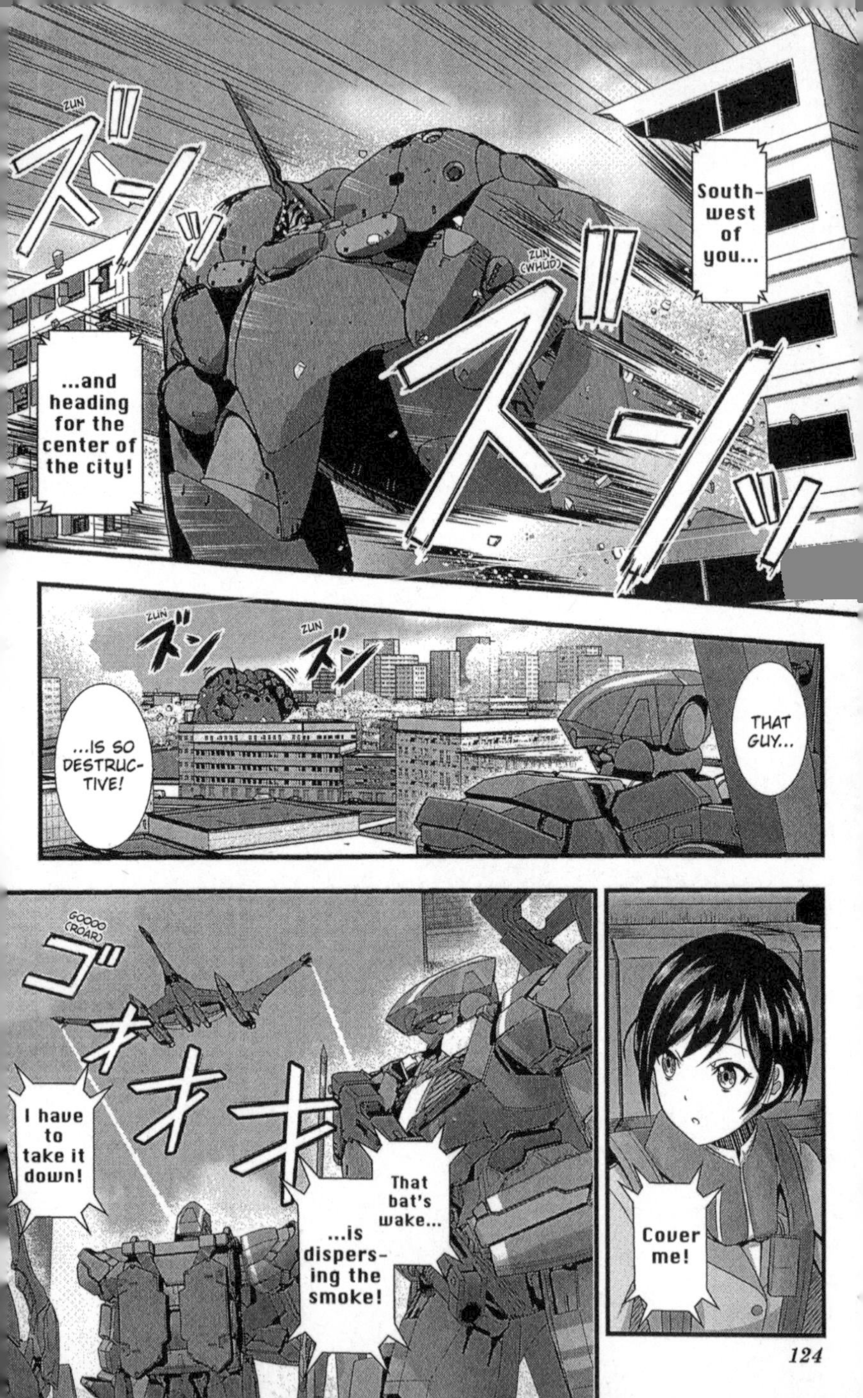
South-west of you...
ZUN (WHUD)
ズーン
ZUN
ズーン
...and heading for the center of the city!
ZUN
ズン
ZUN
ズン
THAT GUY...
...IS SO DESTRUCTIVE!
Cover me!
GOOOO (ROAR)
ゴオオオ
That bat's wake...
...is dispersing the smoke!
I have to take it down!

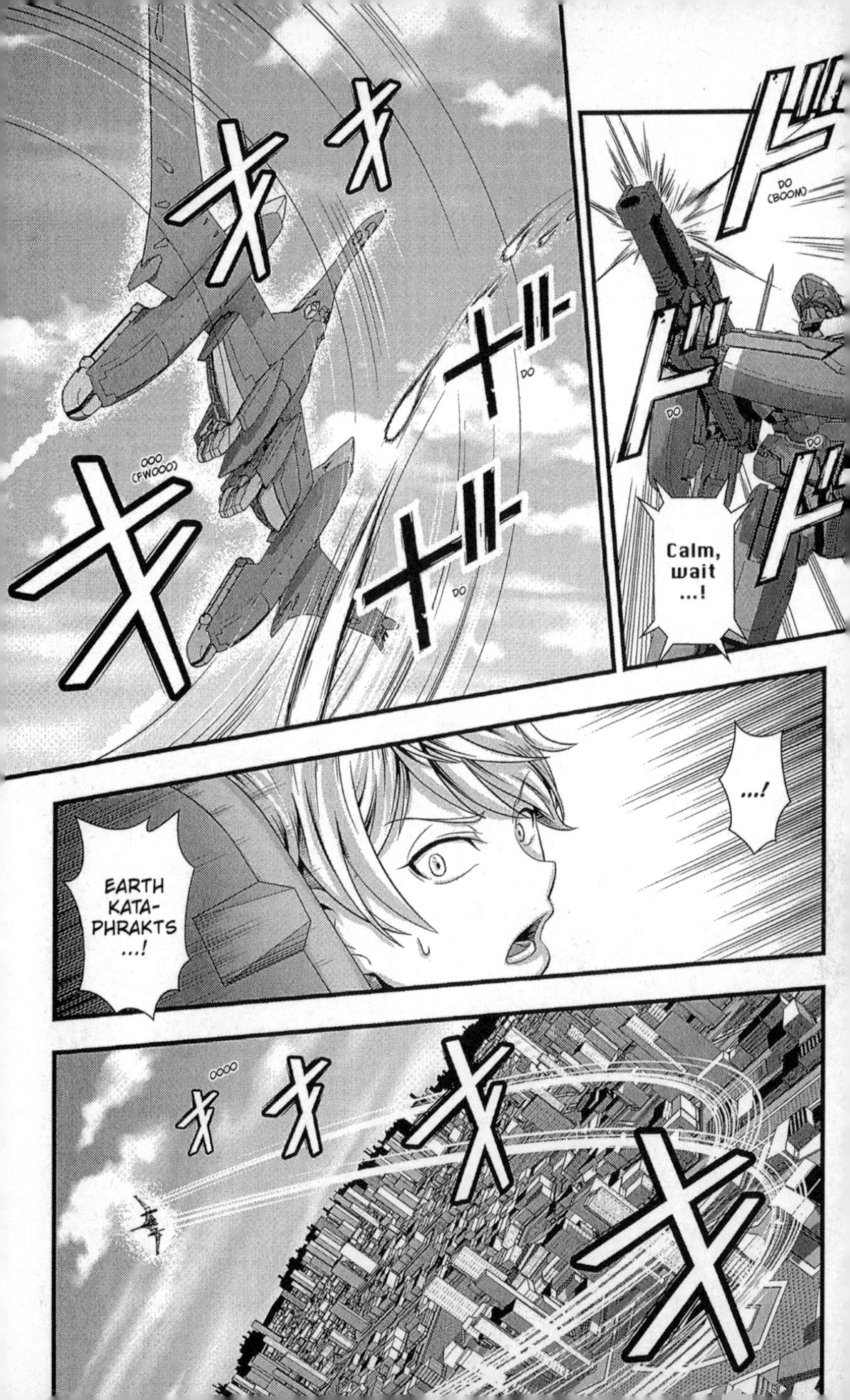
DO (BOOM)
DO
DO
Calm, wait ...!
DO
OOO (FWOOO)
DO
...!
EARTH KATA-PHRAKTS ...!
OOOO

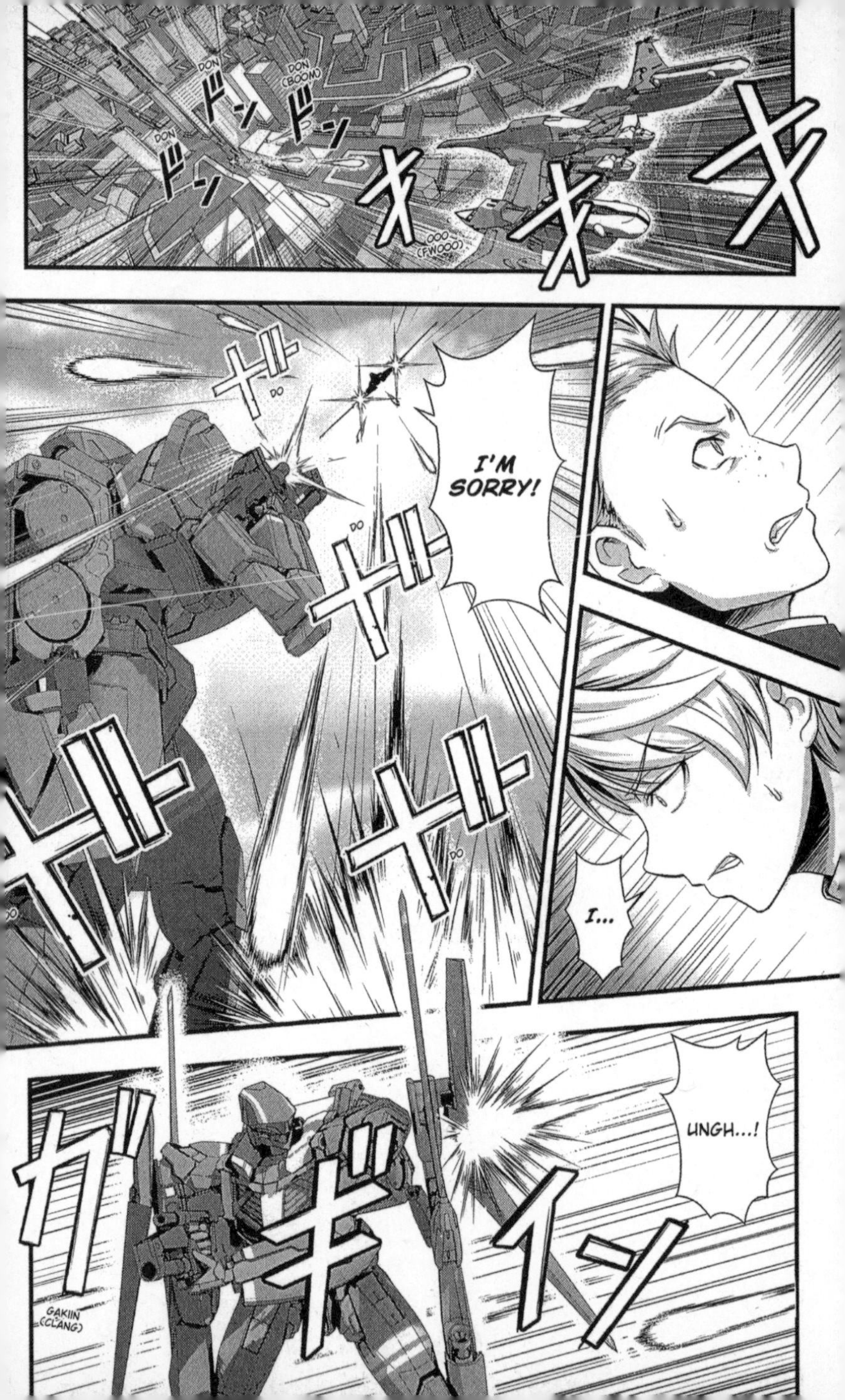
DON (BOOM)
DON
DON
OOO (FWOOO)
I...
I'M SORRY!
DO
DO
DO
DO
UNGH...!
GAKIIN (CLANG)

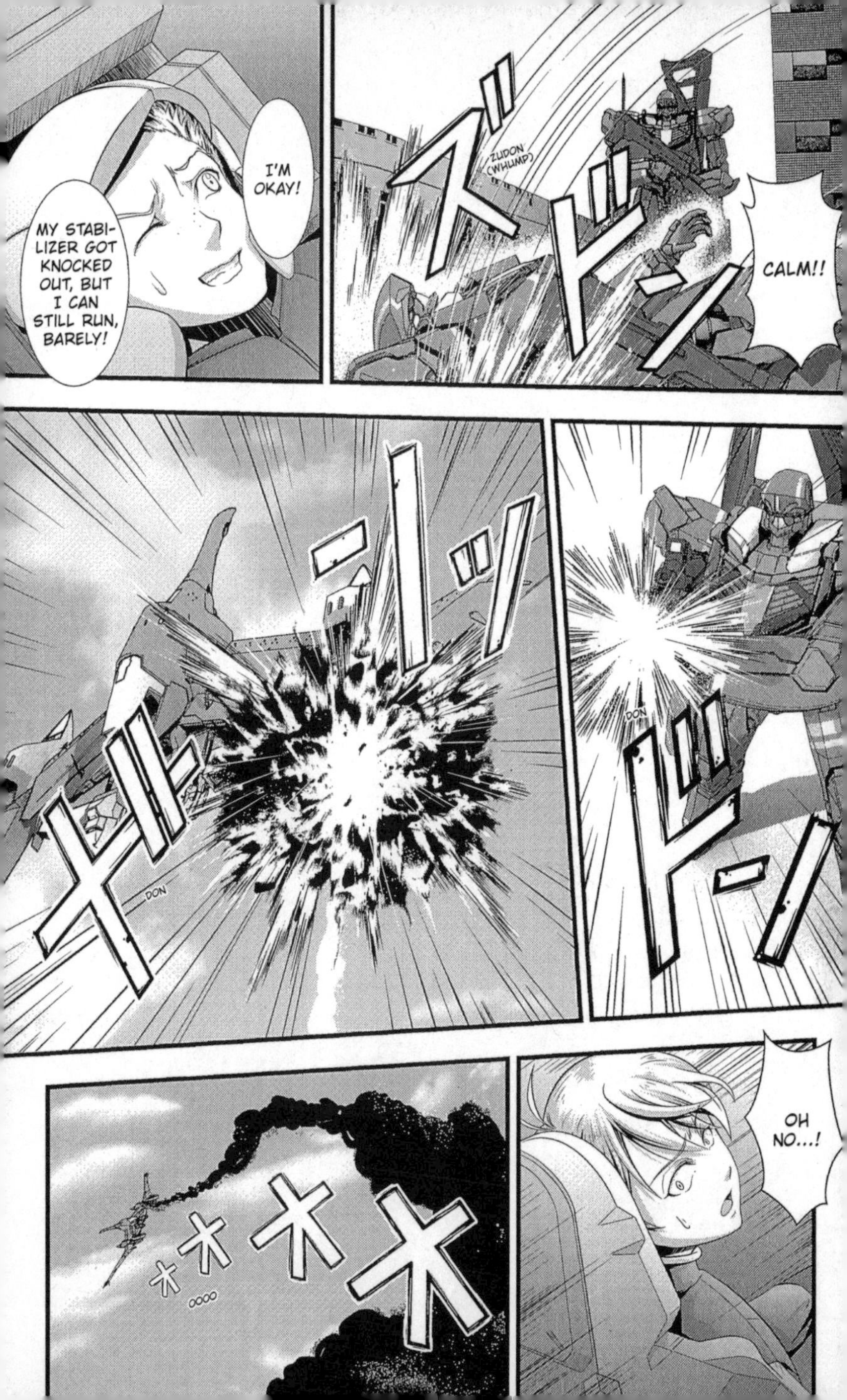
ZUDON (WHUMP)
CALM!!
I'M OKAY!
MY STABILIZER GOT KNOCKED OUT, BUT I CAN STILL RUN, BARELY!
DON
DON
OH NO...!
OOOO

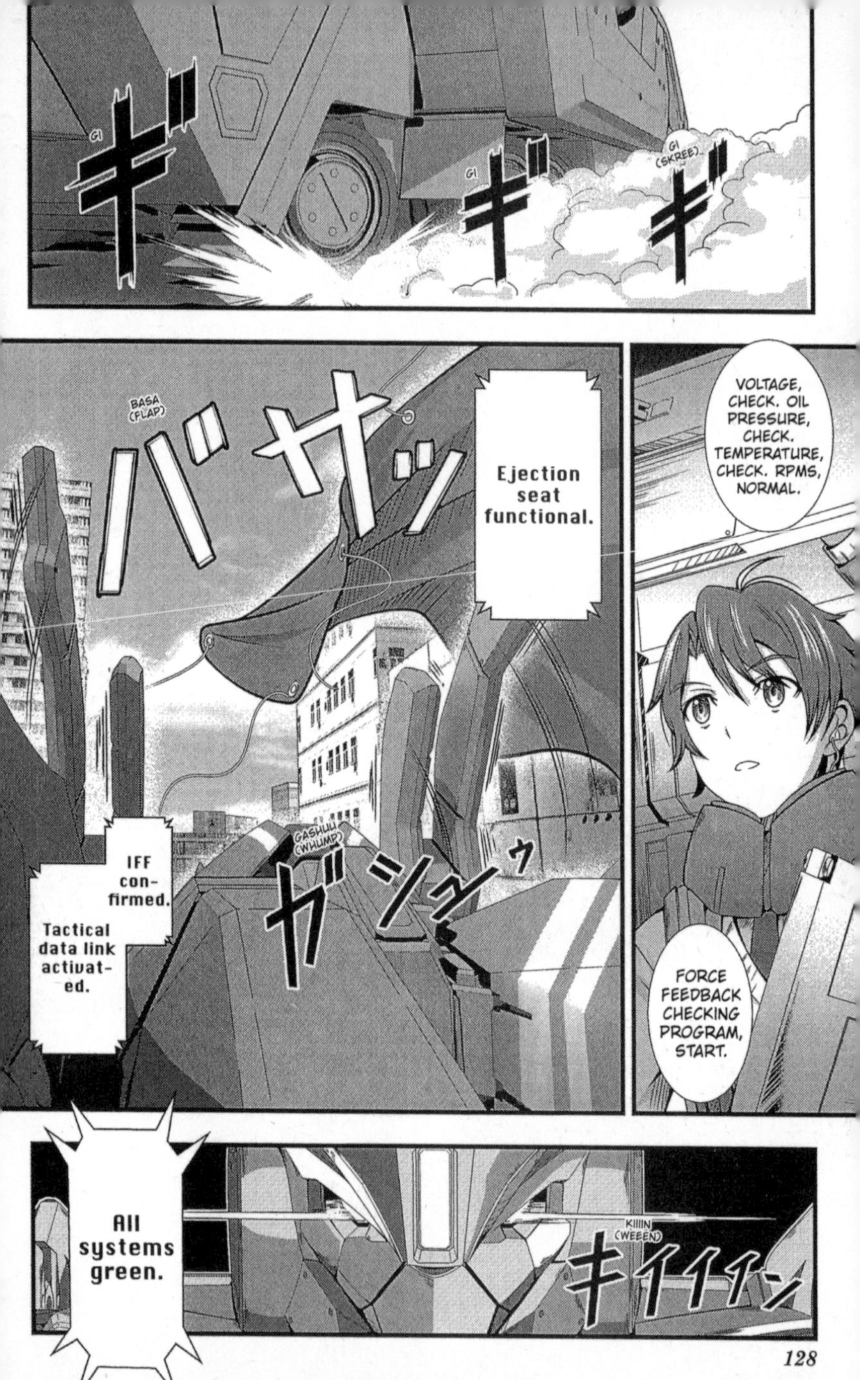
GI (SKREE)...
GI
GI
VOLTAGE, CHECK. OIL PRESSURE, CHECK. TEMPERATURE, CHECK. RPMS, NORMAL.
FORCE FEEDBACK CHECKING PROGRAM, START.
Ejection seat functional.
BASA (FLAP)
GASHUU (WHUMP)
IFF con-firmed.
Tactical data link activat-ed.
KIIIN (WEEEN)
All systems green.

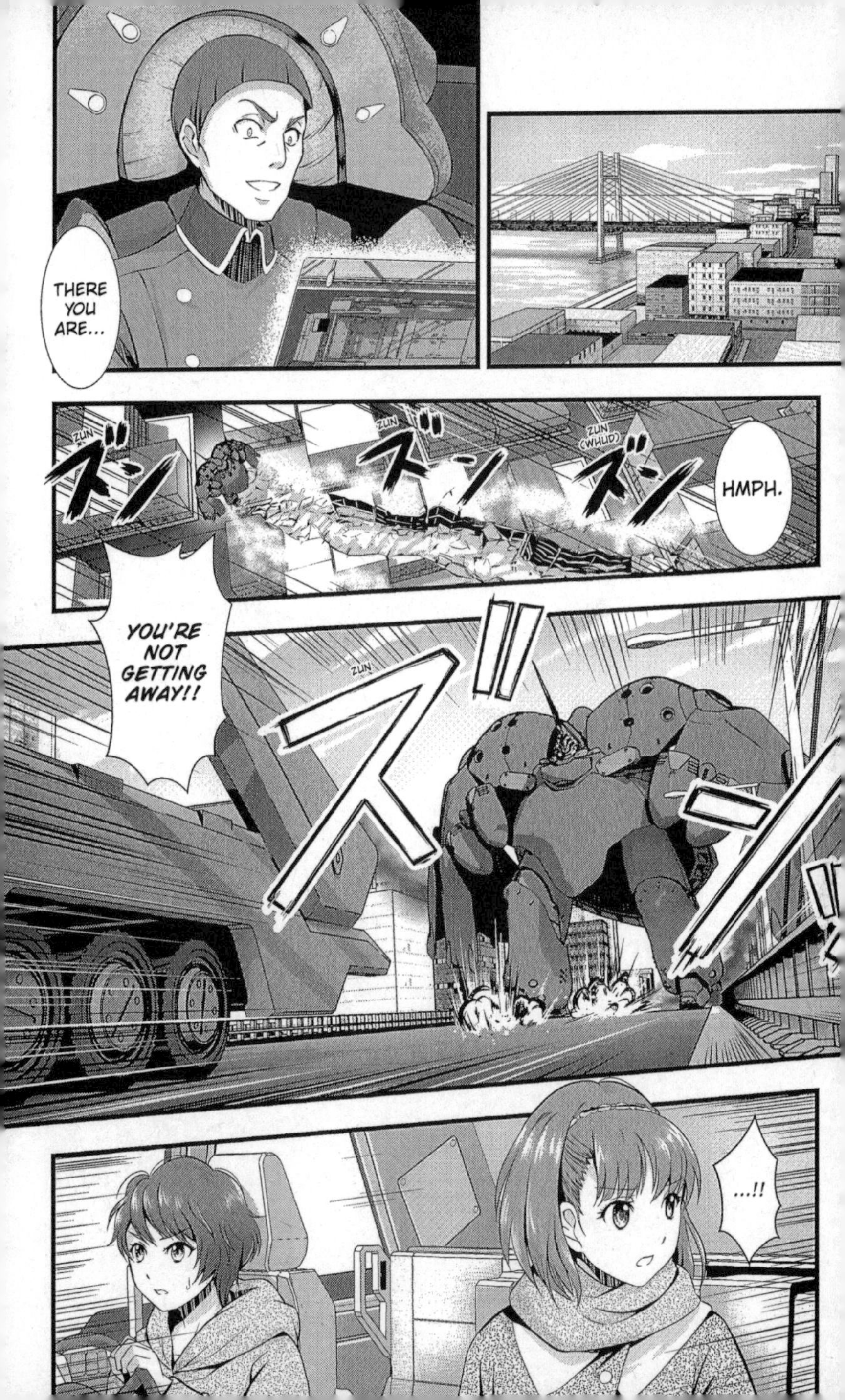
THERE YOU ARE...
HMPH.
ZUN (WHUD)
ZUN
ZUN
YOU'RE NOT GETTING AWAY!!
ZUN
...!!

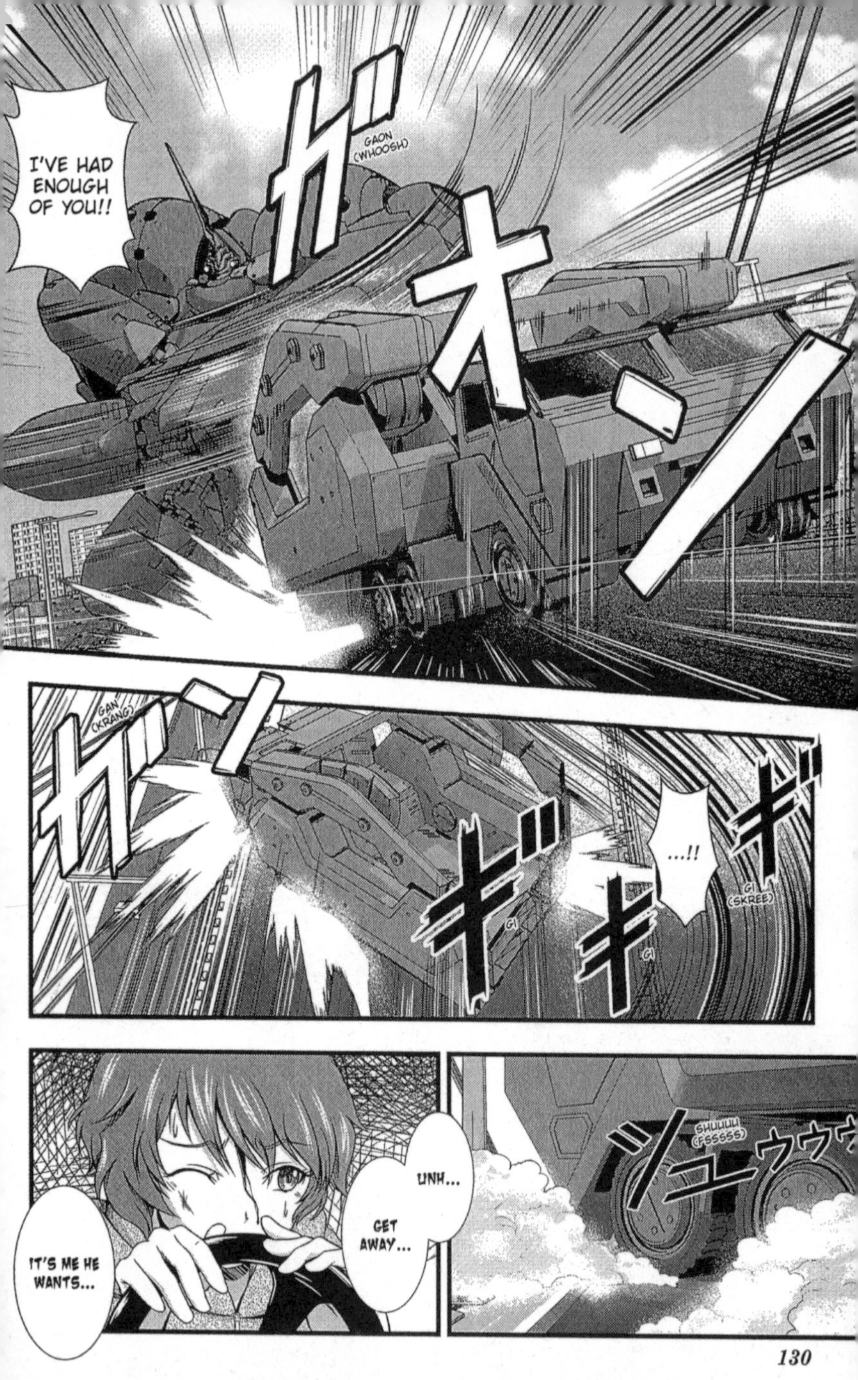
I'VE HAD ENOUGH OF YOU!!
GAON (WHOOSH)
GI (SKREE)
...!!
GI
GI
GAN (KRANG)
SHUUUU (FSSSSS)
UNH...
GET AWAY...
IT'S ME HE WANTS...

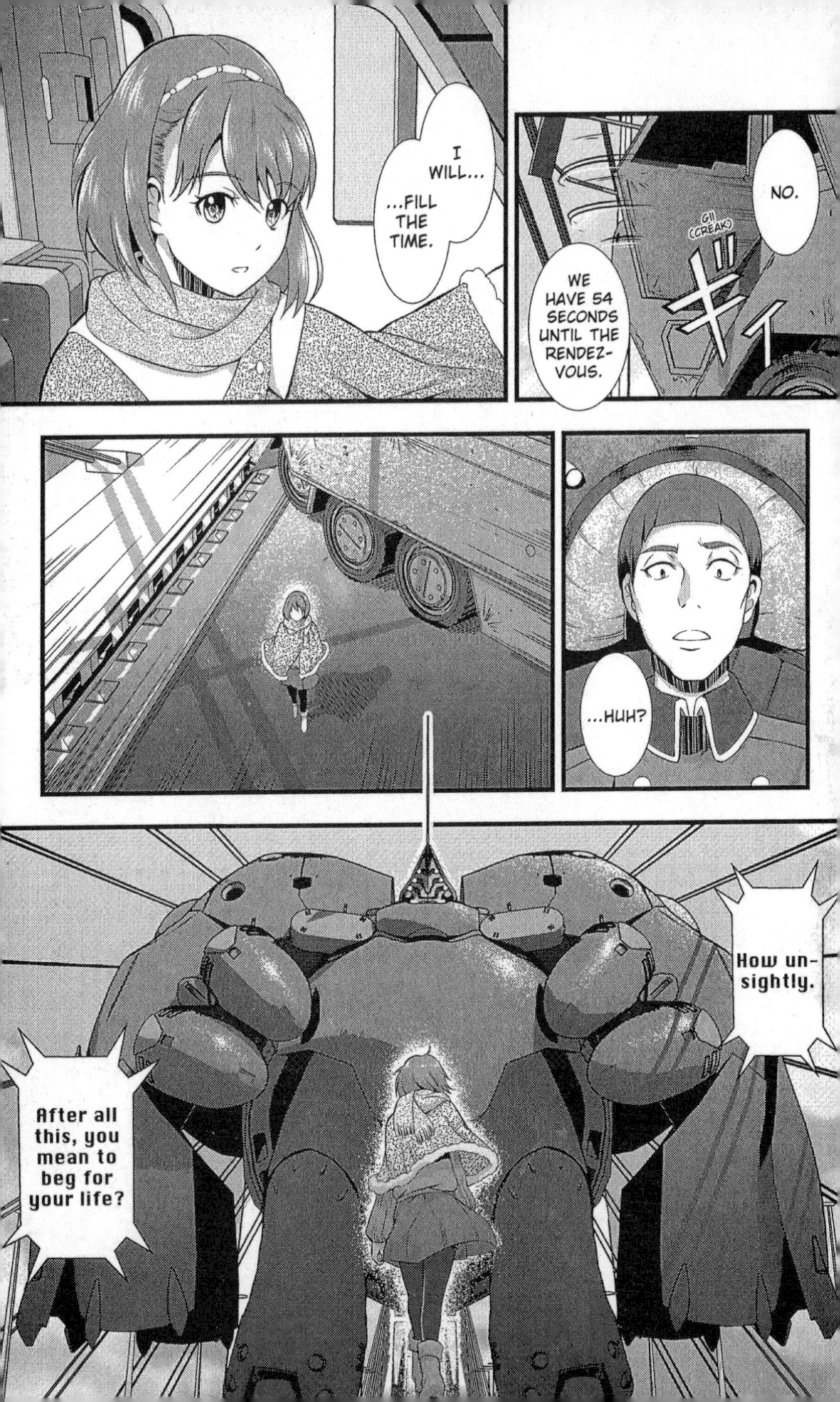
NO.
GII (CREAK)
ギイ
WE HAVE 54 SECONDS UNTIL THE RENDEZ-VOUS.
I WILL...
...FILL THE TIME.
...HUH?
How un-sightly.
After all this, you mean to beg for your life?

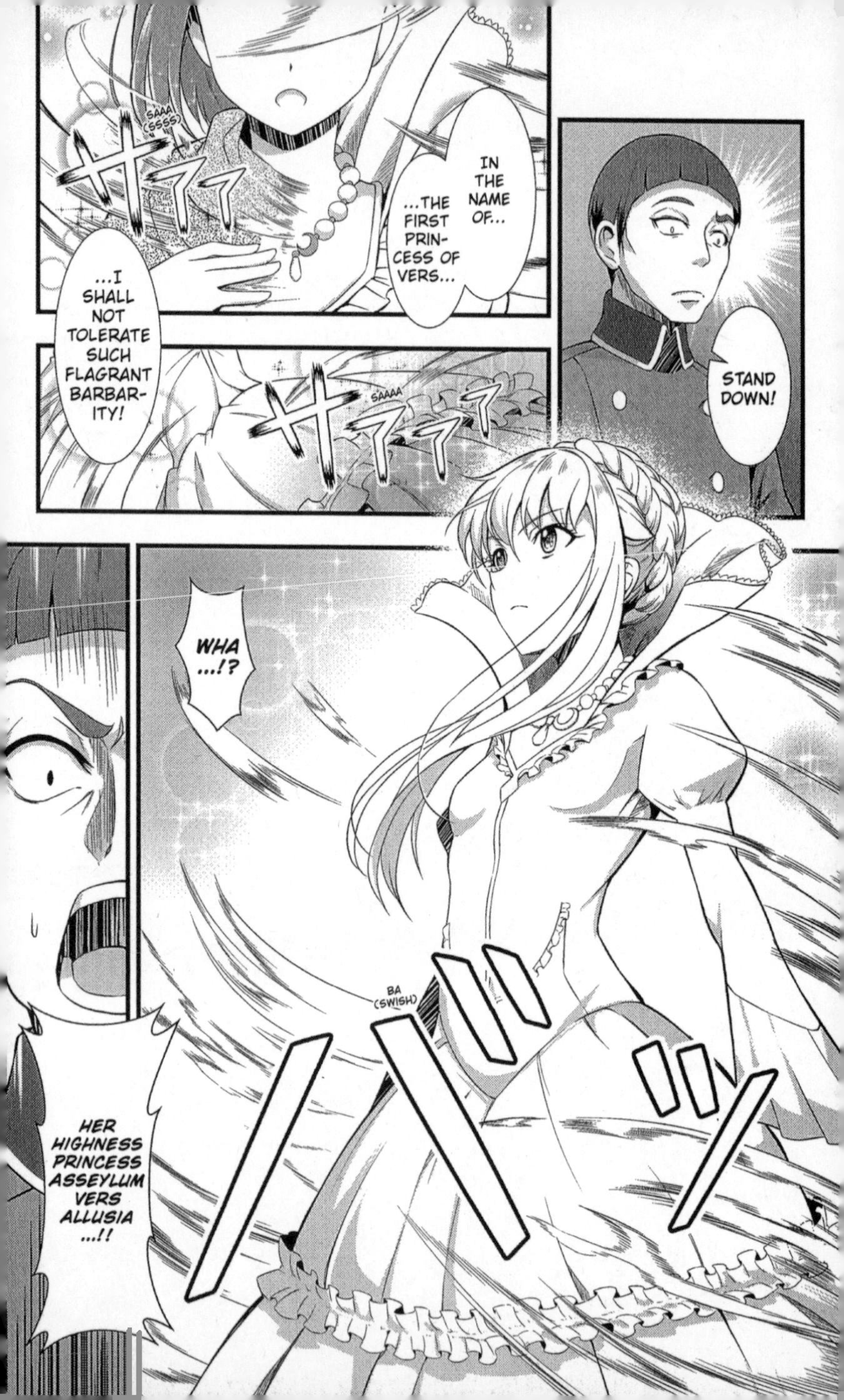
STAND DOWN!
IN THE NAME OF...
...THE FIRST PRINCESS OF VERS...
SAAA (SSSS)
...I SHALL NOT TOLERATE SUCH FLAGRANT BARBARITY!
SAAAA
WHA ...!?
BA (SWISH)
HER HIGHNESS PRINCESS ASSEYLUM VERS ALLUSIA ...!!

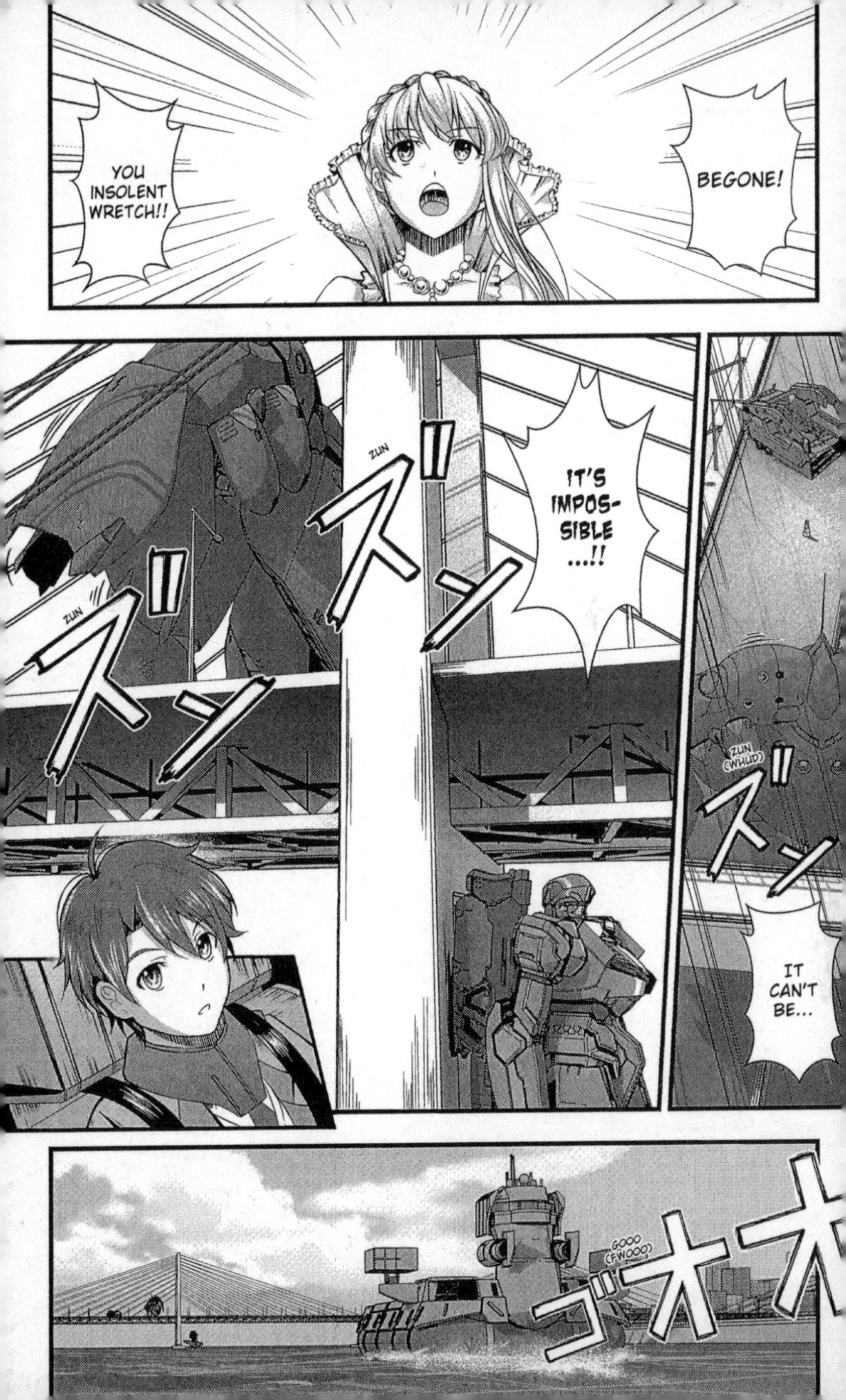
BEGONE!
YOU INSOLENT WRETCH!!
ZUN (WHUD)
ズン
IT CAN'T BE...
IT'S IMPOSSIBLE...!!
ZUN
ズン
ZUN
ズン
GOOO (FWOOO)
ゴオオ

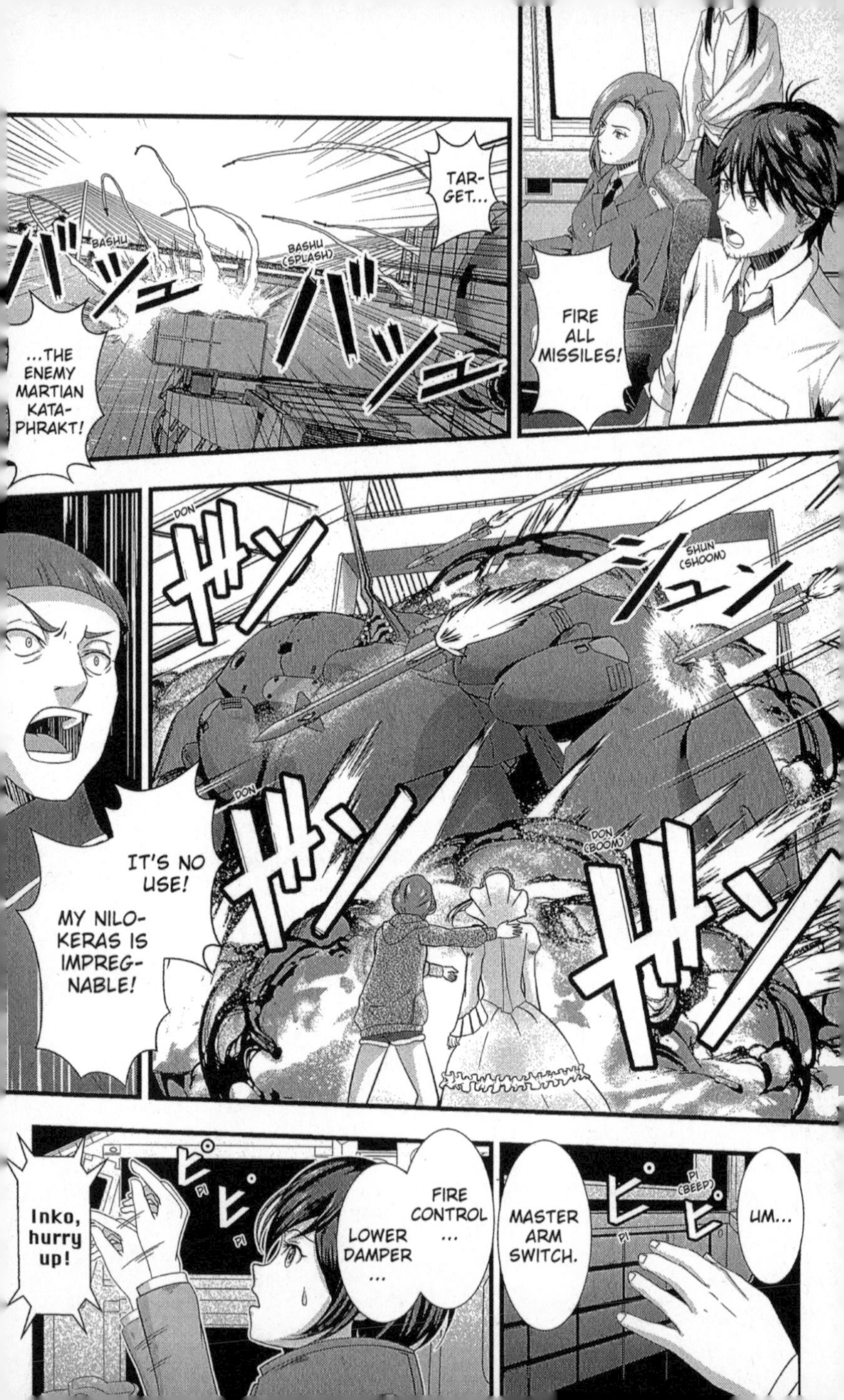
FIRE ALL MISSILES!
TAR-GET...
BASHU (SPLASH)
BASHU
...THE ENEMY MARTIAN KATA-PHRAKT!
SHUN (SHOOM)
DON
DON (BOOM)
DON
IT'S NO USE!
MY NILO-KERAS IS IMPREG-NABLE!
UM...
PI (BEEP)
PI
MASTER ARM SWITCH.
FIRE CONTROL ...
LOWER DAMPER ...
PI
PI
Inko, hurry up!

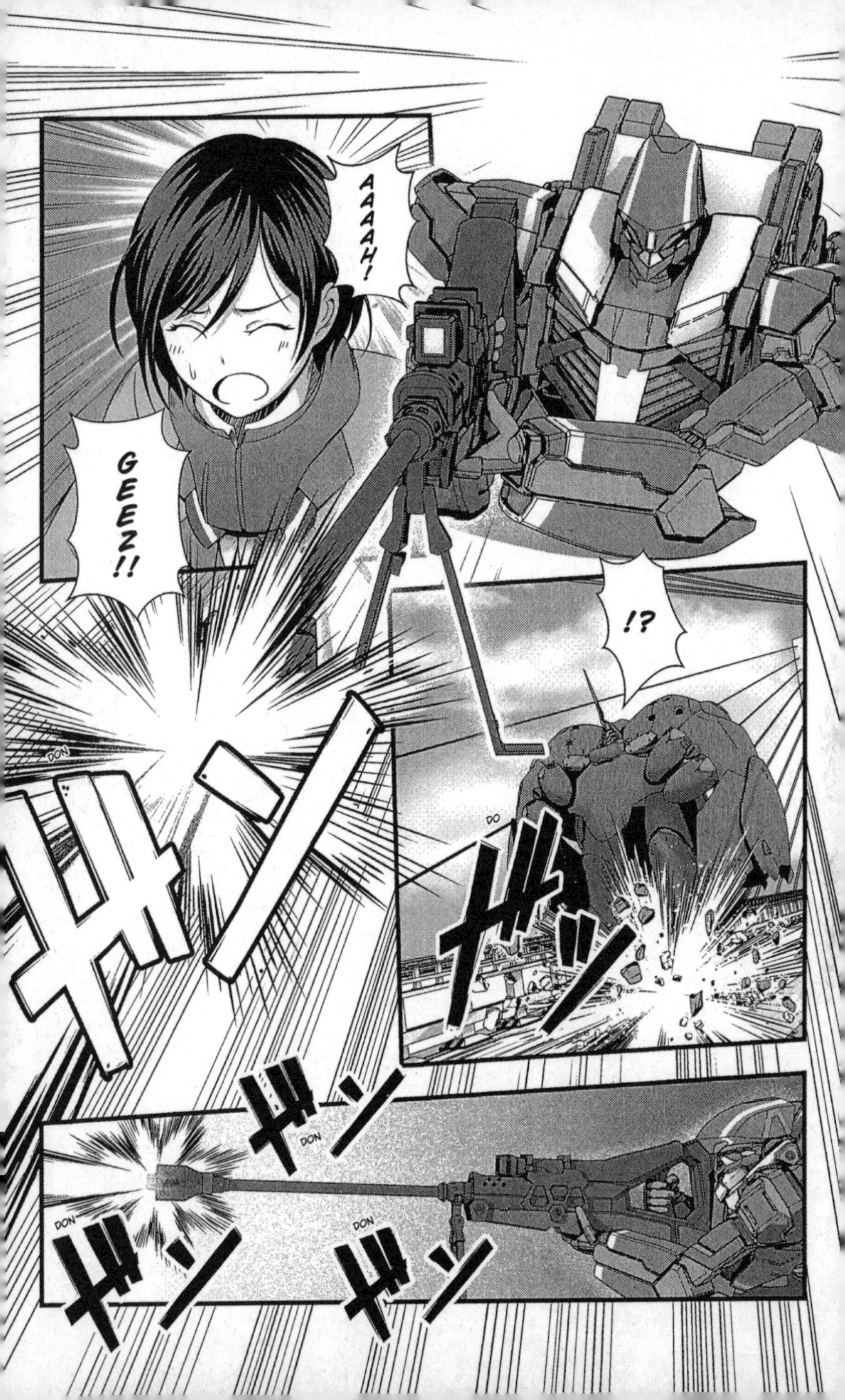
AAAAAH!
GEEZ!!
!?
DO
DON
DON
DON
DON

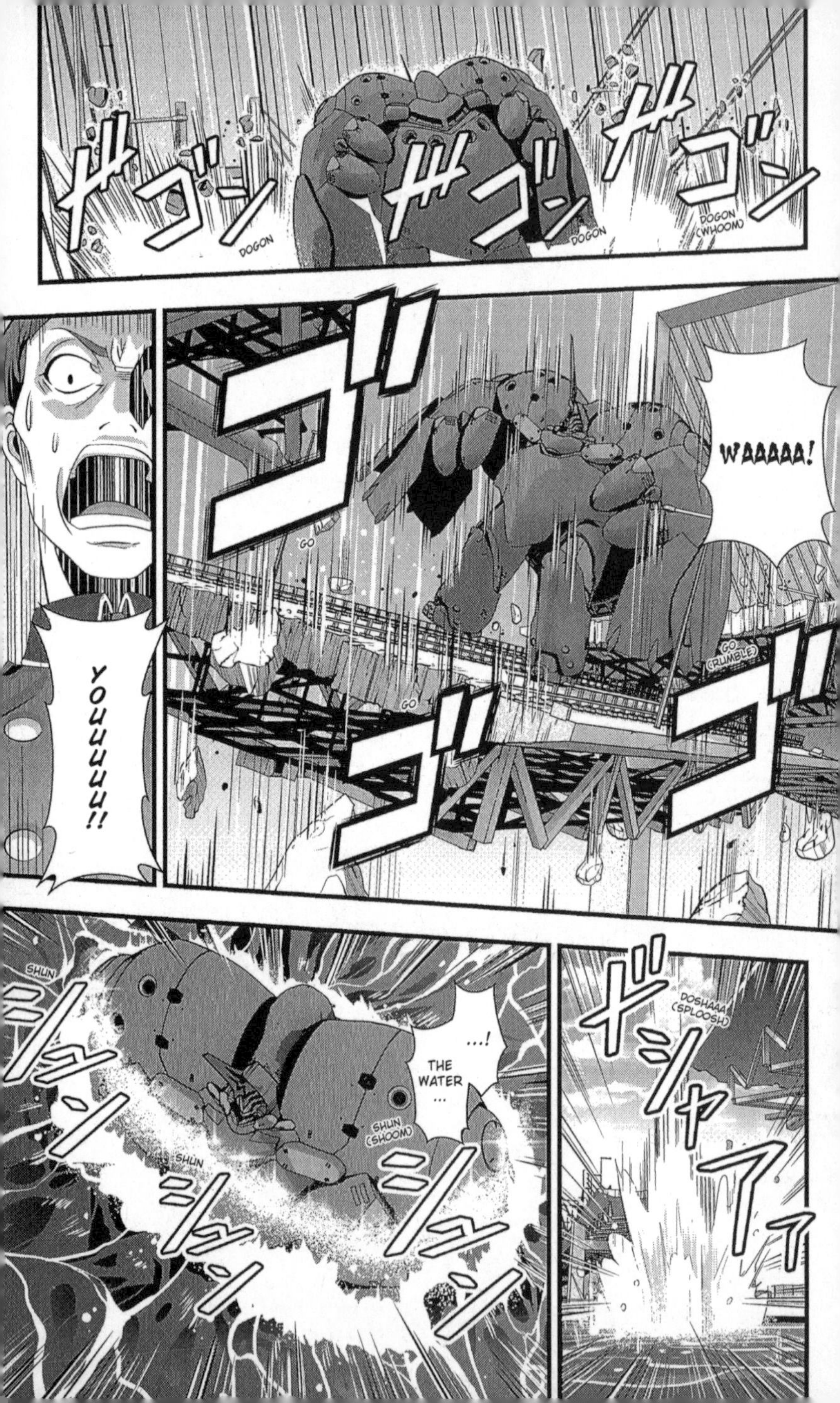
DOGON (WHOOM)
DOGON
DOGON
WAAAAAA!
GO (RUMBLE)
GO
GO
YOUUUUUU!!
DOSHAAA (SPLOOSH)
...!
THE WATER ...
SHUN (SHOOM)
SHUN
SHUN

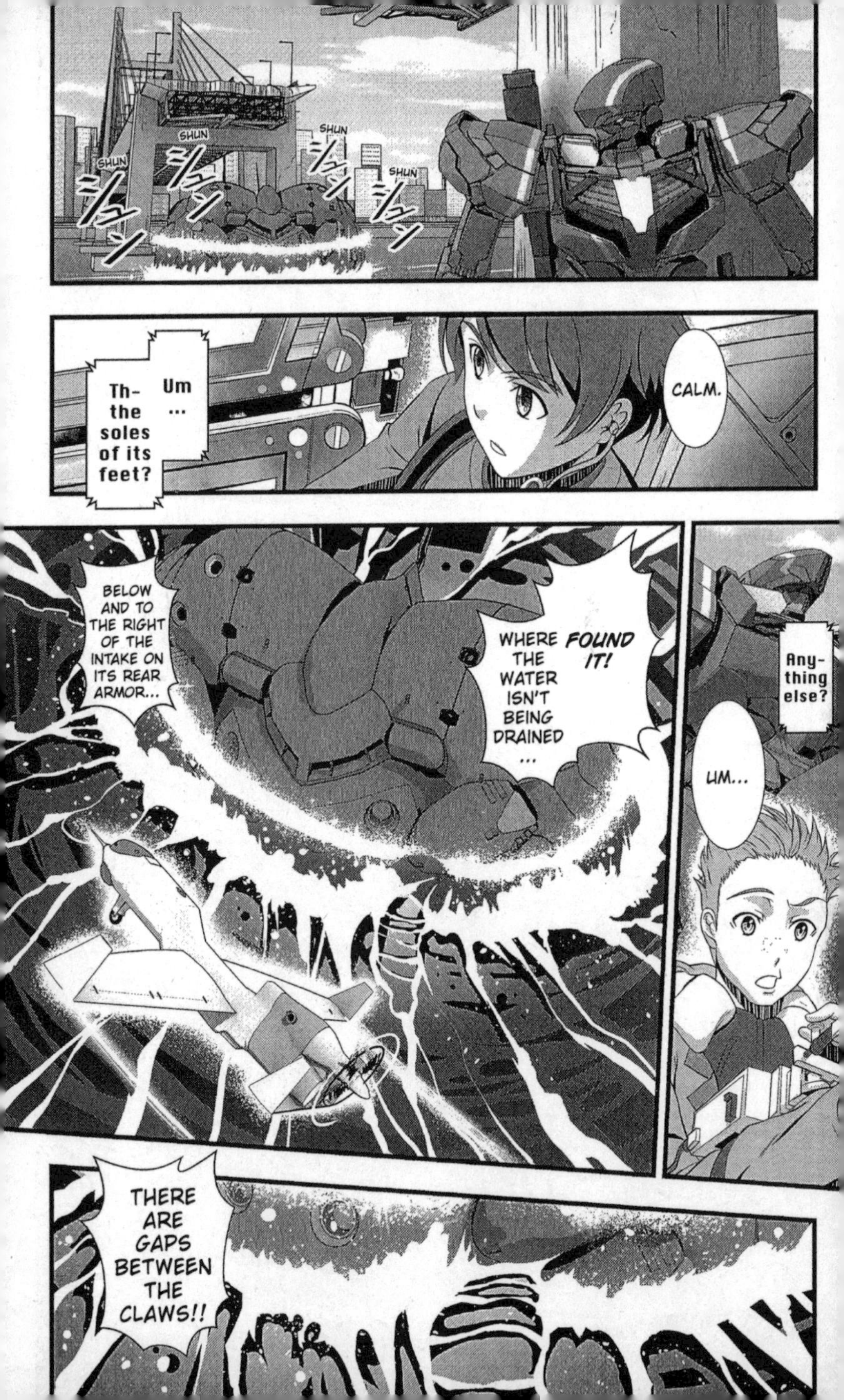
SHUN
SHUN
SHUN
SHUN
CALM.
Um ...
Th- the soles of its feet?
Any-thing else?
UM...
FOUND IT!
WHERE THE WATER ISN'T BEING DRAINED ...
BELOW AND TO THE RIGHT OF THE INTAKE ON ITS REAR ARMOR...
THERE ARE GAPS BETWEEN THE CLAWS!!

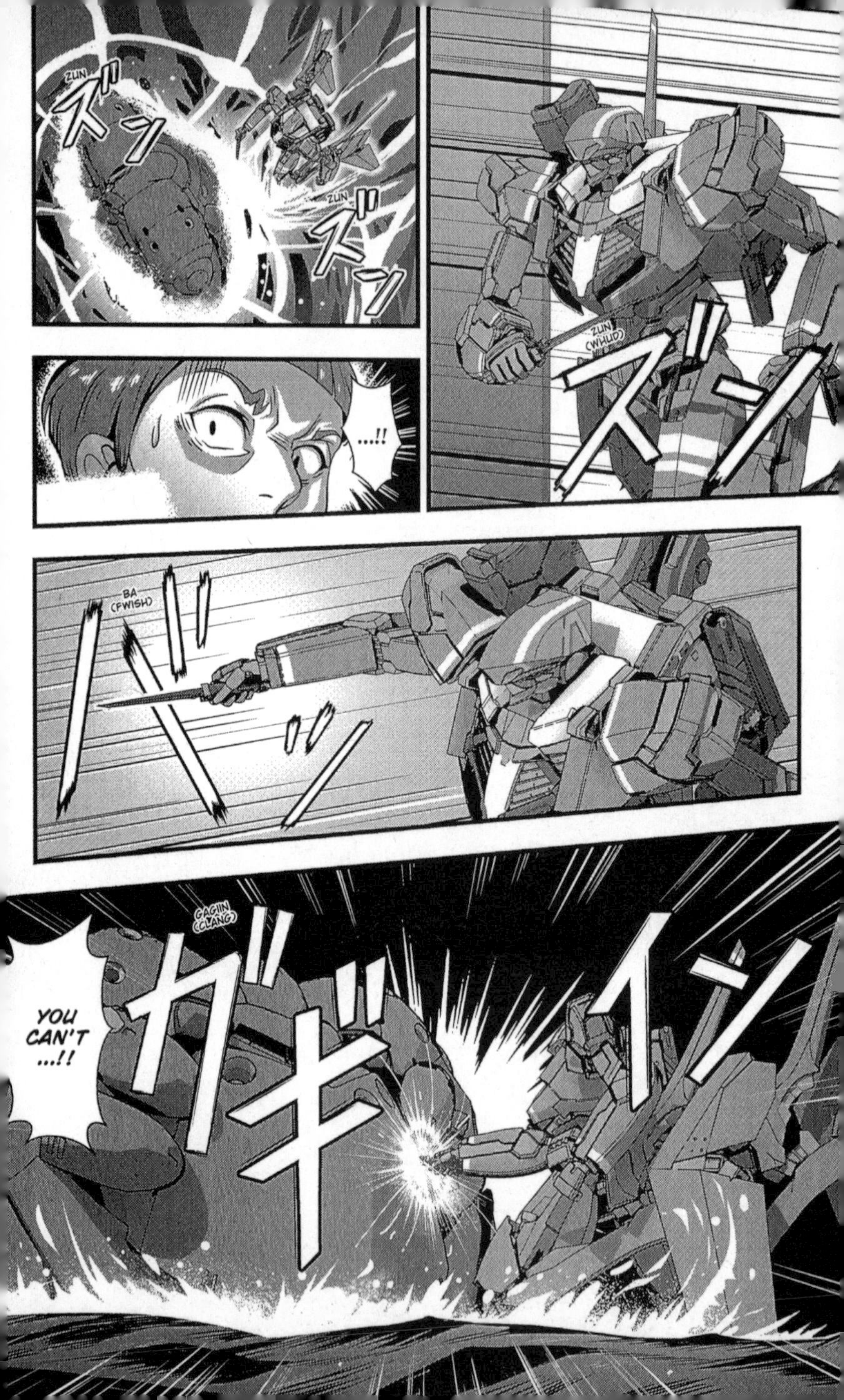

ZUN (WHUD)
ZUN
ZUN
...!!
BA (FWISH)
GAGIIN (CLANG)
YOU CAN'T ...!!

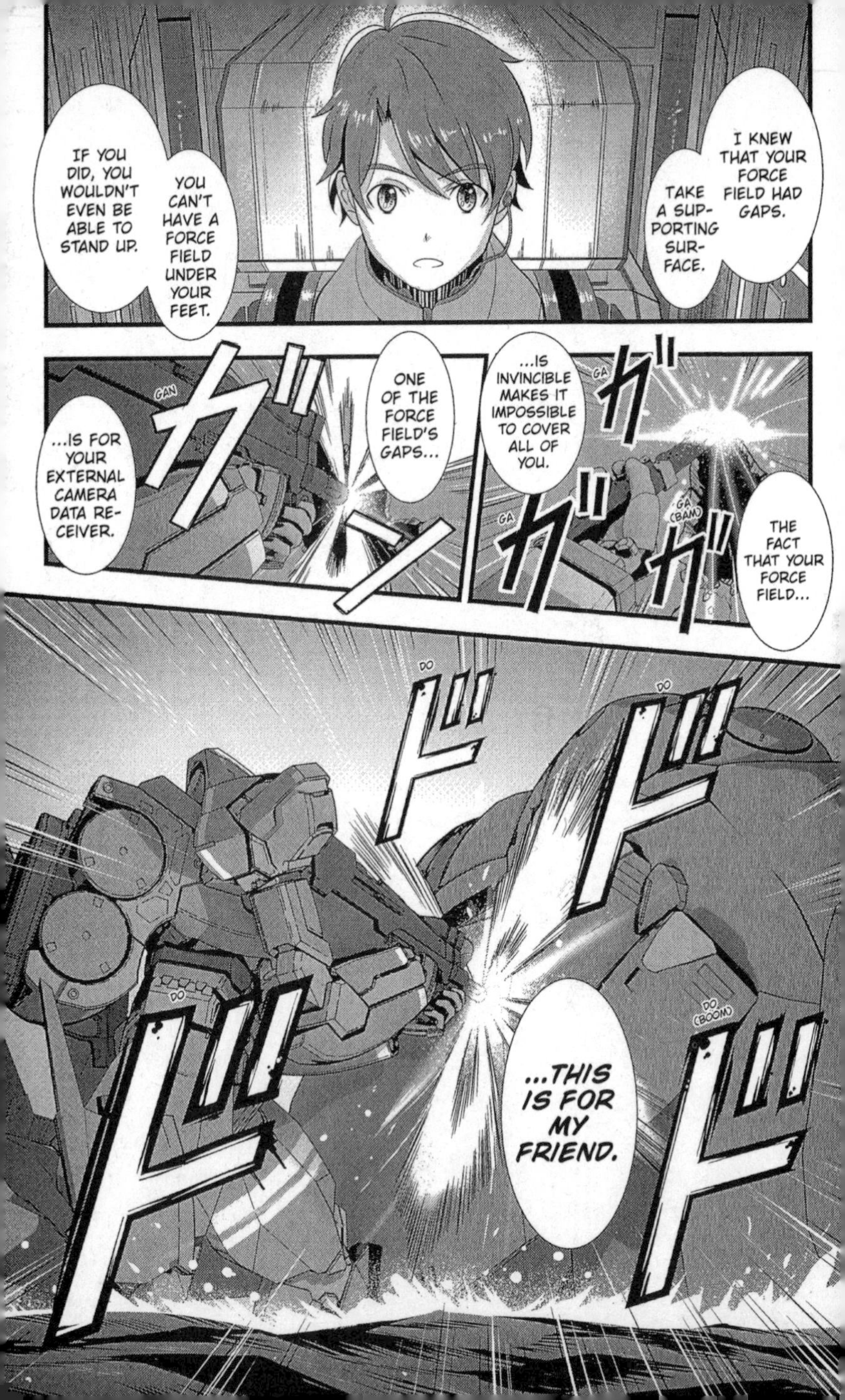
I KNEW THAT YOUR FORCE FIELD HAD GAPS.
TAKE A SUP-PORTING SUR-FACE.
YOU CAN'T HAVE A FORCE FIELD UNDER YOUR FEET.
IF YOU DID, YOU WOULDN'T EVEN BE ABLE TO STAND UP.
THE FACT THAT YOUR FORCE FIELD...
GA
GA (BAM)
GA
...IS INVINCIBLE MAKES IT IMPOSSIBLE TO COVER ALL OF YOU.
ONE OF THE FORCE FIELD'S GAPS...
GAN
...IS FOR YOUR EXTERNAL CAMERA DATA RE-CEIVER.
DO
DO
DO (BOOM)
...THIS IS FOR MY FRIEND.
DO

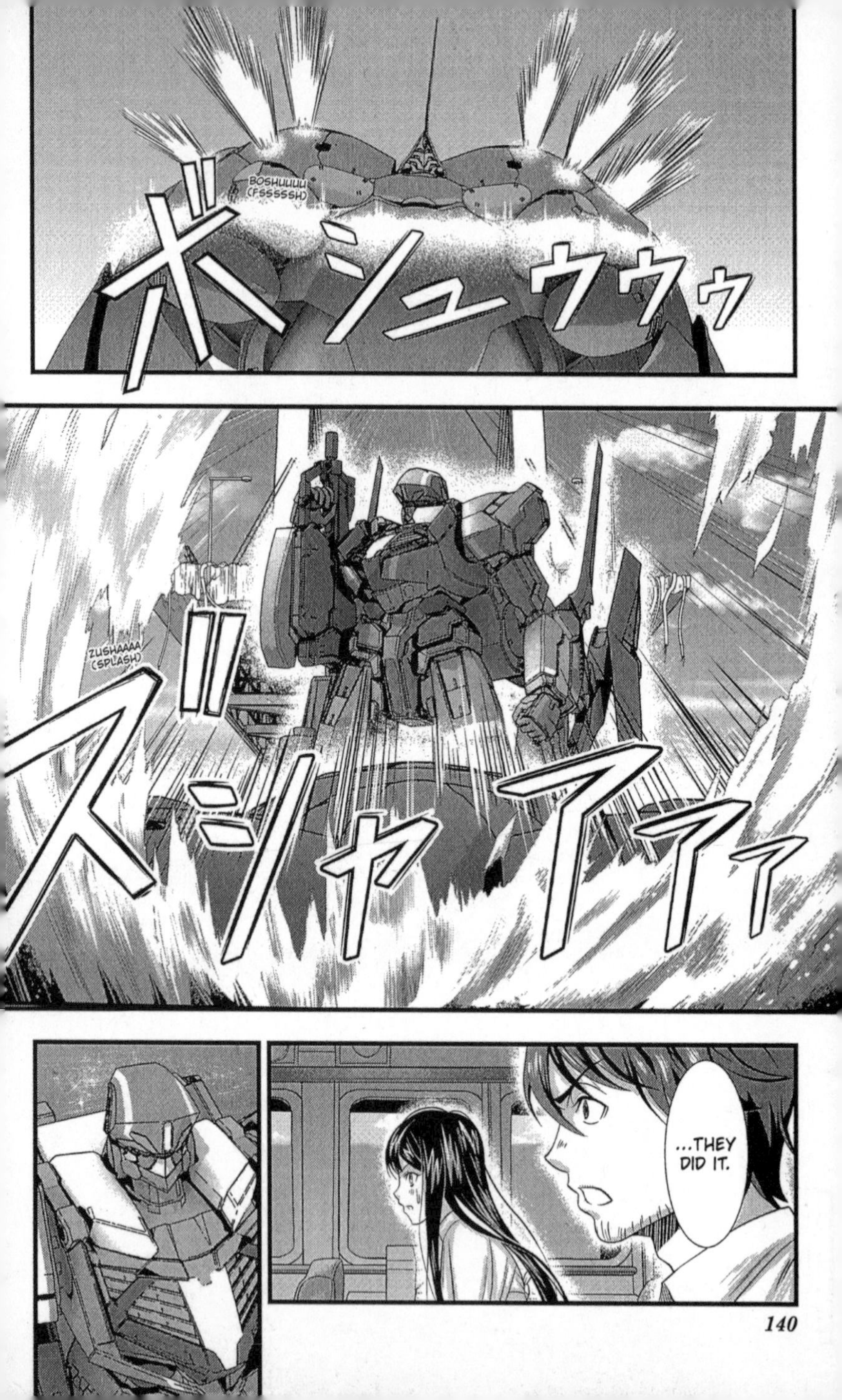
ボシュウウゥ
BOSHUUUU (FSSSSSH)
ズシャアアァ
ZUSHAAAA (SPLASH)
...THEY DID IT.

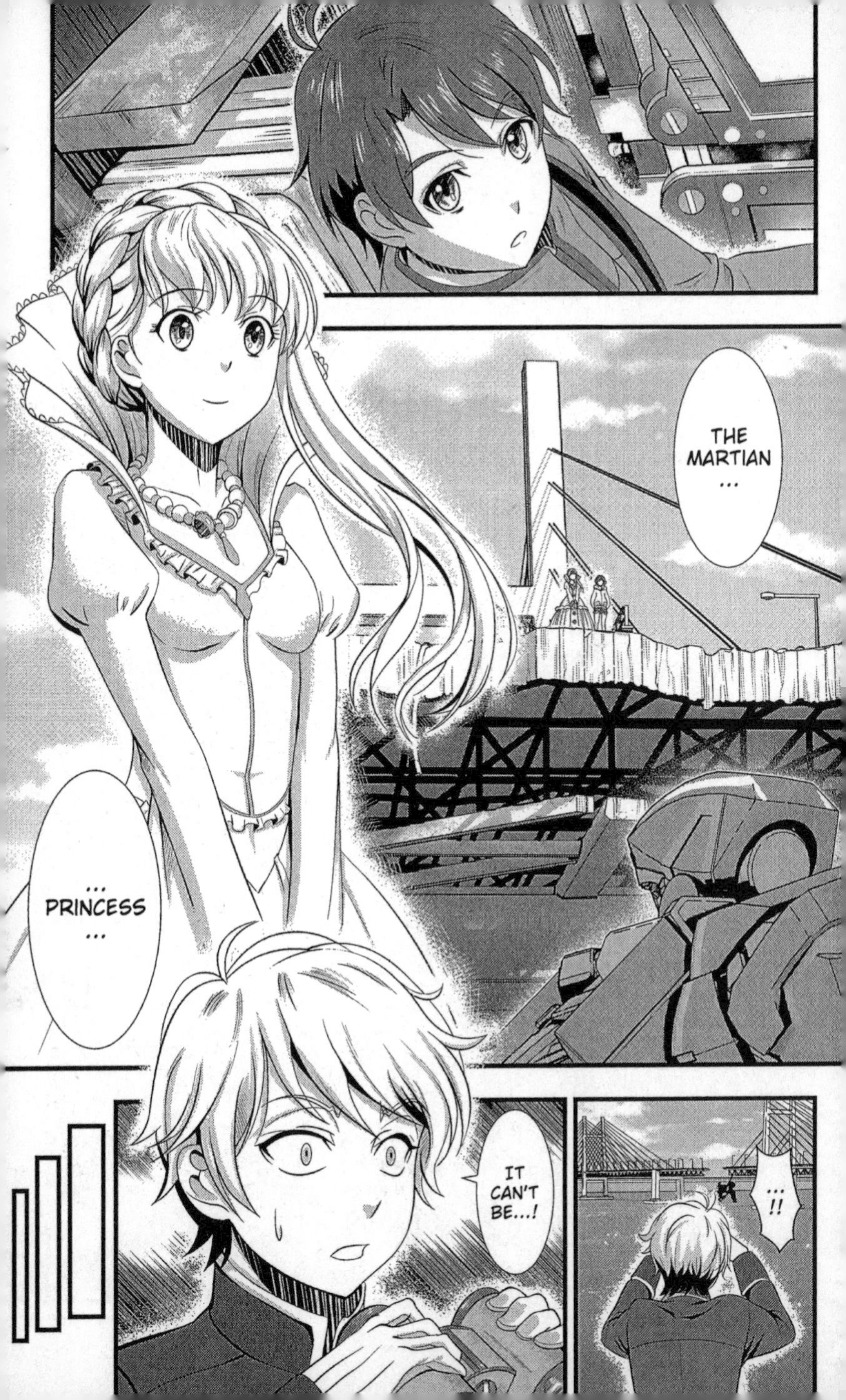
THE MARTIAN ...
... PRINCESS ...
... !!
IT CAN'T BE...!

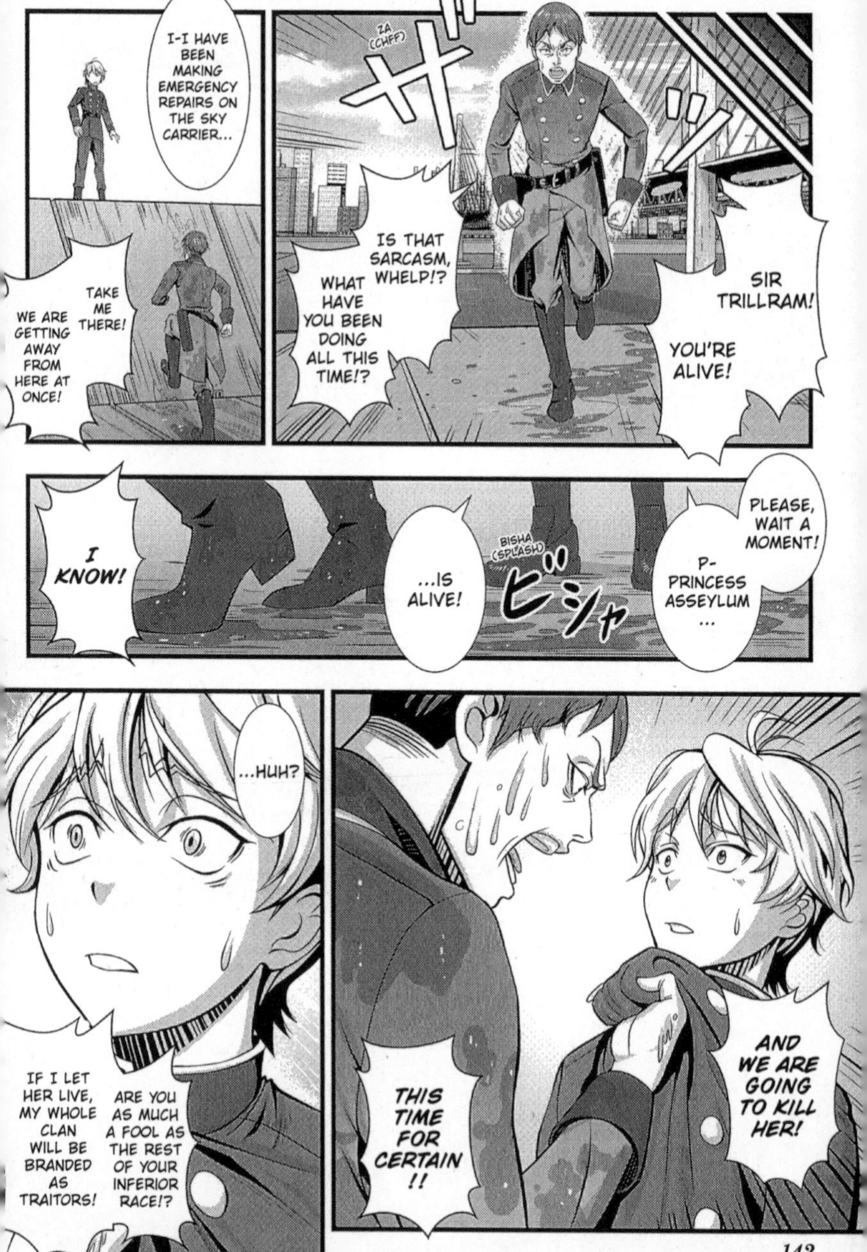
ZA (CHFF)
SIR TRILLRAM!
YOU'RE ALIVE!
IS THAT SARCASM, WHELP!?
WHAT HAVE YOU BEEN DOING ALL THIS TIME!?
I-I HAVE BEEN MAKING EMERGENCY REPAIRS ON THE SKY CARRIER...
TAKE ME THERE!
WE ARE GETTING AWAY FROM HERE AT ONCE!
PLEASE, WAIT A MOMENT!
P-PRINCESS ASSEYLUM...
BISHA (SPLASH)
...IS ALIVE!
I KNOW!
AND WE ARE GOING TO KILL HER!
THIS TIME FOR CERTAIN!!
...HUH?
ARE YOU AS MUCH A FOOL AS THE REST OF YOUR INFERIOR RACE!?
IF I LET HER LIVE, MY WHOLE CLAN WILL BE BRANDED AS TRAITORS!

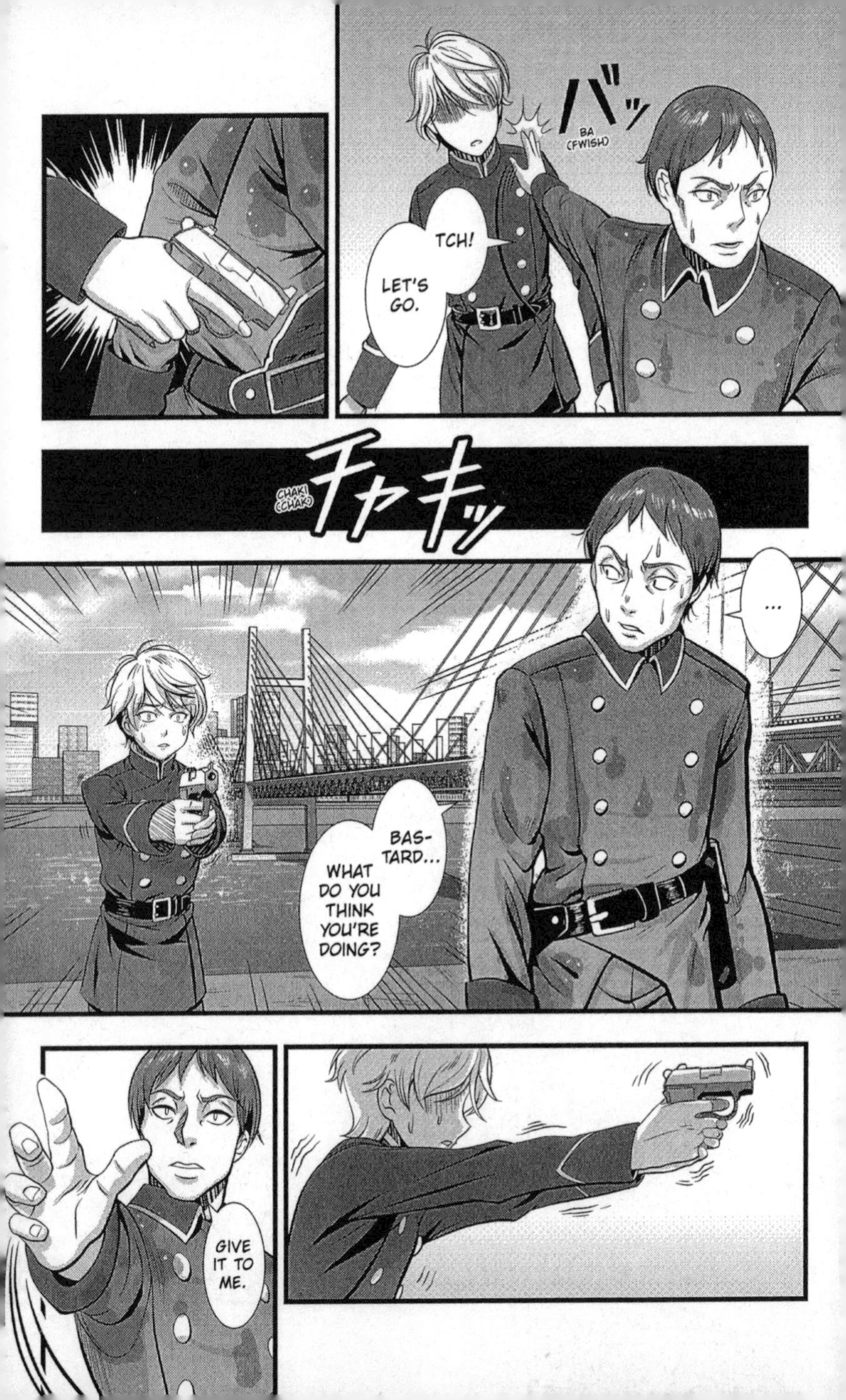
バッ
BA (FWISH)
TCH!
LET'S GO.
チャキッ
CHAKI (CHAK)
...
BAS-TARD...
WHAT DO YOU THINK YOU'RE DOING?
GIVE IT TO ME.

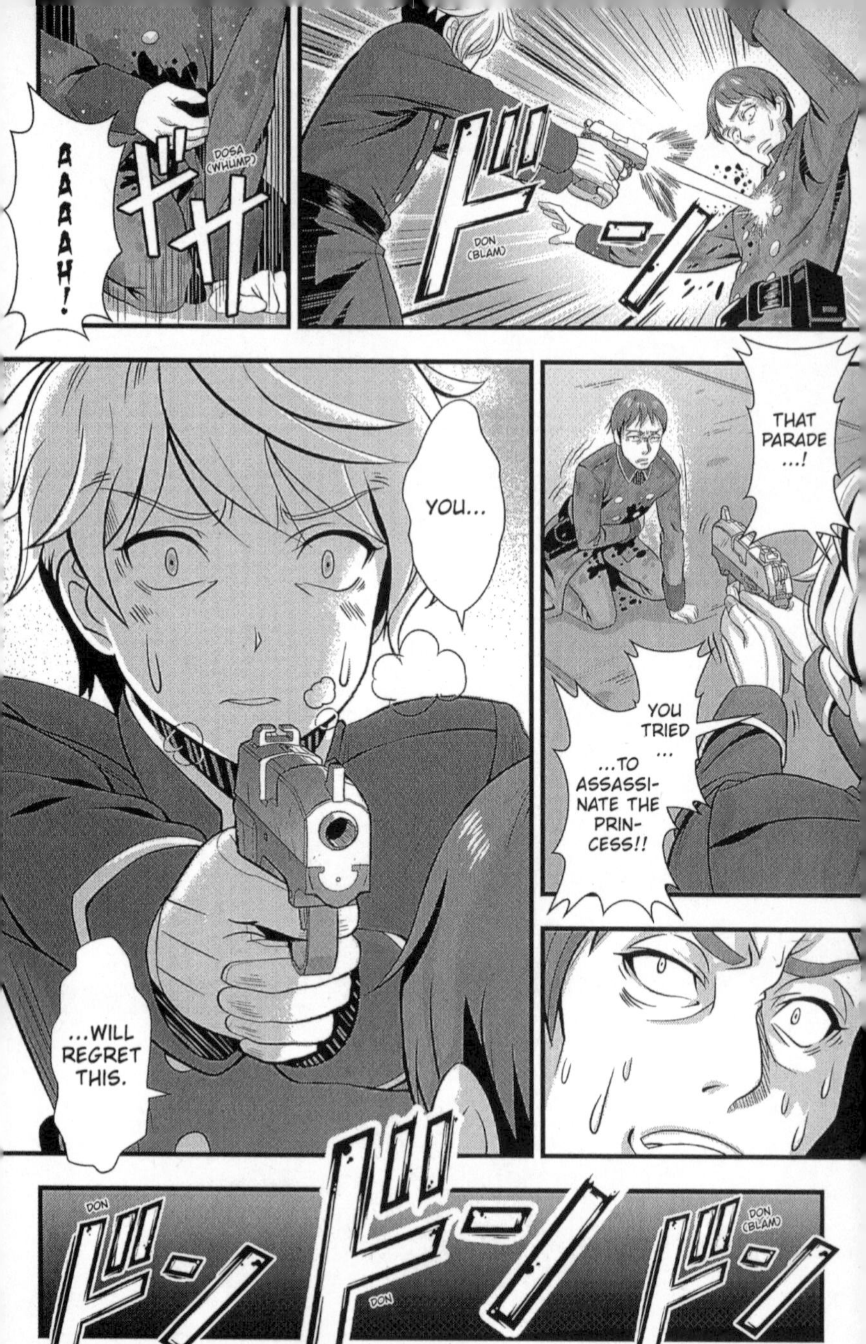
ドーン
DON (BLAM)
ドサッ
DOSA (WHUMP)
AAAAAH!
THAT PARADE ...!
YOU TRIED ...
...TO ASSASSINATE THE PRINCESS!!
YOU...
...WILL REGRET THIS.
ドーン
DON (BLAM)
ドーン
DON
ドーン
DON

To be continued in Volume 2!

ALDNOAH.ZERO
SEASON ONE ❶ WITHDRAWN

OLYMPUS KNIGHTS
PINAKES

Translation: Sheldon Drzka

Lettering: Brndn Blakeslee, Lys Blakeslee

This book is a work of fiction. Names, characters, places, and incidents are the product of the author's imagination or are used fictitiously. Any resemblance to actual events, locales, or persons, living or dead, is coincidental.

ALDNOAH.ZERO Vol. 1
© Olympus Knights/Aniplex · Project AZ. All rights reserved.
First published in Japan in 2014 by HOUBUNSHA CO., LTD., Tokyo. English translation rights in United States, Canada, and United Kingdom arranged with HOUBUNSHA CO., LTD. through Tuttle-Mori Agency, Inc., Tokyo.

Translation © 2015 by Hachette Book Group, Inc.

Yen Press
Hachette Book Group
1290 Avenue of the Americas
New York, NY 10104

www.hachettebookgroup.com
www.yenpress.com

Yen Press is an imprint of Hachette Book Group, Inc.
The Yen Press name and logo are trademarks of Hachette Book Group, Inc.

The publisher is not responsible for websites (or their content) that are not owned by the publisher.

First Yen Press Edition: December 2015

ISBN: 978-0-316-30949-3

10 9 8 7 6 5 4 3 2 1

BVG

Printed in the United States of America

ALDNOAH.ZERO 1
CONTENTS

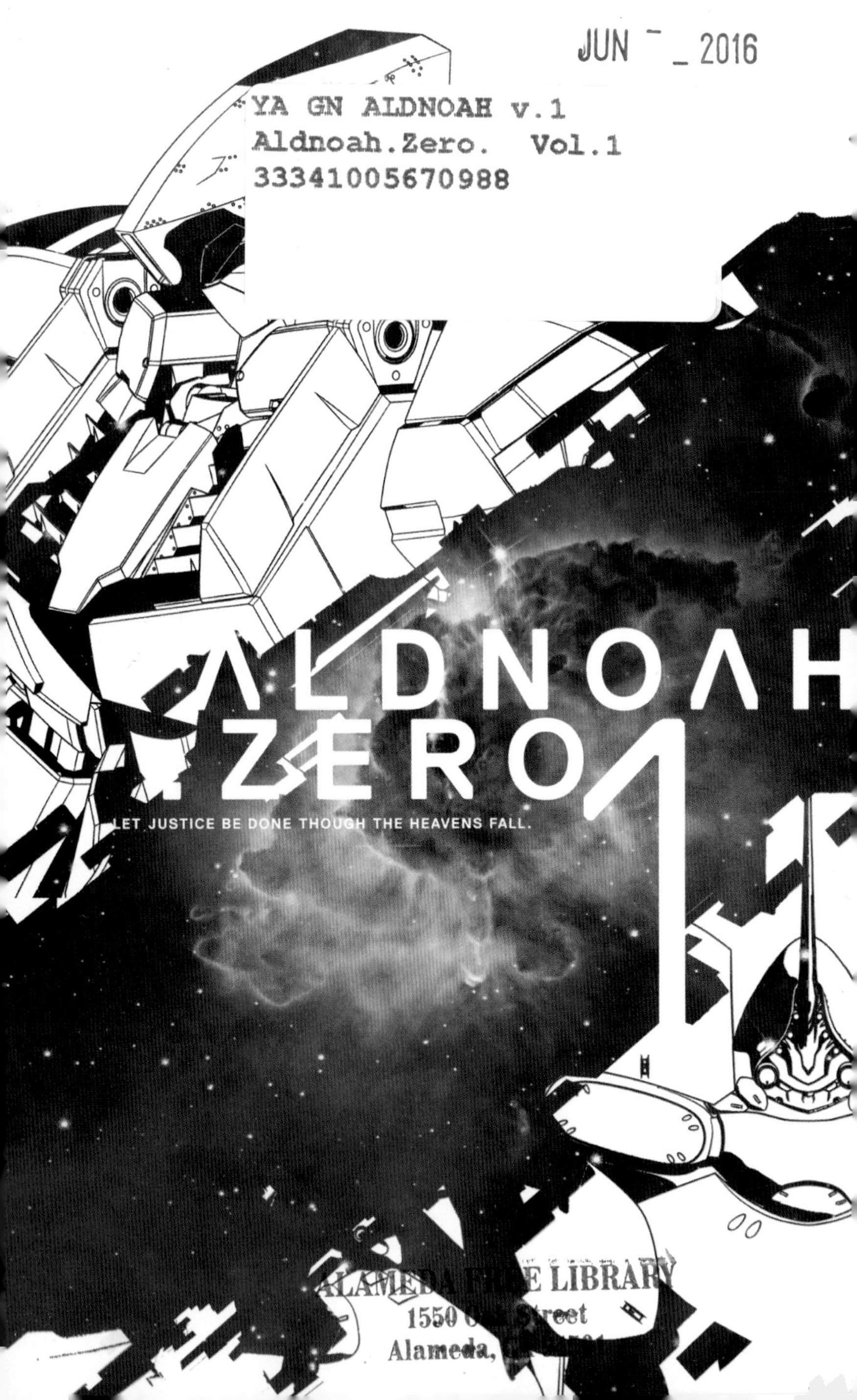
ALDNOAH
ZERO 1
LET JUSTICE BE DONE THOUGH THE HEAVENS FALL.